Essential Guide to Object Monitors

Karen Boucher

Fima Katz

Wiley Computer Publishing

John Wiley & Sons, Inc.

NEW YORK · CHICHESTER · WEINHEIM · BRISBANE · SINGAPORE · TORONTO

Publisher: Robert Ipsen
Editor: Robert M. Elliott
Managing Editor: Micheline Frederick
Electronic Products, Associate Editor: Mike Sosa
Text Design & Composition: Benchmark Productions, Inc.

Designations used by companies to distinguish their products are often claimed as trademarks. In all instances where John Wiley & Sons, Inc., is aware of a claim, the product names appear in initial capital or ALL CAPITAL LETTERS. Readers, however, should contact the appropriate companies for more complete information regarding trademarks and registration.

This book is printed on acid-free paper. ∞

Published by John Wiley & Sons, Inc.

Published simultaneously in Canada.

This publication is designed to provide accurate and authoritative information in regard to the subject matter covered. It is sold with the understanding that the publisher is not engaged in rendering professional services. If professional advice or other expert assistance is required, the services of a competent professional person should be sought.

Library of Congress Cataloging-in-Publication Data:

Boucher, Karen, 1971–
   Essential guide to object monitors / Karen Boucher, Fima Katz.
     p. cm.
   ISBN 0-471-31971-6 (pbk. : alk. paper)
    1. Object monitors (Computer software)   2. Object-oriented programming (Computer science)
 I. Katz, Fima, 1954– II. Title.
 QA76.76.M54B68 1999
 005.7'13--dc21   98-53559
                                     CIP

Printed in the United States of America.

10 9 8 7 6 5 4 3 2 1

Without the support of my family and friends, this book would not have been possible. I dedicate this book to the greatest treasures of my life, my two boys Michael and Jack, who kept me smiling through the creation of "the book that never ends."

—Karen Boucher

This book is dedicated to my family: my son Max, my daughter Victoria, and especially to Nina, my wife, for her enduring support of, and faith in, all my ventures, all my startups (and startdowns), all my wildness, and many, many other things that only she can handle.

—Fima Katz

CONTENTS

When Karen Boucher and Fima Katz first came to me with the idea to write a book about object-oriented technology, I was skeptical. After all, who needs another book on a subject that, while "hot" has more than its share of theorists. But when they described the details of their planned book, my attitude changed. This was what I was really looking for. Many of us have gained experience with object technology. We know how to write objects, how to create class libraries, how to enjoy the benefits of inheritance, and so on. The question is, how to manage the environment. Without industry-wide reliability, availability, and scalability (RAS) we would never be able to fully utilize the power of objects for the mission-critical systems, and objects would remain a tool for the fringe. RAS was the reason for and foundation of the stability that the mainframe-based software (COBOL or BAL using CICS, IMS, DB2, etc.) still possess in all major corporations.

The fact that Karen and Fima planned on using and testing this technology before writing about the system management aspect of object technology indicates that this technology is mature enough to enter the mainstream of software development and be used for the mission-critical applications.

The ways a company can develop new and retrofit older applications has increased exponentially over the last ten years. The move toward distributed applications that run in a distributed systems environment has, however, caused a dilemma: On one hand, there are many more choices to be made (the good news); on the other hand, there are many choices to be made (the bad news). So, why do we continue on this path?

First, the move to distributed computing is a result of an urgent need. In the world of the Internet, we can no longer assume that very few mainframe or some UNIX or NT servers servers can support the huge number of concurrent users now accessing the systems. Vertical scalability (SMP, MPP) is not sufficient. What used to be an elegant and sometimes cost-effective way of computing became a must. We must use distributed computing. In addition, the emergence of effective, fast, and (relatively) cheap development tools in lower-cost infrastructures has enabled new players to enter the marketplace and compete head-on against the establishment. Look at mortgages: At a relatively low cost, an aggregator can offer its customers the lowest possible cost for a loan. Previously, this market was dominated by the big players and by middlemen hunting for deals. Now the Internet is the middleman. Brokerage has shifted from total dominance by the full-service players (Merrill Lynch) to the discount brokers (Schwab) and the deep discount brokers (E*Trade). None could have made it without an alternative computing model. And to survive the expected retaliation of the big guys, rapid application development and reuse of components is a must. Both the newcomers and the earlier leaders need to use distributed technology and its sibling, object technology, to compete.

This book helps all the players in the relatively new field of object technology understand and prepare for the real test: whether their early accomplishments are sustainable. It is often difficult to find qualified people who can point out the essential product information to help users make an informed selection. This book will give you a solid grasp of the technology, along with the necessary information to determine the right product for your business needs. This book also offers important contributions to the way companies look at all distributed technology and the many facets involved in making a sound choice.

In other words, this book is a practical guide to the mysterious world of modern middleware. It leads readers through the why into the how, and helps us all understand how to build the necessary environment to ready ourselves for the new era.

I am sure you will enjoy it as much as I did.

—Tsvi Gal

Executive Vice President
North America Applications
ABN AMRO Bank

Recently one of your authors was speaking on the subject of Object Monitors. The essence of the speech was to define the key characteristics of this new middleware technology and to tell where this segment of the IT marketplace is heading. After the forty-five minute presentation, complete with the latest acronyms and key phrases, a hand rose from the back of the audience. A question was asked which eventually led to the creation of this book. While a seemingly obvious question, it took your author by surprise. It was the simple question, "OK, but what is middleware?"

Like a ton of bricks your author realized the rest of the world does not live and breathe middleware technology. I was reminded once more that, particularly with the newest technology available on the market, it's easy to lose the business benefits that can be found behind all the great acronyms and fancy jargon. Couple this with the difficulty of understanding the differences between the plethora of available products, and it's easy to understand why both the creators and the consumers of middleware products latch on to, and often overuse, the same descriptions for products.

The after effect of this however is confusion about what the real differences are between solutions from different groups of products, and the individual products within these groups. For anyone who has fallen victim to this trend, it may be somewhat daunting to learn that middleware products vary greatly in the needs the product can fulfill. While it's easy to give a simple definition of what middleware or an Object Monitor is, it becomes more difficult to explain exactly how a particular company or application can benefit.

This book was written to clear up that confusion. It is intended as a source for valuable information that will not only teach the reader the differences between the leading middleware products in the market, but to lead the reader through a complete process for choosing the right product to fit his or her corporate business and system requirements.

By the end of this book the reader will not only have a firm grasp on Object Monitor technology benefits, and individual product sets, but will be prepared to further understand a variety of products this technology will effect in the future. The information contained in this book is intended to provide enough information for readers to make informed decisions for choosing products which will help reach business and specific application goals.

Overview of the Book and Technology

The question of middleware is one that has puzzled the minds of Information Technology executives since the creation of the client/server computing model. Initial discussion was heavily centered around two-tier vs. three-tier distributed computing models. Early arguments led way to heated disputes over which architecture was best for the corporate computing world. Over the years IS staff began to realize that ultimately the three-tier model would win out for the large majority of corporate IT structures. As predicted early on, two tier models became inefficient and difficult to change.

Today there is little discussion concerning the two-tier vs. three-tier debate. While three-tier has become the model companies have turned to, debate still exists relative to which middleware is appropriate for which problem. Vendors in the middleware space have only fueled the fire. These vendors promised the moon and offered only confusion as to the differences between products. This led way to hasty decisions and wrong choices. Lucky for vendors and users, even this is now fading. The explosion of the object-oriented programming model to main stream IS shops, as well as the users' need for a more defined middleware product has led to the invention of a new bread of middleware. This new middleware goes under a few different names: Object Monitor, Object Transaction Monitor, Application Server, Universal Middleware. Call it what you wish, the premise is ultimately the same: the creation of one middleware product to serve all application infrastructure needs.

Sadly, with these new products comes the heartache of understanding how well these products are suited to the application needs of corporate America today. The new breed of middleware is designed to handle the demands of every application. But is that really the case? Speculation abounds as to whether these new universal middleware products can be used efficiently for all types of applications. Middleware experts concede that a mixture of products may be required to fulfill all the application requirements of corporate information systems. Until now, however, no independent source has taken the initiative to uncover the core application competencies of the new products coming to market.

This dilemma has prompted your authors to further investigate the claims of universal middleware vendors and offer real solutions for potential customers. Between the covers of this book, readers will get the inside scoop on the differences between these new products, the applications each product is best suited for, the current state of the market, and where these products are heading.

How This Book is Organized

Our intent with this book is to proceed in a logical fashion by first reviewing the overriding characteristics that define products which are part of the Object Monitor market. Part One will introduce the reader to the background which led these products to emerge and the standards that directly affect the way these products work. We'll then take the reader through a brief introduction of the functionality which puts a particular product into the Object Monitor market segment. This introduction will inform readers of key services that make the products comparable with each other.

Part One concludes with Chapter Four which wraps up with information that will prepare the reader for a closer look at each product which is currently playing a key role in the Object Monitor market. Chapter Four also provides essential background information for understanding the way your authors looked at the products and shows how the product chapters can assist with choosing the right product for current corporation and application requirements.

Part Two introduces the six hottest products in the market and describes each product's unique value contribution. The reader is left with a firm foundation of information on the products (such as skills requirements, architecture effects of the product, and means of using the products services). Information is structured to provide information for both the general reader, as well as those who will be involved in a choosing a product for specific application or business requirements.

Part Three provides further information on the current state of the overall Object Monitor market and will prepare the reader for future product evaluations. Part Three will wrap up with insight on the future of the market and what to expect next.

Who Should Read this Book

While one of the least understood products in the industry today, Object Monitor technology is playing a key role in how applications will be created as we enter the next phase of distributed computing systems. The technology is designed both as a common base for multiple corporate applications as well as a product to serve the needs of individual projects. With this in mind your authors of course feel that everyone involved in Information Technology should read this book!

In particular the book is geared towards Senior Level Information Systems professionals who are involved in making corporate-wide systems architecture standards decisions, or anyone involved in this process. These readers may want to skim through Chapter Four and the conclusion charts of each product chapter.

We have also geared the information towards readers that are making decisions based on a particular application requirement. For these readers we've included a complete process in Chapter Four for creating a "short list worksheet" and using this as a basis for deciding which products are most suitable for further evaluation. At the end of each product chapter we have organized the product information to help these readers with filling in their own criteria information and for future reference.

We have written the book in such a way that no prior middleware knowledge is required and tried to stray away from the overuse of acronyms and "middleware expert only" phrases. Our glossary also includes descriptions on a variety of middleware terms that can be referenced throughout reading this book and also for future endeavors. We suggest that these readers start right at the beginning of the book and work their way through from cover to cover—as the information is presented in as a teaching guide and information source.

Readers with more experience in the middleware market, and who are only interested in finding out what each individual product offers as well as where the industry is heading, may want to skim right over the first three chapters and start with Chapter Four.

What's on Our Web Site?

The technology products covered in this book are brand new introductions to the field of distributed computing (many of the products were in fact only available in pre-release form during our writing). Knowing this is the case, and that all of the products are undergoing constant updates and changes, we urge readers to use our accompanying web site as an additional information source.

Our site is located at: www.wiley.com/compbooks/boucher. The information contained at this web address is designed to provide timely information on new product enhancements, links to other sites of interest, upcoming trade show information and general updates to all the information on the state of the Object Monitor market as presented throughout this book.

In addition to providing a source for updated information, the site is also designed as a starting point for gathering time-stamped feature/function information that was not appropriate to include within the product chapters of Part Two.

Up Next

We're glad to introduce you to the market of Object Monitor technology. The products and services described in this book are one of the most interesting aspects of the distributed systems marketplace today. Be prepared to become an expert in these products as we begin our investigation into the six hottest new products in the middleware market.

Coming up next is Chapter 1, an introduction to the key technologies and standards that have prompted the creation of this particular breed of product. We'll start with a gentle introduction to middleware and why readers should care about this technology. Thanks for joining us—read ahead!

ACKNOWLEDGMENTS

It would have been impossible to publish this book without the help of a great many people that assisted us along the way. We pray we haven't forgotten anyone in our long list of helpful people.

- To Denis Ulyanov and Herman Gorra, this book would not have been possible without their Herculean technical research efforts that formed the basis for much of the book's content.

- To the vendor representatives that assisted us with this process. Many of them provided us with free copies of their products for our evaluation. They deserve even more credit than we can give here. While it is impossible to thank everyone that assisted us, the following provides a list of those that have held our hands along the way:

    IONA Technologies: Colin Newman and David Clarke

    BEA Systems: Patti Dock and Jay Fry

    Inprise Corporation: Randy Hietter and Steve Yellenberg

    IBM Corporation: Alastair Rennie and Valerie Olague

    Microsoft Corporation: Pat Helland and Jim Gray

    Hitachi: Shimpachi Ogata and Michael Hicks

- To the various people at Concorde Solutions Inc. who provided both technical ideas and comments combined with continued support especially:

    Gregory Katzman, his support and friendship during this time was truly priceless. Felix Soyferman, technologist and pretty good tennis player, for giving us lots of very helpful technical ideas and comments. Our good friend, Isaac Applbaum, for real life lessons about business, technology and how it is related to people.

- To Jeri Edwards and Bob Orfali for their on-going words of encouragement.

- To Karim Raad of Cornerstone Software for his assistance on the message oriented middleware research.

- Norman Smith of the Contra Costa Software Business Incubator, for helping Fima keep his business stabilized during a period of heavy "multitasking."

- To the people at Wiley that somehow survived our personality quirks and worked with us to see this through, especially Bob Elliott and Pam Sobotka.

- The entire staff of The Standish Group for coping with Karen's on-going edginess throughout this process and for providing invaluable data points throughout this book. We especially thank Jim Johnson for his infinite wisdom.

PART ONE

The Object Monitor World

You are about to enter a mysterious corner of the IT world, a place where objects roam, some free, others contained and managed by forces known as application services. This is the world of Object Monitors.

How did these beings come into existence and how have they evolved? Chapter 1 introduces you to the middleware that produced the Object Monitor (OM): *transaction processing monitors (TPMs)*, *message-oriented middleware (MOMs)*, and *object request brokers (ORBs)* each plays a vital role in the application services the Object Monitor provides. You'll learn the traits of each applicable characteristic in the middleware marketplace and each product's role in the creation of the Object Monitor product.

Chapter 2 explains the standards that play a key role in this world. This chapter summarizes in a few pages all competitive differences between the CORBA and DCOM standards, which have been argued about for years. No matter at what IT level you work, this chapter will give you the information about and insight into the standards that divide the Object Monitor market, to aid you in your choice.

Chapter 3 officially introduces the Object Monitor, and defines how it can help you with your current projects. You'll learn what to expect from this new breed of product and the role it can play in your corporate computing environment.

Chapter 4 is a prerequisite for choosing from products in the Object Monitor market that meet your specific application requirements. This chapter will give you a new way to look at middleware, without overwhelming you with acronyms and confusing terminology.

This book is designed for readers who plan to go cover to cover and for those who only need specific information. So feel free to skip through any chapters that contain information you are already familiar with—although it may not hurt to read them and perhaps gain a new perspective.

CHAPTER 1

The Great Middleware Convergence

W e are witnessing a remarkable change in the world of information technology: the exposure of IT infrastructures. This change is being fueled by the broader access to and realization of what computer technology is capable.

Not too long ago, computing applications could "hide" behind business personnel—the call center or customer service representative, the salesperson or point-of-sale clerk. This layer of "people over technology" could keep many application details from the customer. Today, the customer wants greater access to these applications. The idea is not to bring the customer to the company, but vice versa. The Internet is perhaps the most widespread example of bringing customers closer to our IT structures, in effect eliminating the layer of independence created by corporate personnel.

Over the years, corporations have spent billions of dollars creating fast, secure, and available systems to perform necessary business tasks. These applications have become the lifeline of these corporations. But they must change, because they were built with the assumption that trained personnel would operate these systems, and hide functionality and, yes, defects from the consumer. Now, however, the consumer must be given the ability to take advantage of and easily understand how to access and use IT resources. At the same time, this access must be controlled and managed to ensure the corporation will not suffer. This requires the delivery of new services to new delivery channels and insurance that corporate systems can handle the demands of unanticipated numbers of users and undefined user requirements.

Revealing once-internal corporate infrastructures to the outside world is a daunting task facing IT executives around the globe who must figure out how to connect and share information among multiple applications, how to easily connect new user interfaces to existing applications, how to move data from one back-end system to the next, and so on. These questions affect the ability of a corporation to remain competitive in a self-service society.

Middleware technology is ideally suited to ensure that customers will have access to systems that cannot be hidden by trained personnel. Middleware is *application infrastructure software*. According to the Standish Group International, Inc.'s *Internet Goes Business Critical* report (1997), infrastructure software comprises an estimated 70 percent of an application and provides the necessary foundation to perform a business task. Middleware gives applications the facilities to join disparate applications and systems, share important application services, and even to reuse in-house resources.

Due to the differences in the types of service infrastructure software provides, middleware comes in many flavors dependent on the need the product is trying to fulfill. There are in fact 12 different types of middleware (Figure 1.1), and this chapter provides an overview of the three types that have resulted in the design of today's Object Monitors. These products are:

- Transaction Processing Monitors (TPM)
- Message-Oriented Middleware (MOM)
- Object Request Brokers (ORB)

This chapter is not intended to provide an in-depth technical description of all these middleware products, but rather to give the necessary background information to guide the discussion of Object Monitor technology.

Defining Middleware

For most companies, the middleware of an application may be difficult to pick out, as the infrastructure code is written into, and therefore closely

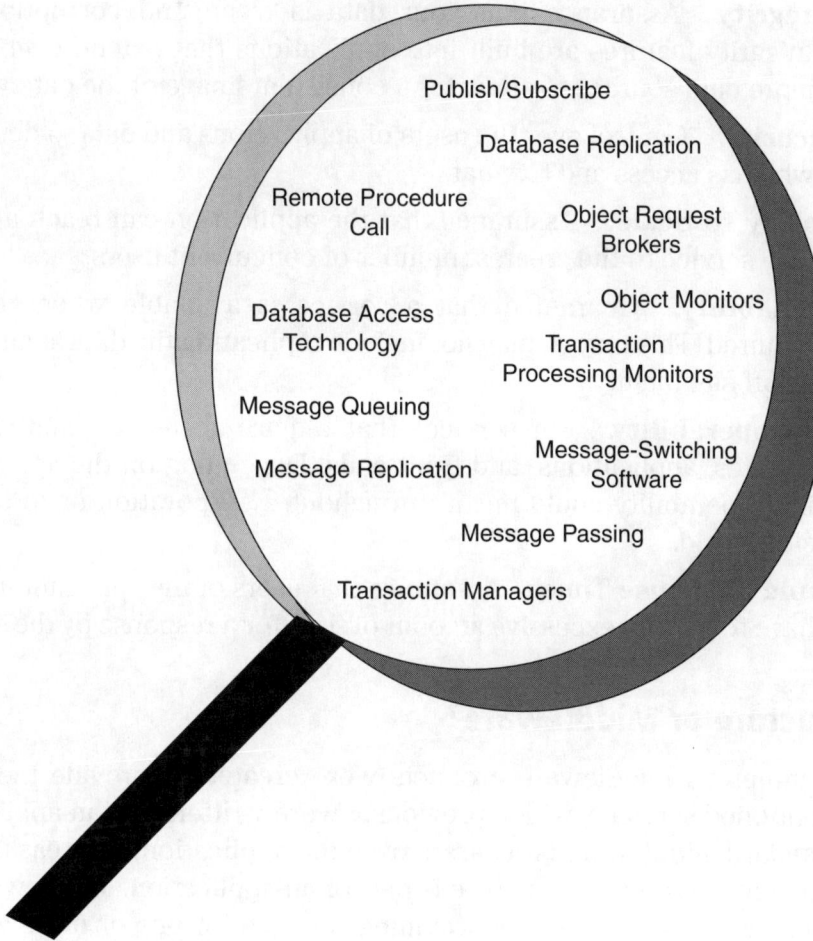

Publish/Subscribe

Database Replication

Remote Procedure Call

Object Request Brokers

Database Access Technology

Object Monitors

Transaction Processing Monitors

Message Queuing

Message Replication

Message-Switching Software

Message Passing

Transaction Managers

Figure 1.1   The 12 types of middleware.

tied to, the rest of the application. To reiterate, application infrastructure is the essence of middleware, as it provides a foundation on which new applications can be created and existing applications can be better utilized.

Infrastructure code is an essential part of every application, and the services the code needs to provide will vary according to the needs the application is designed to meet. Because of this, infrastructure code is often built into the program directly tied to business logic. To understand the value of middleware, it is important to realize that this is not necessary. Infrastructure code does not directly represent a *business* need; rather, it provides for an *application* need. The following are some examples of the services infrastructure code can provide:

Integrity. Assurance that your data is clean and corruption free. Integrity features are built into applications that extend over two or more data sources to allow for a consistent image of the data.

Security. Control over the users of applications and data to determine who has access and to what.

Ability to Scale. Assurance that the application can reach and provide service to the greatest number of concurrent users.

Availability. Guarantee that a service is available whenever it is required. This may or may not include replicating the data at an on-site or off-site facility.

Interoperability. For services that require access to multiple data sources, applications, and front ends. Depending on the application, interoperability could mean throughout a corporation or to the outside world.

Rapid Response Time. Assurance that users of the application do not have to wait an excessive amount of time for a response by the service.

Infrastructure or Middleware?

Commercial middleware products were created to provide the aforementioned services, which previously were written into an application. Standard middleware is separate from the application, whereas the custom application infrastructure is part of an application. Middleware is a standalone software entity providing services for one or more applications; it is a *product* that separates *infrastructure services*. This is a very important concept to understand, because it helps to clarify what middleware actually provides. Often, company executives can be confused as to what middleware is because they are accustomed to creating their own infrastructure services as a necessary step in the creation of an application. Thus, the key to understanding middleware is to view applications not as whole, but as a series of procedures that work together to accomplish a business task. These procedures naturally vary in the type of service they provide. For example, some sections of an application may address the way a user will view the application, while others may address how a segment of business logic is computed, while still others may address how data is transferred to a back-end system.

This no doubt sounds familiar: It is the essence of distributed application design. As the client/server model of computing became more popular, it became commonplace to view the distributed computing model as centering around the capability to divide processing of procedures among many machines. All this work was done in an effort to fully utilize new machine capabilities. Middleware is the evolutionary next step in a distributed system model. Rather than separate processing based on a simple "client device" versus "data source" model, a middleware product takes this one step further and logically separates infrastructure services into an "application service source."

However, defining what that "middle" piece is can be more difficult to grasp then discussing a client device or data source. In the middleware world, that middle piece is a logical base of services of which all applications may take advantage. Take a look at a few of your existing applications and you may notice quite a few similarities. For example, many applications may be accessing the same data on the same machine. Likewise, many applications may be using the same type of access control or availability procedures. However, these actions are most likely built into each application. In contrast, middleware provides the ability to separate business logic from application infrastructure, thereby allowing the application developer to focus on the business task of the application and not the infrastructure, as seen in Figure 1.2.

This separation makes it possible to easily introduce infrastructure changes across many applications, rather than one at a time. For example, if a company is in the process of moving inventory data from a mainframe system to a relational database, it may affect many applications. Middleware allows changes to be made to the infrastructure product, rather than requiring a reengineering effort on a per-project basis.

Figure 1.2 Where middleware fits in an application.

The Middleware Value Proposition

Often, middleware technology is referred to as "plumbing." And in following that metaphor, an example of the value of middleware often includes the following question, "When you're looking for a new house, would you rather buy plumbing materials already made or build the pipes yourself?" A custom-built home with custom plumbing could be a wonderful thing, especially if you're only going to have one home. Custom designing and building will more likely get you exactly what you need (although it will be more expensive). But what if you need several homes, and you need them faster than your neighbor? True, the metaphor falls apart somewhat here since few of us need multiple homes and in a competitive timeframe, but follow the logic for the purposes of this discussion.

If you need to build only one application to satisfy your business requirements, purchasing standard middleware may not be necessary. Generally, however, one application is never enough. To remain competitive, IS shops are under tremendous pressure to deliver new services, in new formats, faster, every day. Luckily, middleware is here to help. Using standard middleware as a base for new applications (and for updating existing ones) can enable users to gain the competitive advantage they require. It is the separation of application infrastructure from application development that makes this possible, providing the following benefits:

Easier Adaptation.   Using middleware allows for easier adaptation of an application based on changing business demands. The separation of infrastructure code from business logic allows changes in data sources or client types to be made simply by addressing the middleware, not each application affected.

Increased Interoperability.   Standard middleware allows for access to multiple types of data sources, other applications, and front ends. This interoperability will often be beyond the application's initial requirements, thereby allowing for future changes and future growth.

Affordability.   Dollar savings are provided through the ability to extend existing applications and to cost-effectively create new ones, thus providing a standard, flexible platform for change.

Management Services.   Middleware products promote the ability to manage application infrastructure for multiple applications together, rather than one at a time.

Faster Development and Rapid Implementation.   Custom-coding an application infrastructure into each application is a difficult and time-consuming exercise. Making use of middleware not only speeds up development time, but delivers new services for the corporation faster.

Once the difference between business logic (code that directly provides for a business service) versus infrastructure logic (code that provides services for the running of the application) is understood, the benefits of middleware become clear. The next logical step is to determine how your company should start taking advantage of these benefits. Like all software, middleware is just code; and anyone can create this code if they work at it long enough. However, the good news is that many vendors have performed this work already and have perfected the technology along the way. These vendors and their products make up the growing middleware market.

Build versus Buy

But can you build infrastructure better yourself? Clearly, the major competitor to off-the-shelf middleware products is the creation and re-creation of new application infrastructure on a per-project basis. And though the benefits of creating a solid infrastructure for change are becoming more widely appreciated, there's still wide adherence to the "Scarlet O'Hara mentality": "I can't think about that today; I'll think about that tomorrow." Middleware has become a product companies turn to in times of distress, which becomes unbearable when changes to multiple existing applications are necessary or when the need to use many applications together is desired or required.

As an alternative to purchasing middleware products, many IS shops may create their own custom middleware. Certainly, this will solve some of the aforementioned problems, but creating a custom middleware product is not the most cost-effective solution because the IS shop becomes, in essence, a middleware vendor. Purchasing middleware from a respected vendor offers additional benefits, such as:

- Product feature upgrades and new features are delivered by the vendor and typically require a simple upgrade install.
- Upgrades to standards that may affect existing and newly installed products are typically delivered in a timely manner.
- Maintenance cost for purchased middleware can be much less than for home-grown middleware. (The Standish Group states that maintenance costs for an in-house development infrastructure can range

from 20 to 25 percent yearly in addition to the original development outlay. In contrast, vendor-supplied middleware maintenance is typically 15 to 20 percent of the purchase price.)

- Documentation is available and updated with the product (something often lacking in IT shops).

- Testing is completed not only by the vendor, but also by beta, alpha, and production users!

The use of standard middleware products can offer these benefits across applications, resulting in significant time, money, and stress reduction during both development and deployment of applications. For those reasons, the products covered in this book are *not* home-grown creations, but off-the-shelf middleware for your applications.

The Illusive Application Server

Most discussions of Object Monitors include the new marketing buzzword *application server*. To prevent this term from causing you the headaches it has caused us, we want to clarify this overused term.

The term application server is not new, having been used to describe the power of middleware technology for many years. What is new is the way the term is being used today. The simple definition is that an application server provides *services* for *applications*. That is not very useful today, as there are several products now referred to as application servers (including object-to-relational mapping products, Web-based development tools, object databases, relational databases, etc.).

Furthermore, the claim, "My product is an application server," means little as there are several types of products that fall into this category. A more useful description might include some prefix determinants, such as "Web application server" (a product that provides services for Web-based applications) or "legacy application server" (a product that provides services for legacy-based applications).

The point is, as of the writing of this book, a good definition for application server has not been agreed on.

Therefore, this book avoids using it entirely. Readers should be aware that it is very important to get additional information on any product described as an "application server." Middleware is the original application server; it is a separate product that provides *application services* independent of *system* details.

The Middleware Personality

Contrary to popular belief, all middleware is not created equal. Once you know that middleware establishes application infrastructure, it's easy to guess what these standard middleware products are intended to provide. That said, each type of middleware product has been created to provide varying infrastructure properties to an application. Knowing the intended use of each product can help you to accurately choose among products that on the outside may seem closely related. Let's go over the common themes of middleware and define the differences.

All middleware products are intended to provide reusable standard infrastructure for many applications and make use of application programming interfaces (APIs). APIs address how a developer "talks" to the middleware. These APIs are not the same across types of middleware, but are the same for each application that will use the chosen middleware. Middleware treats applications and systems as logical pieces that can be combined into a set of functions. For example, a transaction processing monitor will view a set of actions (retrieve data, update data, perform integrity check, etc.) as part of a transaction. Similarly, ORBs connect multiple objects into a whole application. And though MOMs don't join a series of actions on behalf of an application, they do control the way applications are joined through messages.

The differences among types of middleware lie in the services the products provide, the standards they support, and architecture and use methods in each product. To understand the mind-set of the creators of these products is to understand their intended use. To begin our discovery, we'll start with the earliest entry into the middleware marketplace: the transaction processing monitor, the TPM.

The Transaction Processing Monitor: The Pessimist

> Transaction: a logical group of actions through which a change in the state of the business is made (updating data, exchanging funds, etc.). Transactions adhere to the four ACID properties: Atomicity, Consistency, Isolation, and Durability.

Defining a transaction as a separate unit of work is very important as it is the base from which all other middleware products branch. The goal behind defining a transaction as a separate entity is to bring an infrastructure service to a business level. A transaction is paramount to a company's survival—the result of a transaction is always a direct change in some facet of the business. This is true in every industry and is not limited to the exchange of funds; any change to a company's assets can be protected in the context of a transaction. For example a change in the status of inventory for a manufacturing company, or a change in the availability of seats in a theater alter the state of a business, but do not directly indicate that money has been exchanged.

Transaction processing middleware is designed to protect the integrity of these changes and to provide services for the timely and reliable execution of all processes involved as the result of these changes in a distributed systems environment. It is very important to repeat that middleware is designed to separate the services it provides in a more distributed manner. For example, database products can provide integrity services for direct interaction between client devices and a particular database. The difference lies in the fact that transaction processing products provide these services regardless of the back-end data source. In other words, it doesn't matter where the change is made; the transaction processing monitor will manage these changes at a higher level.

Transaction processing products were created to serve the needs of corporations that live and die by transactions, that could shut down (or at least suffer severe monetary disablement) should the transaction processing application fail. Such companies include banks, airlines, and retail stores. To create a system for these companies, designers of transaction processing products had to imagine the worst fate that could befall a transaction and come up with ways to handle each of them. The result? TP monitors. They manage all of the bad situations imagined by TP system designers.

Transaction processing software is the most mature kind of middleware. The TP monitor market was initially dominated by mainframe class systems with proprietary solutions built directly into the operating system, such as MVS and VSAM. This later gave way to TP products that were removed from the operating system but were still mainframe-based, such as CICS and IMS. The new TP monitor market has changed. Today's TP monitors support a flexible design and open architectures, as seen in Figure 1.3.

But TP monitors remain true to their heritage, They provide a breadth of services required by mission-critical applications. Now, however their use need not be limited to a traditional "transaction processing" applica-

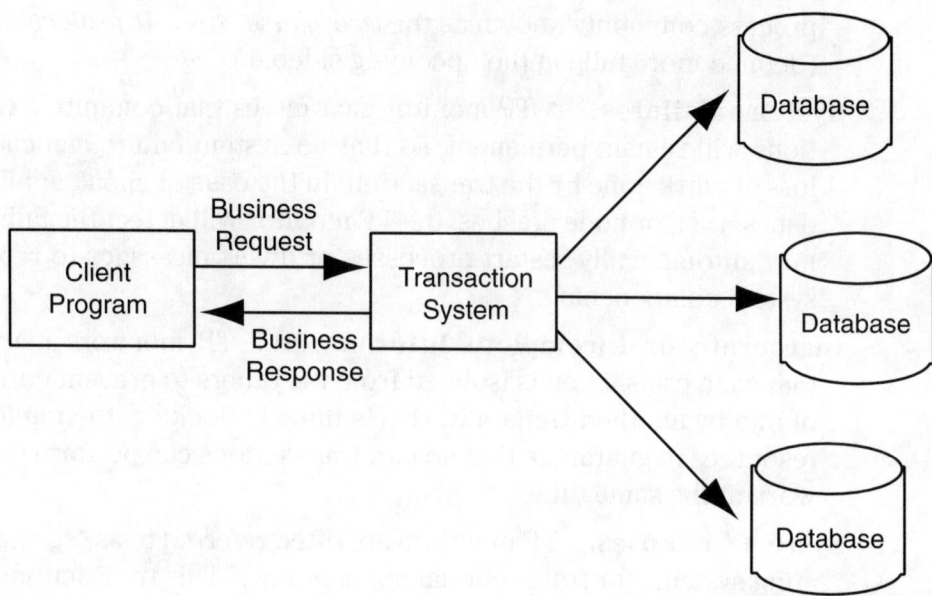

Figure 1.3   The transaction processing monitor.

tion (such as consumer banking or point-of-sale). For example, if we were creating a customer service application, it would include data from a couple of varying RDBMSs, as well as a mainframe system. The users of this application would have to have accurate, up-to-date information in order to do a good job. In addition, the work performed by the customer service representatives could not interfere with other account activity and would have to be available to associated applications to maintain integrity. To fulfill the user's request, a TP monitor would evaluate all the steps necessary as a logical unit of work called a transaction. The TP software would provide a full development, deployment, and management environment for the transactions it was in charge of.

To summarize, the TP monitor protects the transaction in the following situations:

Loss or Corruption.   The TP monitor remains in complete control of the transactions it is in charge of from inception to completion. Should the transaction get lost along the way or somehow become corrupted, the TP monitor will prevent that transaction from completing. All work of the transaction (such as updates to a database) would then be entirely committed or completely undone. And to guard against the TP monitor getting confused, integrity is guaranteed via the voting process commonly known as the *two-phase commit protocol, or 2PC* (defined more fully in the upcoming sidebar).

Systems Failures. A TP monitor guarantees that committed transactions will remain permanent, so that no system failure can cause the loss of work done by the transaction. In the case of client, application, data server, or node crashes, the TP monitor will detect the failure and may automatically restart processes or divert messages to replicated system components.

Inaccurate or Incomplete Information. TP monitors make sure that each transaction is isolated from the others to prevent corruption of one by another. Generally, this is done by locking, then unlocking, resources to guarantee that no two transactions can perform the same work at the same time.

System Collapses. TP monitors are often referred to as "special operating systems for transactional applications." This transactional operating system multiplexes requests of concurrent users of shared resources. (This works in much the same way as a time-sharing operating system, which divides CPU cycles among users that share copies of the same frequently used applications.)

Information from Multiple Disparate Systems. The TP monitor provides facilities that enable the transaction to connect to all types of resources, such as multiple types of databases, mainframe systems, and so on. All of the resources required by the transaction are under the control of the transaction management features of the TP monitor, thereby ensuring a consistent image of data across systems.

Transaction processing monitors offer a wealth of application functionality, and should be considered a necessity for transactional business-critical applications. This is proven middleware that has advanced over the years into the ultimate application service provider. The advanced application features of a TP monitor are essential for the new computing models of the Internet age.

But because these products were created prior to the object era, changes to the products must occur to support emerging development models. Even more crucial, their use is somewhat confined to new or redeveloped applications, due to the nature of introducing a TP monitor. Though it is possible to take advantage of the features of a TP system for existing applications, this often requires a major reengineering effort. Therefore, a transaction processing monitor should be incorporated into the application at time of development, not after the process.

2PC and the All-or-Nothing Myth

The two-phase commit (2PC) protocol enables a single transaction to update multiple resource managers while guaranteeing integrity. The 2PC ensures that all participants in the transactional unit either all agree or all abort, through a democratic voting system.

The transaction manager (a central element of the TP monitor) coordinates the 2PC protocol by starting, receiving, and reviewing protocol messages either through message interchange with child transaction managers and/or directly with the participating resource managers. (Note: the resource manager controls the actual resource; for example, an RDBMS.)

This voting process is achieved in two phases (hence the name). In phase 1, the parent (or coordinating) transaction manager polls all participants about the intent to commit. If all the child TMs and RMs vote affirmative, the parent TM commits the transaction. In phase 2, the parent TM informs all children that the transaction has been committed. The children then can move on to other tasks. However, should the result of the initial vote result in a negative reaction by any of the children, all participants are told to "roll back" the results in phase 2.

With the parent TM remaining in control of all the activity over a network, the application can readily access and update many resource managers and manage their computation. This action relieves the programmer of having to develop the complex code associated with implementing custom compensating or coordinating logic.

One of the great myths surrounding the 2PC protocol is the "all-or-nothing" attribute, the idea that should a resource be unavailable the transaction will fail resulting in the loss of business. In practice, the two-phase commit protocol allows for the commitment of transactions even when a resource is unavailable. This is performed through a logical agent mechanism representing a resource (known as a *heuristic commit*). If a resource is unavailable, using the agent as a communication point for the parent TM allows the business transaction to be completed in its absence.

Message-Oriented Middleware: The Gossips

> Message: A sequence of bytes, which represent a unit of work (such as a database record update or sound and video images, etc.) to the applications that send and receive it.

Every application has good information to share with other applications, and often it is crucial to performing a business task. An example might be the need to send a message from an ordering system to an inventory system to protect against a customer's demand not being met by supply. It bears repeating that in the context of a MOM middleware product, this need to share information among applications is regardless of the application that sends and receives it. In a typical application, a developer may include code that executes a set of calls to another, complementary, application. When the need to share information between two existing applications is an afterthought, many companies create proprietary ways of linking information between the two systems. In contrast, MOM products provide this functionality as a separate process, not as part of a particular application. Should a company decide to change the way two or more applications communicate, it is not necessary to change the actual code of the application or the proprietary interfaces; instead, the same messaging structure can be used for every application.

This type of middleware operates under the premise that information should be able to be shared in a variety of ways. MOM products provide services for sending messages between applications. These messages can be guaranteed, queued, broadcast, published and subscribed to, and deferred. In fact, just about any type of application-to-application interaction can be achieved through the use of message-oriented middleware products. MOMs also provide a separation of application from communication protocol, allowing interoperability across heterogeneous environments, as shown in Figure 1.4. This is possible through the use of common APIs designed to mask protocol differences from programmers and applications.

Several types of message-oriented middleware products are available on the market today, including message passing, message queuing, message replication, broadcast, and publish and subscribe. Depending on the level of message features required, MOM products can range from extremely easy to use (with a simple-to-follow API and easy-to-remember rules for engagement) to extremely difficult (elaborate APIs with literally hundreds of complex rules). Let's say that you are creating an Internet banking application that includes an electronic customer service option. Using this service, the customer can change information about his or her account, such as update their mailing address. Though this notification must be delivered, the customer does not require an immediate reply. Instead, he or she may want to move on to another area of the site and perform a different type of transaction. So rather than make the customer wait for a reply, the service can inform the customer that an e-mail notification will be sent to acknowledge the change. The MOM in this application would guarantee message delivery and allow the customer to move on to other tasks. Once the change has been made,

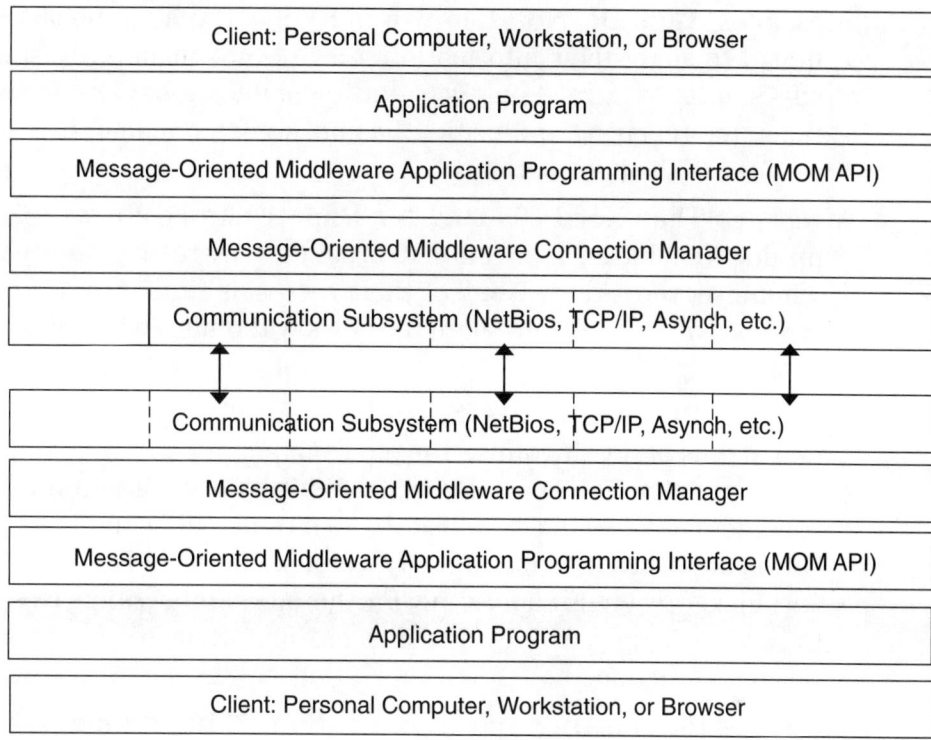

Figure 1.4   Base message-oriented middleware function.

the MOM product could be configured to send a message to another application prompting the creation of the customer's e-mail notification.

Because MOM messages are sent and responded to at an application level, these interactions can occur over varying types of protocols and systems, and may be location-transparent. Creators of MOM products have considered all the possible ways an application should or could share information and have attempted to account for them. And though not all products are the same, the following application communication needs may be provided for by MOM software:

Messages That Require a Reply.   MOM products aren't necessarily in a rush. They allow for an application to continue without requiring an immediate response to every query. This is contrary to a traditional application messaging structure that requires a response to every query before continuing. The MOM product will insert a piece of code as a placeholder, thereby permitting the continuation of work; when a message arrives, the piece of code is executed with the response (in "MOM-speak," this is the callback).

Messages That Do Not Require a Reply. Some applications just intend to share their information; they do not require a response at all—similar to a read-only system for applications. For such situations, the receiving application has no way to respond; it is just the receiver of the information.

Messages That Need Sharing for Undetermined Reasons. MOM products enable an application to broadcast interesting information to whomever they want. Think of this process as similar to news broadcasting, where reporters share the news without knowing exactly who is receiving it.

Messages Broadcast to a Specific Type of Application. MOMs may act as a clearinghouse for publishers and subscribers based on subject matter. For example, applications that require notification on specific trade events can subscribe to a trade publisher, whose application publishes information only to subscribers—this is *narrowcasting*, in contrast to broadcasting. Furthermore, subscribers may access only those application events that are important to their particular business function.

Messages Shared Only in the Event Something Happens. MOMs allow applications to be selective. Users can configure a MOM product to react only in the event something occurs, as in our previous example, where once the address information is updated, the coordinating application prompts the e-mail notification service.

All Messages Must Have Guaranteed Delivery. MOMs often will guarantee that messages will be delivered. And if the resource is unavailable at time of delivery, some MOM products hold the messages in a queue until the resource is available, as indicated in Figure 1.5.

In general, most message-oriented middleware products minimally affect the existing application and therefore can be used with existing or new applications. (The exception to this rule is messaging software designed for high availability through message replication, which can be extremely intrusive to the application.)

MOM products were originally created to solve the problem of creating applications without requiring knowledge of underlying transport or communication protocols. And although this is still MOM's primary function, due to the wide use of TCP/IP, the solution is less important today. Now a MOM product is typically brought into a company for the asynchronous guaranteed message delivery or advanced messaging services

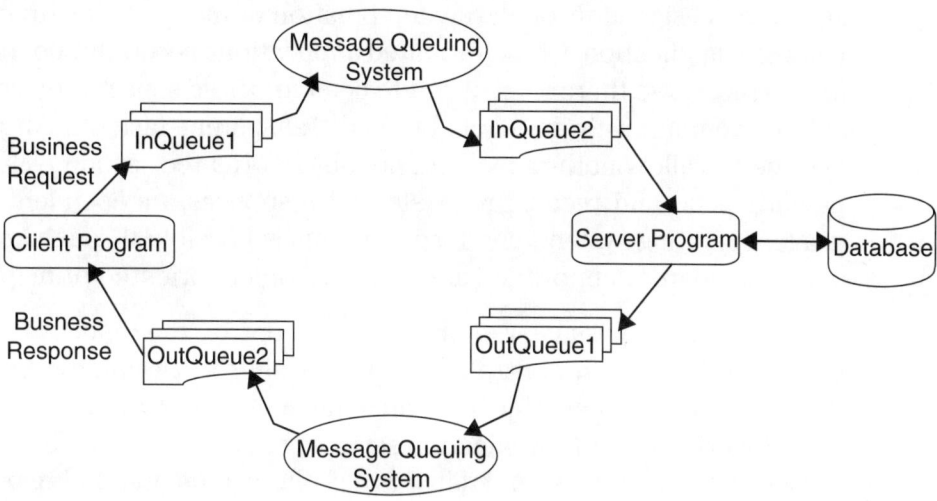

Figure 1.5　Message queuing system.

they provide. While this functionality is important, obviously it is not recommended nor required for every application. Some messages between applications must be delivered immediately (before further processing), as in changes in status of the customer's checking or savings account balance.

In addition to MOM products' limited appeal, a problem with the technology has been a complete lack of standards among the available products. Consortiums have been formed to promote the use of messaging products, but to date none offers standards enabling the various products to work together. Therefore, only applications taking advantage of the same MOM product are interoperable. Consequently, companies that use MOM products become fairly dependent on the particular vendor they have chosen. Using a replacement is a difficult (sometimes impossible) and time-consuming option.

The Object Request Brokers: The Optimist

> Object: A logical self-contained entity containing both data and operations, which can be performed on said data. Objects support the notions of inheritance, encapsulation, and polymorphism.

If TP monitors were created for the pessimist, ORBs were created for the optimist. They were designed for those who follow the adage "Don't tell me how you do it, just get it done." It is a given in the ORB "world" that applications should be massively distributed; in other words, applications should be designed through the combination of many objects to create a complete application. Object-oriented applications naturally separate into logical pieces, so there is an absolute need for these separate pieces to be able to communicate in a reliable and transparent fashion. An ORB is designed to allow both object and nonobject-oriented resources to transparently send and receive requests and responses, independent of language, operating system, and location. This is possible through an ORB's object standards support and adherence to object-oriented principles.

The ORB is very passive; rather than take control, the object initiating a request is the one in control. The ORB is simply the middle broker. It takes the request of an object, locates the appropriate target object (perhaps throwing in some application services requested by the first object), passes off the response, and delivers a reply, as indicated in Figure 1.6.

The benefits of an ORB can be summed up in two words: *reuse* and *abstraction*. The ORB allows a company to use extant code for one application in another simply by calling its name. For example, a call center application may share code written for a customer service application. Through the ORB's abstraction layer, this code can be shared whether the application is written in the same language, resides on the same type of system, or is object-oriented. To do so, ORBs follow these rules of engagement:

1. *All objects must be able to communicate with each other.* This is one of the most important assets an ORB can offer, the separation of interface from implementation. All the pieces of an ORB's world communi-

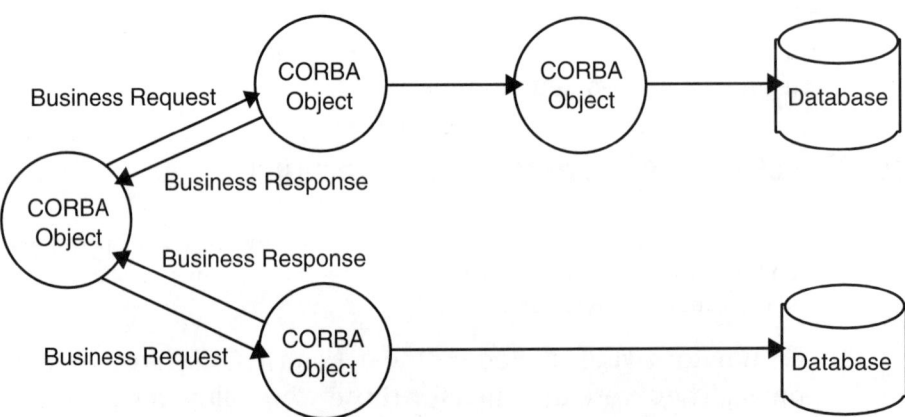

Figure 1.6 The object request broker.

cate through the same interface language. Likewise, an ORB can communicate with all these pieces using the same communication mechanism. It is unnecessary that the ORB know how the object will perform its function; it is only necessary that the function is able to be called in a language the ORB understands (that is, the same interface).

2. *Any system, application, protocol, or process should be able to communicate with an object.* This notion of interface versus implementation continues beyond the object world. A nonobject application can be covered in the interface familiar to the ORB and suddenly become part of the ORB's world. In addition, the ORB always communicates with these resources in the same way (via the same protocol).

3. *Anything that can be reused, should be.* Like objects themselves, ORBs support reuse (the type of reuse available varies according to object model and architecture standards, as detailed in the following chapter). This "take it where you can get it" attitude allows users of an ORB to expand the notion of reusing application infrastructure beyond the actual middleware functions to business, presentation, and data access code.

4. *All objects have the right to privacy.* Being object-oriented, the ORB operates under the notion of encapsulation. Similar to isolation for transactions, encapsulation guards against the corruption of objects by other objects and by the ORB itself.

5. *An object invoked by the same method name, need not react the same.* The object technology notion of polymorphism extends to the ORB. Since the ORB holds object location information, communication among objects is not limited to unique messages for each object. For example, the message: "retrieve account information" can be sent to both a checking account and savings account object each responding with different information. The ORB couldn't care less.

6. *Each object has the right to choose its own services.* An ORB allows users to define which extra services the object may require based on the action being executed. For example, an interaction between objects that will result in the alteration of data would take advantage of the ORB's transaction and security services, whereas a read-only interaction (the object only needs to display the data) would not require the management control a transaction service provides, but would rather save the processing time. ORBs allow for this service choice at an object-to-object level.

An object request broker offers many benefits to the user, not the least of which is tremendous interoperability. In addition, an ORB takes the value of object technology and broadens both the scope and appeal to allow for increased reuse potential. So, what's the downside? Objects are anarchistic by nature, and the ORB is no different. The good news is that this allows for an amazing degree of flexibility to the object developer and the user. The bad news is that there is no central point of control when one is required. The laissez-faire attitude of an ORB, while beneficial at times, opens the doors to possible data corruption, loss of work, and security loopholes.

Overlap of Middleware Products

As we reach the end of this chapter, you may be wondering what causes all the confusion over middleware products. Simply, the differences among products are not as cut and dried as they may appear. Many middleware products offer overlapping services, causing a quandary, because upon first glance, the products appear to be providing the same functionality. The confusion can be divided into three factors: transaction, messaging, and object.

The Transaction Factor

Many messaging products provide transaction messaging as part of their plethora of services. What may not be instantly apparent, however, is that this feature is designed to work with a TP monitor, and is not a standalone transaction processing product. Used as a standalone product, the transactional messaging services of a MOM will help to guarantee consistency among messages, but they are still messages, not transactions.

In addition, many ORB providers now offer what is known as an *object transaction service (OTS)*. The addition of an OTS to an ORB allows for the use of the 2PC protocol to ensure transactional integrity. Often this is provided through a segment of an existing TP monitor, the transaction manager. However, there is much more to a TP monitor than the transaction manager, which only accounts for about 10 percent of a monitor's code; and its use is limited to roughly 15 to 20 percent of the applications that use a TP monitor. The 2PC does not help with availability attributes or with the multiplexing of requests, nor does it provide access to multiple systems and load balancing of these interactions.

The Messaging Factor

TP monitors can perform messaging that is part of a transaction; this is referred to as *transactional messaging*. The messaging the TP monitor performs is done in the context of the transaction for which the product is trying to provide service. One example of this is the queuing of transactional messages to resources that were unavailable at commencement. It's important to note that this TP messaging is not separate from the transaction; the messaging is part of the transactional unit of work. MOM messaging is removed from the transaction context and acts alone.

Likewise, ORB providers are beginning to offer advanced messaging among objects. An important distinction today, however, is that this messaging power (delivered as a feature of the ORB) is not to the extent as that of a MOM. This messaging may include asynchronous delivery (no need to wait for a reply) but generally it does not include a guarantee of delivery, nor does it include multiple methods for deliveries (i.e., publish and subscribe or broadcast).

The Object Factor

TP monitors are beginning to emerge with "object-aware" interfaces. This simply means that a programmer can write to the TP monitor in an object-oriented (OO) language, and may or may not be able to invoke reusable object classes to create the application. However, the TPM does not provide the same level of object services that an ORB does, nor does it support the object principles that enable wide-scale reuse in a transparent fashion.

MOM products that offer an OO interface are basically in the same situation. This, coupled with the usual lack of support for ORB standards, diminishes their value as a suitable replacement for an ORB. At the time of this writing, work is being conducted in the MOM world for using a standards-based "MOM-style" transport mechanism for object-to-object communication. This will be offered initially as an alternative transport layer in place of a traditional ORB synchronous communication model.

Up Next

TPMs, MOMs, and ORBs each provides functionality important to different types of applications, thus, taking advantage of multiple middleware products is often appropriate. Because each product was designed to meet a specific type of application need, none of the products can convincingly be swapped for another. In addition, functional differences, architecture variations, and use methods make the products difficult to use together. This, combined with multiple standards (or, in the case of MOMs, no standards) among the different products creates havoc for developers who want to combine application services at an infrastructure level.

As we showed in the examples in this chapter, an object-oriented customer service application can provide a great deal of reuse potential to a call center application (provided by the ORB), and these applications could be made available to Internet banking applications as well. All three applications may have instances where messaging among the applications must go beyond immediate request/reply (provided by the MOM). In addition, any changes to the state of the business must be protected against integrity corruption (the TP monitor).

Prior to the introduction of the Object Monitor, a customer would need to create his or her own "universal middleware," scale down the services of the application, or attempt a custom integration/cooperation among multiple middleware products (a nontrivial task). The Object Monitor is intended to provide a better solution. Knowing how this has been done and how to take advantage of these new products is the purpose of this book. It is our intent to show what Object Monitors, the new breed of middleware, provide and how to take advantage of their functionality. Certainly these new products, features, and functions will be enhanced over the years as products mature, but the architecture of the products will remain the same, so join us as we examine the architecture of each product and inform you on how best to take advantage of them.

The Standards Divide: CORBA versus DCOM

M aking use of a separate product—middleware—to provide a variety of services for many applications can offer a long list of benefits, as covered in Chapter 1, but these services must be transparent to system details. Unfortunately, each of the middleware options we've covered so far has its own way of handling this layer of transparency. Fortunately, Object Monitors adhere to industry middleware standards.

The standards covered in this chapter establish a common method for vendors to deliver products; these standards also directly impact the decision-making process, as well. Remember that middleware is a separate process designed to provide the *infrastructure service link* between clients and servers in a distributed system. But it cannot provide a wide breadth of services for a company unless it is first able to communicate with the many varieties of front-end clients and back-end data sources a company may use. Without this capability, the application services that middleware can provide are worthless.

This is not to say that all is perfect in the world of Object Monitor standards. A conflict over the best way for this interoperability to be achieved separates these products into two camps: the Object Management Group's (OMG) Common Object Request Broker Architecture (CORBA) and Microsoft's Distributed Component Object Model (DCOM). In this chapter, we'll explore the world of object architecture standards and the important role they play in the Object Monitor market. You'll learn the way CORBA and DCOM differ on a variety of levels, from a high-level architecture view to a developer mind-set.

The Value of Object Architecture Standards

For most companies, the single-system environment is a distant memory. Today, new operating systems, communication protocols, front ends, databases, and the like are part of the corporate systems' architecture. And with the recent drive in development shops toward the object-oriented programming model, enabling pieces of an application in the form of objects or components to work together is now a necessity. Making all these disparate systems work together has become nothing less than an art form. Standards are the media enabling the practice of this art.

As just mentioned, there are two competing standards that affect the Object Monitor product your company will choose: the Object Management Group's Common Object Request Broker Architecture (CORBA) and Microsoft Corporation's Distributed Component Object Model (DCOM).

Understanding Object Interoperability

Object interoperability standards define common interfaces and invocation strategies for the way the various pieces of your application architecture will work together. This interoperability can be thought of as the glue that combines your code elements into a real business application. Understanding the "glue" choices available to you is a necessary step in determining how well suited your company is for the introduction of an Object Monitor. For example, does your company have the right talent pool, or will you need to bring in outside help or hire new employees? Do you know how each standard works? There are four ways to evaluate this glue. Ask yourself:

- What does the glue look like?
- How does the glue work?
- What's the glue made of?
- How is the glue applied?

Depending on your job description, you may care only about the answers to the first three questions. But those of you involved in "applying the glue"

Is There a Third Standard?

At first glance, it appears JavaSoft's Enterprise JavaBean (EJB) is another competing architecture standard. This is both true and false. True, EJB is designed to provide much of the same benefits that both CORBA and DCOM are positioned for. However, the key difference is that EJB is designed for communication among multiple *Java-only* applications, and does not promote the ability for multilanguage interactions. To provide cross-language functionality, EJB works with CORBA.

As defined by JavaSoft, "JavaBean is a component model for the visual construction of reusable client-side applications in Java." An Enterprise JavaBean (EJB) is designed to provide this "visual contruction of reusable Java applications" for the server-side as well. This includes Java application services and facilities for distibuted Java object communication.

JavaSoft defines the Enterprise JavaBean as "a cross-platform component architecture for the development and deployment of multitier, distributed, scalable, object-oriented Java applications."

At the time of this writing, EJB is a fairly new standard with no implementations available. It is expected in the future that support for JavaBeans will be provided by multiple vendors. In fact, the majority of vendors covered in this book plan to provide some level of support for the EJB model. However, it is important to point out that none of the products covered in this book plans to exclude CORBA or DCOM in favor of the EJB standard; EJB will be used as a third standard that works with the products' main object architecture support (CORBA or DCOM).

It is unclear currently how Microsoft and its DCOM model will support the EJB specifications; in contrast, many CORBA vendors have drawn road maps for future support, once the specifications are more clearly defined. Support for Enterprise JavaBeans in addition to CORBA standards will give users easier portability of applications across operating systems. Therefore, for many corporations, the combination of CORBA and Enterprise JavaBeans will be a powerful one.

To track the support of the products covered in this book for the full EJB specifications check the book's companion Web site at wiley.com/compbooks/boucher.

will need the answers to all four questions. To help answer these important questions, we've included comparison tables for easy reference. Feel free to skip through the parts that do not apply to your situation.

What the Glue Looks Like

From the perspective of a high-level, "power," user or a programmer in charge of combining objects, there are no apparent differences in how to use either CORBA or DCOM, the "glue" options. Both models follow the same logical steps.

1. Find the object.
2. Start the object.
3. Connect to the right target object.
4. Issue a request.
5. Receive a reply.

At this level, neither the user nor the programmer will notice any significant difference between the options. Both CORBA and DCOM provide facilities to locate objects, communicate with other objects, and issue and receive responses.

The only noticeable difference at this stage would be the client machine the user or programmer is using. At the time of this writing both CORBA and DCOM support all the flavors of Windows, as well as Apple machines, though only CORBA supports multiple flavors of UNIX and mainframe clients (DCOM does support UNIX on a limited basis through a third-party partner, Software AG). Depending on the client reach of your application, if you're considering DCOM, please check current client support.

How the Glue Works

If you are fixing a broken vase, and are sure you have all the pieces, you know they will fit together. In contrast, in the object world, we often must piece together objects that have never been part of the same whole application. If the objects are written in the same language and run on the same machine, it's easy to make all the pieces fit. But in a distributed object world, objects may never have been part of a whole application, and they may live on different systems and communicate in different languages.

So, how do we fix this problem? The solution is in the separation of interface (how the object communicates with others) from implementation (how the object performs its job). This is done using an Interface Definition Language (IDL). An IDL provides a nice covering for our objects to make them appear the same, or at least as pieces of a whole application, as seen in Figure 2.1.

Practically speaking, an IDL could be likened to a highly sophisticated header file. This header file is written in the same language (the IDL) and includes information about which tasks the object can perform and how to make the object perform these tasks (in object speak, how to *invoke*

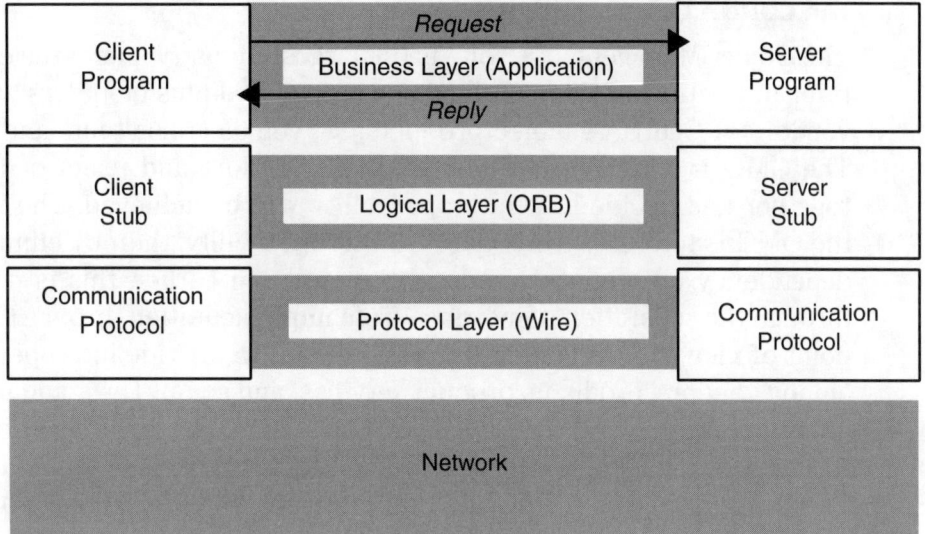

Figure 2.1   Standards-based object communication.

the object's services). This is where DCOM and CORBA part ways. Both have their own version of IDL: Microsoft's is MIDL and OMG's is CORBA IDL. You can begin to see what this means for an enterprise of objects: The goal of IDL is to mask the differences between objects, but there are two different "masks" to choose from. Trying to combine multiple objects with different masks is the fastest way to get a migraine.

Furthermore, these look-alike objects also need to be able to talk to each other across a network. Here again, CORBA and DCOM have a difference of opinion. The OMG camp uses a CORBA Object Request Broker (CORBA ORB), and Microsoft uses its DCOM product. Multiple CORBA ORBs communicate via a standard communications protocol known as the Internet Inter-ORB Protocol (IIOP); Microsoft uses the DCOM protocol. (Under the covers, EJB uses its own standard communication for Java-to-Java communication called Remote Method Invocation (RMI). However, for cross-language applications, EJB supports CORBA's IIOP.)

The difference from a high-level corporate architecture point of view (beyond the fact that these two solutions use different standards) is mainly political: One of standards by committee versus a single-vendor solution. We'll attempt to tell both sides of the story and leave it to you to decide which camp you want to join.

The CORBA Camp

The Object Management Group is the largest industry standards consortium, at the time of this writing composed of 800-plus members who are vendors of CORBA-enabled products, as well as consultants and users. The OMG is a forum in which multiple vendors and users can come together and decide how interoperability will be achieved. The goal of the OMG is to create a standard of interoperability, thereby eliminating dependency on any one vendor. As mentioned earlier, this is possible through the separation of interface from implementation. From a CORBA point of view, object standards were created to provide interoperability among vendors' products, product services, and so on. The standards the group sets go beyond the CORBA IDL and CORBA communication protocols; they also define how services are to be invoked. This will lead us to our common goal of mixing and matching "best of breed" software based on the business task of each application.

However, CORBA standards and products were around for several years before Microsoft created DCOM, making them more mature and, therefore, more proven. In the past, the OMG has avoided problems with other standards consortia in two ways: standards were created *before* the products (not in an attempt to standardize already popular products), and it does not sell any product to achieve the interoperability goal. Object architecture standards are about more than bringing in a new product; they're about protecting your company from dependency on one vendor's solution. CORBA proponents believe that true interoperability can be achieved, and that the OMG is making it happen.

The Microsoft Camp

Object standards are about enabling objects to communicate in a standard fashion, and Microsoft provides this through COM/DCOM. And though CORBA started work on object architectures before Microsoft, by eliminating a voting process, Microsoft can deliver new products and product functionality faster.

DCOM is at its best when combined with MS middleware (which you'll learn about in the Microsoft Transaction Server (MTS) chapter). The services are provided through other Microsoft products such as MTS, Microsoft Message Queuing (MSMQ), and MSCS clustering technology. The Microsoft operating system, NT, enables all of this functionality in one product, thereby increasing performance and allowing for the delivery of new services cheaper and faster.

CORBA is not vendor-independent, users become dependent on the CORBA vendor they choose. Despite the hype, interoperability among CORBA ORB vendors is not as easy as it seems. Like DCOM, CORBA is at its best when combined with services, but these services are proprietary to the CORBA ORB vendor and are not interoperable. Trying to avoid lock in by choosing CORBA products will not work; you'll just get locked into your ORB vendor.

Microsoft proponents believe that true interoperability is a dream that won't come true. They prefer to use a product that can be enhanced faster and delivered cheaper. That product is available from Microsoft.

The Authors' Camp

Like most of our counterparts in the middleware world, we have argued frequently over the positions of the two camps. But for the sake of our readers, we felt we had to come to an agreement. It is this: Though we understand Microsoft's position and give credit to the company's compelling viewpoint, we are nevertheless partial to CORBA. Why? Simply because we believe standards are tremendously important, in particular when they relate to infrastructure software.

We also believe that object architectures are designed to become corporatewide standards for how applications, services, programming languages, systems, and protocols talk to each other. For this reason, we contend that no company should put all its eggs (or in this case, objects) in one vendor's basket.

Being able to mix and match off-the-shelf with in-house-created objects/components can bring tremendous benefits to the user. Ask yourself why you should accept the security service your corporate vendor is providing, rather than choose the best service for your application needs? This is a major difference between DCOM and CORBA: DCOM may run on platforms other than NT (though we are skeptical this will be true in the long run), but the services will not. We believe this dependency on Microsoft will go beyond the object architecture. DCOM and its services (provided by MTS, MSMQ, and Wolfpack) are available only for the NT operating system. Therefore, companies using DCOM must be committed not only to the Microsoft object "standard" but to an operating system as well. No doubt in time this will also extend to Microsoft-only databases, development tools, and so on. This limits a company's choice to Microsoft-only solutions, which essentially means settling for one vendor's idea of how a company's infrastructure should be run. This is dangerous at best.

True, CORBA ORBs from different vendors have not yet reached the "holy grail" of interoperability, but they do work together, if not always easily. The bigger problem remains with the services, which are often more proprietary than open. But this dependency is still limited to the ORB vendor services, not beyond. CORBA ORBs are not tied to any operating system, and can run on a wide range of platforms. In addition, advancements are being made to the CORBA standards on an ongoing basis in the effort to achieve interoperability, a significant advantage to having a large standards consortium that includes users as well as vendors.

That said, it is important to have two competing standards. Probably, Microsoft's DCOM is the best thing that could happen to the OMG's CORBA standard, and vice versa, because competition prompts vendors to continually enhance their offerings and fuels innovation, which in turn makes better products available for the entire user community. And if you happen to be more comfortable on the Microsoft side fence, rest assured that this book examines the MTS option fairly.

What the Glue Is Made of

CORBA and DCOM both rely on a remote procedure call (RPC) method of communication, meaning this architecture consists of three logical layers. We'll explain the generic RPC method first, then show how both CORBA and DCOM handle communication.

At a high level, our applications will use an application programming interface (API) to invoke the communication between applications or objects. This layer of the RPC architecture defines how a programmer will call the application it's trying to reach. At the second level, the RPC model uses a logical connection to its target. This layer of the architecture includes services for the packaging and conversion of parameters and different sizes of integers across systems. The RPC mechanism creates what are typically referred to as *stubs*, to which the programmer will logically connect through the APIs.

Client stubs and server stubs communicate via the next logical layer, that is, the communication protocol the RPC model will use. The RPC service handles details associated with how a message will be sent from one stub to another, such as how to negotiate between different wire protocols, directory services, operating systems, languages, and so on. The RPC's communication protocol is a layer above the wire protocol used through the systems architecture (e.g., TCP/IP, SNA LU6.2, etc.).

CORBA and DCOM both offer requests and replies based on the same communication model (RPC), but each model uses different pieces (Figure 2.2). In CORBA, the programmer uses the CORBA IDL to call the stubs. (Note: In the CORBA lexicon, client stubs are called stubs, server stubs are called skeletons). The CORBA implementation repository (IR) contains all the required information about object interfaces. The client stub then links to a CORBA library, uses the server-side CORBA library known as the Basic Object Adapter (BOA), handles conversion, and passes requests off to the server skeleton, which then handles the passing of the request to the target server object.

In contrast, DCOM uses the Windows Registry (instead of the IR), with client and server stubs linking to DCOM libraries (see Figure 2.3). DCOM uses what is called a Service Control Manager (SCM). Table 2.1

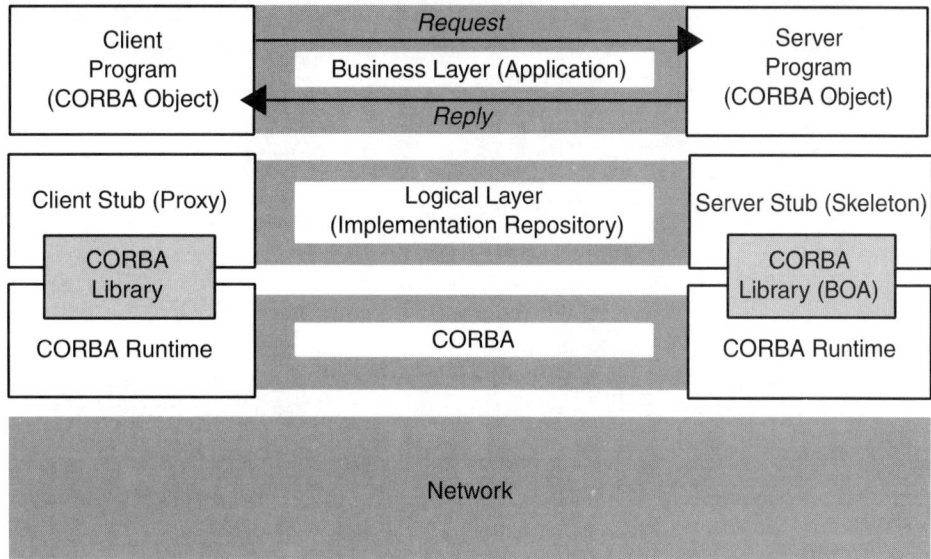

Figure 2.2 CORBA communication model.

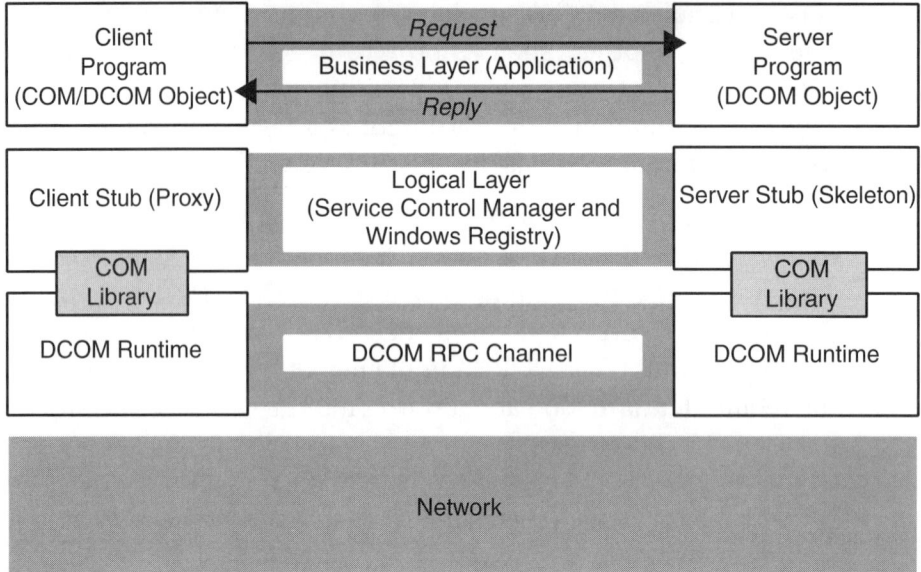

Figure 2.3 DCOM communication model.

gives a comparison of CORBA and DCOM from an application architecture perspective.

Table 2.1 Application Architecture*

FEATURE	DCOM	CORBA
Architecture paradigm	Component-based programming.	Component-based programming.
Platform support	Windows, Apple, and limited UNIX support through third-party vendor (Software AG).	Windows, Apple, and multiple UNIX platforms. Some mainframe implementations available through select vendors.
Access to component	Via external interface with properties accessible through methods.	Via external interface and by direct access of IDL-defined attributes.
Component location**	Location-independent.† In current release, this is heavily based on static definitions in Windows Registry (both on a client and on a server).	Location-independent. Static and dynamic definitions available from all vendors.
Interoperability	Only with DCOM. Bridges between DCOM and IIOP are available through some CORBA ORB vendors.	With any IIOP-based CORBA implementations; some DCOM interoperability available through CORBA vendors.

Table 2.1 *(Continued)*

FEATURE	DCOM	CORBA
Deployment	In current release, each client machine must know server object location (by customizing the Registry).	No specific info on client site required. CORBA has an Implementation Repository plus forthcoming CORBA component XML-based deployment description.
Runtime management	Allows reference counting and component pinging.	No specific runtime management facilities defined by specifications. Each CORBA ORB vendor has its own tricks.
Security	Supports access control lists on COM components. For a finer level of security, DCOM provides programmable APIs.	Based on CORBA security specs; defines a variety of security options (ranked via levels by support). All vendors provide some level of security; however, implementations vary among CORBA vendors.
Support for multithreading	Limited; needs a lot of hand-written code for controlling threads. When used with MTS, much more control over threads can be achieved.	Vendor-specific (not addressed by standards); however, nature of CORBA model allows for three forms of multithreaded servers: pool of threads when all threads from pool shared by incoming calls; thread per client, where thread is created for each active client; thread per object, where thread is created for each object.
Load balancing	Not in DCOM. Will be available through MTS.	Exists primitively in CORBA implementations. More advanced implementation could be implemented on a top of Trading Service or through the use of a CORBA Object Monitor.
Location management	Allows only static location management based on client and server registries.	Trading service allows location management based on policies (rules). Currently not available from most vendors or in very primitive format. (Many vendors offer proprietary solutions.)
Directory services	Currently based on Windows Registry. Future releases will be based on Active Directory.	Naming services defined and available from CORBA vendors.

Continues

Table 2.1 Application Architecture* *(Continued)*

FEATURE	DCOM	CORBA
Asynchronous communication	DCE-type one-way calls. Potential integration with Microsoft's MOM product, MSMQ, available in the near future.	One-way calls. CORBA messaging RFP currently in progress. Some vendors provide primitive functionality.
Publish/subscribe mechanism	Not available, but could be be implemented using one-way calls. Support may be forthcoming through integration with MSMQ.	Event Service allows easy implementation of publish/ subscribe architecture. Becoming widely available from CORBA ORB vendors or through relationships with third parties.

* The information in this table, current at the time of this writing, is subject to change.

** Both technologies from an architecture perspective are location-independent; however, they are implemented in different ways and using different techniques. Microsoft plans more dynamic component location features with the release of NT 5.0.

† Mechanism for resolving initial object reference needs to be put into place.

How to Apply the Glue

CORBA and DCOM differ in how a programmer makes the objects ready to take advantage of the architecture standard—how to apply the glue.

This is not a programming book, so we examine the differences from an experience perspective, describing how difficult each model will be to implement. For IT executives, this is important for determining to which architecture model current in-house staff is better suited; for programmers, this is important for determining which model better coordinates to past experience.

The CORBA standard is based on a "pure" object model, and therefore follows the procedures of a natural object-oriented language such as C++, Smalltalk, or Java. The CORBA IDL is a natural for experienced programmers of OO languages, particularly those who program on a UNIX platform. Objects can inherit the properties of any other class and raise exceptions where necessary. In contrast, the DCOM IDL is a derivative of DCE IDL with syntax similar to C. Therefore, DCOM is a more natural choice for C programmers and those with DCE experience. In addition, users of products that incorporate Microsoft desktop component models (OLE, ActiveX, COM), such as those in Microsoft's Visual Basic development tools, will respond more easily to DCOM.

The differences between the DCE IDL and DCOM IDL are in the numerous extensions that Microsoft has added to support component-based programming. DCOM is based on Microsoft's COM object model, thus DCOM objects can inherit the interfaces of other DCOM objects as defined via MIDL (Microsoft IDL) constructs.

At an object model level, CORBA and DCOM vary as outlined in Table 2.2. And because of these different approaches to object/component development, the steps a programmer follows when using the products are slightly different, although they result in the same outcome, allowing distributed objects to communicate.

The steps a programmer takes when creating a CORBA interface are:

1. Define interface in the CORBA IDL.
2. Generate stub.
3. Derive and implement server skeleton through inheritance.
4. Invoke main server program to create a new object and notify the ORB.
5. Client binds to remote object. It can then make requests and receive responses.

The steps a programmer takes when creating a DCOM interface are:

1. Define interface in the MIDL.
2. Generate proxy/stub and implement server through class factory.
3. Take care of reference counting.
4. Invoke main server program to create a new class factory, which signals an event and waits until object gets deleted by COM library.
5. Invoke client to create interface pointer through an instance of a DCOM class, then query for additional interfaces.
6. Exchange requests and responses are through interface pointers.

Both models and architectures are designed to support the notions of component- or object-based programming, so the features provided by these two options are similar in service but differ in implementation and availability. Table 2.3 lists their implementation differences.

Table 2.2   Object Approach

FEATURE	DCOM	CORBA
Interface inheritance	Achieved through interfaces grouped together; COM model.	Similar to C++ type of inheritance.
Multiple interface inheritance	Not supported.	Supported.
Exceptions	None. Each call returns HRESULT, the value of which must be interpreted by client programmer.	Limited functionality compared to C++.
Attributes in IDL	None.	Accessible similar to attributes of C++ class.

Table 2.3   Programming Languages and Concepts*

FEATURE	DCOM	CORBA
Client languages	C++, Java, OLE-enabled tools, COBOL.	C, C++, Java, OLE-enabled tools, COBOL, Smalltalk, and ADA (varies among vendors).
Implementation-languages (for server side)	Language-independent. Components written using different languages could be mixed and matched even within a single server process. Currently supports C++, Java, Visual Basic and COBOL.	Language-independent. Components written in different language can communicate with each other but cannot reside in the same address space (on the same server). C++ and Java primarily used for server implementation.**
Programming paradigm	Reflects COM's binary architecture, based on class object paradigm (metaclass).	Similar to C++ programming paradigm.
IDL	MIDL. Based on DCE IDL(syntax similar to C) with numerous extensions to support component-based programming.	CORBA IDL with OO features; very similar to C++.
Component paradigm	Set of DCOM interfaces grouped together. Grouping/packaging could be done in very dynamic way.	Allows for static component definition. No grouping allowed in current CORBA. Component RFP, in progress, probably will be very similar to DCOM grouped mechanism.

Table 2.3   *(Continued)*

FEATURE	DCOM	CORBA
Portability	Not an issue.	OMG standards define a portable object adapter (POA) instead of existing basic object adapter (BOA). Support of this standard will increase portability among CORBA implementations.

*The standards listed in this table are part of an evolving process, and thus subject to change.

**Official mapping exists for C, C++, Smalltalk, Ada, Cobol and Java. Availability varies among vendors.

Up Next

In Object Monitor technology, object architecture standards are fundamentally important; they define how all the objects and nonobject resources of the Object Monitor's world will communicate with each other. These standards also define how the programmer will write to the Object Monitor, including the method to choose services.

If you've chosen the DCOM route as your object architecture, the only Object Monitor you can currently use is Microsoft's Transaction Server (MTS), so you can skip ahead to the MTS chapter. If, on the other hand, your corporate structure will call for both DCOM and CORBA, or if you've chosen the CORBA option, your choice of Object Monitors is much wider, and your next step is to determine which product best suits your current application needs. You should probably read all the chapters in sequence.

Much like everything else in our industry, standards evolve and adapt over time based on user requirements (and vendor preferences). Many CORBA ORB vendors currently offer bridges to DCOM architectures and will no doubt, over time, offer a way for CORBA users to take advantage of Microsoft's Object Monitor product. The reverse may also happen, although less likely. Still, because of the use variations between CORBA and DCOM, and because these standards are so important to the Object Monitor product, it is unlikely the mixing and matching of Object Monitor solutions across architecture standards will over be a widely used option. Of course you could choose which object architecture (CORBA or DCOM) you will use based on Object Monitor preference. However, we hope by the end of this chapter we have convinced you that the standards preference in relation to this set of middleware products is far greater than the middleware itself. It's important to continually recognize the difference between architecture standards and product implementations.

The next chapter introduces you—finally—to the Object Monitor, and explains what this new class of middleware product offers to meet your business computing needs.

Introducing the Object Monitor

Previously, no middleware product has proven ideal for every application, nor have any two provided the same application services. With each introduction of a new middleware product, new functionality has been added, fueling the growth of the middleware marketplace. The Object Monitor is intended to change all that. This technology is an attempt to take us through the next phase in the ongoing middleware evolution cycle by combining all the lessons learned and the product sets created into one product.

The goals of the Object Monitor product are twofold:

1. To make middleware more accessible and useful by providing many application services under one name.
2. To enable middleware products to work together more easily.

Let's review how TP monitors, MOMs, and ORBs work:

- TP monitors break up applications into pieces of code called transactions, then manage their progress.
- ORBs connect already broken-up pieces of code (objects) in a transparent fashion.
- MOMs allow for more advanced communication (messages) among applications (or pieces of code).

Together, these products can combine their strengths into the ultimate middleware product. The result is the Object Monitor. Object Monitors expand the scope of all three middleware products. In a sense, they are expected to provide a nonplatform-specific operating system for objects. Object Monitors are also designed to perform application services for interacting objects regardless of platform, language, or any system aspect not part of the object's interface.

This chapter will answer the following questions:

1. What is the Object Transaction Server (OTS)?
2. What is an Object Monitor (OM)?
3. What can I expect an OM to deliver?
4. How do I choose between products in the OM market?

What Is OTS?

We begin with the Object Transaction Service (OTS), defined by the Object Management Group (OMG) as a service for the Common Object Request Broker Architecture (CORBA), to be invoked (activated) to serve objects joined through the ORB. The creation of the OTS service was the first step in the middleware convergence between ORB and the TP monitor. The CORBA OTS service provides or allows for the following to the ORB:

- Support for the two-phase commit protocol (2PC) for interacting objects, including objects of multiple ORBs that may participate in a single transaction.
- The cooperation between object transactions and procedural transactions through support for TP standards (X/Open DTP).

As shown in Figure 3.1, OTS combines the transaction coordination method (2PC) of traditional TP monitors with the standard object interfaces of an ORB. Doing so allows for the easy transformation of a plain distributed object into a distributed transactional object. This transformation is performed through the object's capability to inherit the properties of a transaction service object. But OTS alone does not make an Object Monitor. Remember, 2PC provides a mere subset of the functionality a TP monitor provides; it does not address the features a MOM product brings to the table.

NOTE — The Java Transaction Service (JTS) is a standard mapping of the OMG's Object Transaction Service using the CORBA-defined standard IDL to Java language mapping. As specified by JavaSoft, JTS "defines a standard transaction management API for the Java platform."

What Does an Object Monitor Do?

As just stated, Object Monitors do more than allow objects to communicate (this is the purpose of an ORB). They also manage more than transactions (this is the purpose of a TP monitor). And—you guessed it—OMs do more than provide a variety of methods that enable objects to share interesting information (this is the purpose of a MOM product). Object Monitors are designed to perform *application services* for interacting objects, in a variety of configurations, regardless of platform, language, or any system aspect not part of the object's interface.

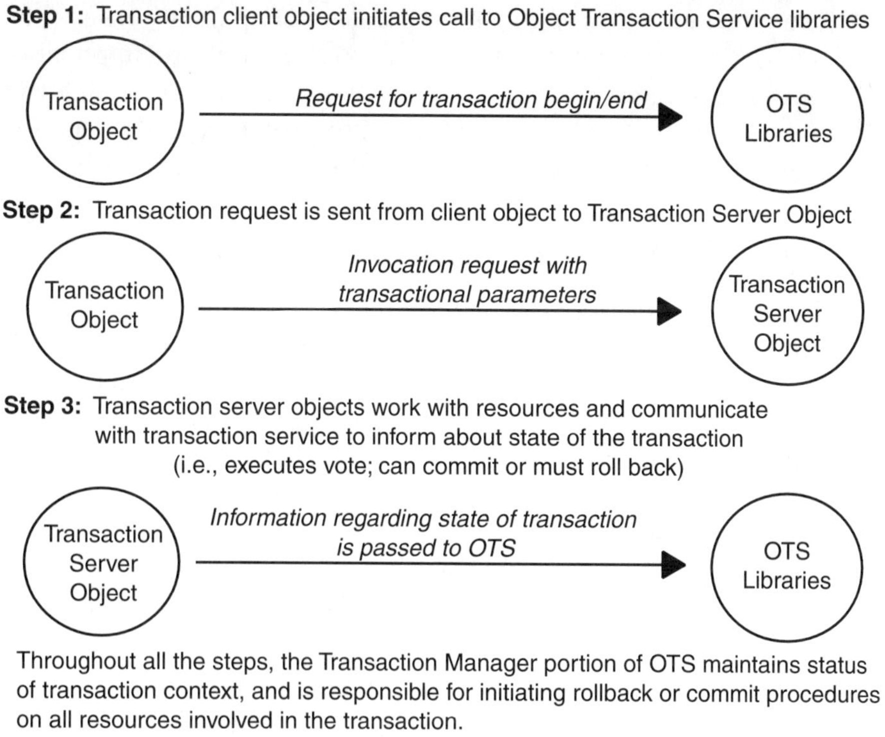

Step 1: Transaction client object initiates call to Object Transaction Service libraries

Transaction Object → *Request for transaction begin/end* → OTS Libraries

Step 2: Transaction request is sent from client object to Transaction Server Object

Transaction Object → *Invocation request with transactional parameters* → Transaction Server Object

Step 3: Transaction server objects work with resources and communicate with transaction service to inform about state of the transaction (i.e., executes vote; can commit or must roll back)

Transaction Server Object → *Information regarding state of transaction is passed to OTS* → OTS Libraries

Throughout all the steps, the Transaction Manager portion of OTS maintains status of transaction context, and is responsible for initiating rollback or commit procedures on all resources involved in the transaction.

Figure 3.1 CORBA Object Transaction Service.

In short, an Object Monitor is designed to provide the foundation for performing business tasks in a distributed computing environment. To do so, Object Monitor products support the concepts of clean layering, object/component-oriented computing, and more as we describe in the next subsections.

Clean Layering

Object Monitors work under the concept that infrastructure should be separated into independent layers of functionality, termed *clean layering*. At an application level, this implies a separation of presentation code from business code and of business code from data access code. This separation means that changes made in one layer do not affect the other layers. One example would include the changing of a client type from PC to browser; or, on the other side of the application, moving data from a mainframe system to an RDBMS. In the middle, a change to business logic (less likely to change but still plausible) would not require alterations to client or data access code.

The clean layering concept in relation to the Object Monitor extends even further, allowing for the separation of application services and system details. This implies the ability to swap out one application service (security, integrity, etc.) for an existing one, the idea being to minimize risk for users of these products and to protect against dependencies on any one piece of the overall application architecture.

Object- and Component-Oriented Computing

Object Monitors operate under the assumption that the value of the object-oriented computing model enables code reuse. Object middleware, including the OM, expands on this notion through the support of object architecture standards. These standards lift reusability limitations formerly imposed by programming language, transport protocol differences, or other system-specific features. It is also through these standards that the OM can provide a common interface and common communication method as the means for interoperability throughout an enterprise architecture. Furthermore, OMs enable reuse of their application services, objects created for use with the OM environment, and existing nonobject application resources and systems.

A Reliable Foundation for the Interaction of Objects and Components

To provide its intended functionality, the OM must establish a reliable software foundation for applications that require high availability, guaranteed integrity, increase in the number of users, and more. Object Monitors are not designed for any one type of application; the OM is intended to provide services to all applications, whether mission-critical or not. To be useful for both situations, Object Monitors must be able to accomplish a number of chores, ranging from establishing a simple means of communication among objects to ensuring bulletproof application services. Obviously, the availability and feasibility of these services will vary among Object Monitor vendors.

How do OMs do all this? The technology to support this new application infrastructure is available today through middleware products: transaction processing monitors, message-oriented middleware, and object request brokers. But as we've already discussed, these products are often difficult to use together within a corporation and frequently require complex custom integration on the part of the corporate development staff. OMs are designed to combine the functionality of these three products into one, resulting in a universal middleware across applications that are more easily customizable.

The next section examines the capabilities each of these middleware products provides for the Object Monitor, to give you an understanding of the functionality promised by OM products.

What TPMs Do for OMs

Transaction processing monitors (TP monitors, TPMs) have proven to provide a strong foundation for mission-critical applications. Over the years the TP monitor has solved many application problems relating to distributed architectures. Their key strengths to the OM market include the following:

Integrity of Data.   As detailed in Chapter 1, TPMs ensure the integrity of corporate data at all times. Without this, OM users would risk loss of business and widespread dependence on invalid information.

Distribution of Data. TP monitors are adept at distributing data across multiple machines. Over the years, the vendors of TPM products have added to their arsenal of data source support and have established standards that are now widely used among data access vendors (XA). In addition, the TP monitor has been perfected to balance the load across multiple servers for the sake of performance and availability.

Performance. *Subsecond response time* is a phrase often used by both vendors and users of TP monitor products.Vendors have worked diligently to ensure that performance need not be sacrificed for integrity.

Scalability. No other middleware product today can scale to the degree a TP monitor product can, because these products were built from the start for applications with large numbers of users, sometimes even unknown numbers of users, and have stood up to the scalability tests of time. Particularly because of the need for more business services to be delivered over the Web, scalability is a nonnegotiable requirement for OM products.

Availability. How many times can we say mission-critical with respect to TPM products? Probably not enough. Availability has always been a major concern of TPM vendors, and, today, the products have multiple means for acquiring hot or warm failover of processes, replication of processes, and data recovery.

TPMs bring mission-critical application services to our object-oriented applications. The addition of the transaction processing functionality to the Object Monitor through TPM services allows for the creation of object-oriented electronic commerce/Internet commerce applications without having to give up the power previously reserved for in-house applications. It is, in fact, the TPM services that enable the Object Monitor to be used for mission-critical applications.

What MOMs Do for OMs

Imagine a world in which distributed objects could communicate with each other across languages and systems, to complete a business task. Consider an object that must send information to multiple sources at the same time (update a database, check inventory, etc.). These sources may not all be available. Furthermore, the need to deliver these messages in a timely manner will differ dependent on the target source. Message-oriented middleware (MOM) brings diversity to object communication and supplies services for the accurate and timely delivery of object-to-object interactions in the following ways:

Nonintrusive Programming.   MOMs have been perfected to enable non-intrusive programming. Most MOM products require minimal changes to the applications for which the product will be used, in contrast to TPM middleware, which should be incorporated at time of development.

Application Flexibility.   MOMs supply a wonderful array of application services through support for such features as broadcasting, publish and subscribe, and so on. This abundance of messaging services allows for infinite possibilities in the way applications work with each other and the way a user interacts with the application.

Message Distribution.   The distribution of messages is a MOM's primary function, and no product does it better. MOMs allow for multiple messages to be delivered to many targets at the same time with optimal performance.

Message Integrity.   MOMs typically guarantee message delivery. In addition, MOMs can work with the TPM features of the OM to ensure that these messages can be part of a transactional unit of work.

MOMs offer new and interesting ways for the objects in the Object Monitor environment to communicate. This means our object applications can be customized at an interaction level. Without MOM, the applications created with Object Monitors could only offer one way to communicate: by sending a message and waiting for a response.

What ORBs Do for OMs

The object request broker (ORB) has brought object-oriented programming from the garages of Silicon Valley to mainstream computing. Having done so, ORBs have increased the value of objects by combining interoperability with reuse, ultimately making its presence in the Object Monitor indispensable. This unique value proposition allows the functionality of all three middleware products to work together, while providing the following to our applications:

Interoperability.   ORBs bring the promise of the ultimate interoperability solution through their support for object/component model and architecture standards. Support of these ORB standards allows for further separation of interface and implementation (more clean layers).

Prior to the broad support for object/component standards, interoperability among middleware products was typically via clumsy gateway interfaces or through custom coding. ORBs bring widely used, simple-to-implement interoperability standards to middleware.

Integration of Existing Applications. Through these same interfaces, ORBs allow for the integration of existing applications into the middleware world. While MOMs and TPMs allow for the passing of information between applications, ORBs allow for the full participation of these existing apps. Like an ORB, the OM will also provide facilities for the incorporation of existing applications through interface wrappering techniques.

Rapid Development. Through the ORB's support for multiple programming languages, teams of programmers using different languages and/or development tools can share existing code across a network. Rather than learn a new language or redevelop difficult code, these programmers can take advantage of in-house resources. This reuse is brought to the OM world through the ORB, which provides the facilities for broad-scale reuse of application architecture and services.

Rapid Implementation. ORBs speed application introduction through more than support for reuse. Perhaps you have heard the phrase "iterative development." It refers to the incremental delivery of new application functionality. Through support for object-oriented programming and object-level services, ORBs make it easy to implement applications in parts. This piecemeal application delivery allows for implementation of new services at a faster rate.

Adaptability of Applications and Services. ORBs create highly adaptable environments, and Object Monitors mirror that approach. Through ORBs' standards support and the objectized nature of OMs, each piece of the product architecture can be object-oriented, allowing for mixing and matching of various pieces of the product among different vendors.

An Object Monitor provides an architecture model that can be used throughout a corporate IT infrastructure in the same way an ORB does, thanks to the product's support for object architecture standards (discussed in Chapter 2). These standards help mask the differences between systems, transport protocols, programming languages, and locations. What these standards do not always account for, however, is the need to integrate or interoperate with existing in-house standards. An Object Monitor will provide facilities for the incorporation of existing corporate standards (i.e., XA or ODBMS).

Up Next

This brief chapter introduced you to Object Monitors. Chapter 4, the final chapter in Part One, will introduce some tools to help you to evaluate Object Monitor products. It will also explain how we evaluated the products in the market and how you can use these same methods for creating your own product "shortlist."

Part Two will present each Object Monitor product in more detail and will give you the necessary background information for the selection of the right product for your corporate or application needs.

4

Creating Your OM Product Shortlist

It is always difficult to choose the right product to meet your business objectives from a new technology market. And because the cost of making the wrong architectural decision or choosing the wrong product is so high, it is inadvisable to play a guessing game when evaluating a new technology. Early problem detection is extremely important especially as it may become impossible to run tests on an existing system because it may be too late in the project's life cycle or because the problem becomes too complicated to fix.

Modern, dynamic systems—including applications, computer networks, hardware and software, and business processes—need to interact in very complex ways that are difficult (almost impossible) to understand. They depend on combinations of different resources, their states, capacity, availability, and many other issues. This complexity typically leads to erroneous design assumptions and implementations, which in turn cost corporations huge amounts of money (as a result of missed deadlines, additional hardware, endless attempts to root out the problems, and so on). In addition to these immediately recognizable costs, the possible loss of current and new customers adds to the cost; in fact, in the long run, it is this potential for losing business and market share that poses the biggest threat.

The critical nature of these issues becomes even more evident in this era of distributed component-based applications for Internet and intranet use.

Applications are composed of distributed components scattered across LANs and WANs with myriad parameters affecting system functionality.

When company executives look at infrastructure-based products, such as middleware, it is easy to understand how they might get wrapped up in specific features and functions, even those features and functions which may not specifically address any application requirements. This can cause them to choose a product that, while it may have a nice check-list of features, may not be the right product for a particular company's distributed system environment.

To prevent making such a costly wrong decision, what is required is a thorough examination of application requirements *before* looking at individual products. That is precisely the purpose of this chapter: To introduce how to choose Object Monitors based on specific application requirements. You'll learn how we evaluated the products covered in Part Two and how to apply the information contained within the product chapters to determine the right product to meet the need in question. We've also included a template for judging products using some fictional applications.

The Infamous Standard Benchmark

To aid customers who have to make these tough buying decisions, some vendors supply results from a standard benchmark test. The most popular standard to cite is conducted by the Transaction Performance Council (TPC), a consortium of vendors who define benchmarks for transaction processing and database domains. The TPC defines how the test should be run, how system price should be measured, and how the results should be reported.

For many professions charged with making these buying decisions for their companies, these standard benchmark results may assist in the initial review, but thereafter become meaningless because each project and each company is so specific. Consequently, such standard benchmarks are often seen as nothing more than another soapbox upon which vendors stand to hawk their wares.

One cause of this problem is that the standard benchmark is limited in what it can show. The tests can indicate whether a product can scale according to the benchmark environment (although some might even argue this point due to vendors making "benchmark tweaks"), but they do not account for differences in the form of scalability that is required for the use of the product. For example, they do not answer such questions as: Does the application need to support multiple concurrent users making quick updates to a single database? Does the application require the capability that enables many users to conduct long sessions using multiple databases?

Corporate Benchmarks

Often, a more meaningful approach is to perform an in-house custom benchmark within a corporate IT setting. Some companies spend huge amounts of money bringing in products from a shortlist, which they then test in-house. Corporate benchmarking involves the execution of artificial workloads on a system with a similar application pattern (a prototype). By varying the benchmark workloads and reconfiguring the pattern system, companies can predict the behavior of alternative designs or plans and help companies choose the "right" technology.

These tests also can provide a reasonable answer to the question, "How will the product react to my application?" Unfortunately, monetary, time, and workforce restrictions often limit (if they are feasible at all) these tests to a chosen few. Those who cannot run custom benchmarks often have to use a checklist method for choosing products. And even those companies that can afford to run such tests often perform them on a dual-product comparison, after a shortlist has been generated through the traditional checklist process.

To assist companies in choosing the right technology for their corporate requirements, this book combines the benefits of both types of product selection methods to ensure that your shortlist includes the right products for your corporate needs.

How We Evaluated the Products

Ideally, we would be able to offer information specific to every application out there, but since that is both time- and space-prohibitive, we have figured out a way to examine the products in terms of the characteristics important to more generic types of applications, to which individuals can apply their specific criteria.

To provide the most useful information on the products currently available in the Object Monitor marketplace, we applied distributed application patterns for a set of target applications. More specifically, we have created prototype applications to examine the way each product tackles a set of infrastructure problems, which vary according to application needs. The product information that follows in succeeding chapters, then, is not a cross-product comparison, but rather a cross-application needs comparison. But to understand the full potential of the product chapters, we suggest that everyone read this chapter first to understand our evaluative process before delving into the product descriptions. And even if you have already made a commitment to a particular Object Monitor product, we recommend you read the product chapters, because they also include information on system configuration requirements to achieve your desired effect.

The parameters of our prototype applications are as follows:

- Each product contains the same procedures, which were run on the same platforms.

- We used Microsoft's NT operating system and the Sun Microsystem's Solaris.

- All test applications were written in C++, and all accessed Oracle databases.

- Our developers did not utilize any third-party development tools; they used straight code combined with the development process provided by the product being tested.

NOTE **These tests were not run to determine final product selection, as your particular computing environment will no doubt differ from our test model. The goal was to give you enough information on how each product handles various infrastructure services at a product architecture level to assist you in deciding yourself whether the product is geared toward your particular type of application and existing staff skills.**

Introduction to Application Patterns

To know which is the right product for your company, you must first identify your business goals. As you know, in practice, product selection is much more than checking off which product has more features, is cheaper, or has the nicest salesperson. You must first determine that the product can help your company provide the services it offers its client/customer base.

Using an *application pattern* as a first step toward product selection can assist in narrowing the field into a more manageable subset. The products in that subset can then be examined with respect to your particular business situation.

As we look at the various types of applications currently in production and those in design, it is of course difficult to identify all the differences in these applications. However, there are some "givens" in the Object Monitor category. Remember that these are infrastructure products, designed to eliminate and reuse as much infrastructure code for your applications as possible.

With this in mind, we were able to determine a product's strengths and weaknesses with respect to each application characteristic. The following is a list of the questions we determined had to be answered to enable correct product selection:

Number of Concurrent Users. Will the application have a large number of customers accessing the same application processes at the same time, or is the number of concurrent users easily manageable?

Length of User Session. Does the application require customers to sustain a long-term connection to the system, or will the access time be short and quick?

User Population Change Rate (Sign-In/Sign-Off Variances). Will the application vary in the number of customers accessing the service, or is the population relatively stable (for example, time-of-day services versus eight-hour customer service applications)?

Number of Data Sources. Will the application require access to three or more data sources, or are the requirements for two or fewer?

Inquiries-to-Update Ratio. What are the requirements for the application in terms of the number of inquiries expected to the number of updates that will be required?

Average Length of Chain of a Distributed Call. Will the application require distributed workflow semantics; and if yes, what is this average length of chain of this workflow?

Connectivity Requirements (Synchronous versus Asynchronous). Does the application require an immediate customer response before processing, or is a more flexible request/reply model required or desired?

Requirements for Maintaining State of Changes.   What are the application's requirements for state management of changes?

Requirement for High Availability/Fault Tolerance.   Are there requirements that the application be readily available, replicated to a back-up system, and so on?

Use of Application Services.   What are the application's requirements for application services (we looked at naming and directory services, event and notification services, and security)?

As you begin the discovery process into both the products covered in the following chapters, as well as new products emerging in the marketplace, your goal should be to clearly identify your particular application needs and apply them to each of the listed product differentiators.

Sample Patterns

To help get you started, we've created some sample generic patterns of popular applications. Within these patterns, you will be able to easily see the differences in the aforementioned application characteristics that we anticipated for our test applications. The pattern names are based on the benefits they are intended to bring your customers, whether they be in-house staff or external purchasers.

Customer Service Direct

A *customer service direct* application is one where the user is, in essence, "driving the application." The primary objective for this type of application is rapid response to multiple customer requirements (such as the purchase of a product, access to account activity information, etc.). For our test application, we used a prototype Internet home banking application. This application could be any Internet or 24-hour purchasing system with an anticipated large number of customers, unpredictable peak loads, and a need for scalability and performance of multiple short transaction updates.

Table 4.1 lists our customer service direct application traits: column 1 is just the feature number; column 2 is the feature description; column 3 identifies the specific business requirements for the feature; and column 4 lists the technology implications for handling these business needs—in other words, what the product will have to do to fulfill the business requirement.

Table 4.1 Customer Service Direct Application Traits

NO.	FEATURE	BUSINESS REQUIREMENTS	TECHNOLOGY IMPLICATIONS
1	Number of concurrent users	Large number (thousands) of concurrent users	Ability to support large number of concurrent users accessing the same object. Effective multithreaded support required for supporting a large number of objects.
2	Level of user interaction	Interactive	Ability to support heavy traffic between the client and server parts of an application. System should be able to manage session information in such a way to prevent frequent save/restore operations.
3	Average session length	Short	Not necessary for system to handle long sessions.
4	User population change rate (number of sign-in/sign-off)	High	System should be able to support effective load balancing because of rapidly changing user population.
5	Number of requests/responses	Small to medium	Not necessary to handle unusual sizes of requests or responses.
6	Session and states	Yes	System should be able to maintain session state between clients invocations.
7	Number of hits	Large	Because of a large number of concurrent sessions, the system should be able to sustain a large number of external hits.
8	Response time	Immediate response	System required to ensure reasonable response time without significant degradation in performance.
9	Inquiries to update ratio	5:1	System should support management of database connection pool.
10	Distributed workflow	Simple	Connection between cooperating components could be resolved statically before making call.

As the table delineates, to handle the business requirements of the customer service direct application, the system must be able to support a large population of users accessing the same objects, as well as multiple instances of the same object, and to provide load balancing among all the objects involved. Because of the large number of hits to the system, the product must provide the capability to effectively multithread requests as well as services to handle a rapid sign-on/sign-off procedure.

Customer Service Indirect

A *customer service indirect* application is one where corporate personnel are in charge of giving information to the customer; the customer will not be directly accessing the system. The business goals for this application are to enable corporate personnel to access information from multiple sources to satisfy a customer requirement or complaint/dispute.

The primary technology objective for this application is to allow access to a lot of information with a high response rate. The number of users for this system is more manageable than in a customer direct application, but the system must be able to handle lengthy customer sessions to prevent forcing a continual sign-on/sign-off approach. Consequently, the information bandwidth requirement is much greater for this type of application, in contrast to our previous pattern. In addition, the application must be able to access multiple types of data sources to respond to customer queries.

Our test application was a generic customer service application prototype, whose characteristics are listed in Table 4.2.

Customer On-Call

In a *customer on-call* application, the customer will be accessing a call center. For the purposes of our prototype application, we replicated a typical banking call center application, as specified in Table 4.3. The main business objective of the system is to offer a means for customers to call in to the system and perform a small variety of common services (for example, retrieve checking account information or transfer funds from a checking to a savings account).

From a corporate standpoint, such an application is intended to decrease the need for customers to contact customer service personnel directly, and the quicker the call the better, to reduce the load on the system.

Table 4.2 Customer Service Indirect Application Traits

NO.	FEATURE	BUSINESS REQUIREMENTS	TECHNOLOGY IMPLICATIONS
1	Number of concurrent users	Hundreds	Must be able to handle a reasonable, yet highly predictable, load of customer service representatives.
2	Level of user interaction	Very interactive	Conversation type of system where each business request might be accessing many forms of back-end sources.
3	Average session length	Very long	System should be able to maintain a certain number of objects in memory during a session to prevent burdening the system with constant sign-on/sign-off requirements.
4	User population change rate (number of sign-ins/sign-offs)	Very stable during work hours	No major requirements for this application; the number of users is highly predictable.
5	Number of requests/responses	Medium to large	System should be able to handle large number of requests and responses.
6	Session and states	Yes	System should be able to maintain session state between client invocations so as not to burden the overall system architecture.
7	Number of hits	Large	System should be able to handle traffic to multiple sources transferring large data volumes.
8	Response time	Varies, but should be reasonable	Technology should be able to handle multiple requests in a timely manner.
9	Inquiries to update ratio	2:1	System should support effective management for sharing database connection pool. Updates may include multiple data systems.
10	Distributed workflow	Complex	System should be able to support various combinations of business components.

Because the primary technology requirement for this application is to handle a large number of requests very quickly using an optimal system path, the product you choose should be able to manage a large number of concurrent requests while maintaining their states and managing the necessary resource load. It is also preferable to pick a product that can maintain queues in order to prioritize requests and to provide some functionality for recovering from component failure.

Table 4.3 Customer On-Call Application Traits

NO.	FEATURE	BUSINESS REQUIREMENTS	TECHNOLOGY IMPLICATIONS
1	Number of concurrent users	May become very large	Technology should provide the capability to handle large volumes of users and to keep the environment "alive."
2	Level of user interaction	Minimal	Usually offers only a portion of "regular" functionality for telephone users.
3	Average session length	Short	Major requirement to make each session as short as possible.
4	User population change rate (number of sign-ins/sign-offs)	High	Should be able to handle a large number of incoming . requests.
5	Number of requests/ responses	Small	This application offers only a subset of the services of a traditional customer service application, so the number of requests and responses is small and therefore manageable.
6	Session and states	Yes	System should be able to effectively manage session states between business requests, as the price for reestablishing a session may be very high.
7	Number of hits	Large	Should be able to handle an extremely large number of concurrent hits on a system.
8	Response time	Minimum	Requirement is to minimize response time for all users.
9	Inquiries to update ratio	7:1	Primarily used for inquiries; update services are rarely required. The main purpose of the system is to provide small amounts of information.
10	Distributed workflow	Medium	The application may have to support component combinations.

Customer with a Vote

The *customer with a vote* application, such as an online auction or bro-kerage firm, has an interesting list of requirements. The primary busi-ness objectives are to handle unpredictable customer requests in a timely manner and to guarantee both that the request is answered and that it has integrity. In the case of an online brokerage or similar busi-ness task, these applications must be easily and readily available, and so must be able to handle system faults to ensure that the service remains active. For our test purposes, we used a prototype online brokerage application, as shown in Table 4.4.

The primary technology implication for this application is to provide up and down scalability and to guarantee both the delivery and integrity of requests. The product should also provide the capability to handle unsynchronized events and high availability and fault-tolerant attributes.

Indecisive Customer

The *indecisive customer* pattern refers to a typical decision support sys-tem application. The user of this service might be conducting various procedures to multiple corporate systems to enable him or her to make an informed decision. For our prototype application, we created a typi-cal loan selection service, as shown in Table 4.5.

The indecisive customer application requires that the system be able to effectively process multiple complicated ad hoc requests to many data sources. The system should also be able to handle intensive calculations; therefore, it is important to establish flexible policies for managing a multithreaded environment. Furthermore, so that a user can make ongo-ing requests without having to wait for responses to previous requests, this application also requires asynchronous communication. Finally, the product must be able to effectively manage memory and CPU-intensive components and provide support for reasonable information bandwidth especially when including graphical data.

Customer with Cash

By far the CEO's favorite, the *customer with cash* pattern refers to an online reservation or purchasing application. The main business objec-tive for this application is, obviously, to be sure the company does not lose reservations or purchasing information, and that the system is able

Table 4.4 Customer with a Vote Application Traits

NO.	FEATURE	BUSINESS REQUIREMENTS	TECHNOLOGY IMPLICATIONS
1	Number of concurrent users	Might be extremely large, and will certainly go up and down continuously	The nature of this application requires that the technology be able to handle varying system loads (from very light to very heavy) in a matter of seconds.
2	Level of user interaction	Medium	Users' requests are fairly manageable as to the type and level of usage to back-end systems.
3	Average session length	Short	System must be able to handle multiple discrete sessions.
4	User population change rate (number of sign-ins/sign-offs)	Might be extremely high	This type of application is very volatile, with a lot of unpredictable picks.
5	Number of requests/responses	Small to medium	Generally no requirement for most information passed in either direction.
6	Session and states	Absolute requirement	Of primary importance for this application, and includes the capability to guarantee delivery and provide transaction integrity.
7	Number of hits	Vary	System should be able to handle highly unpredictable picks.
8	Response time	Reasonable	The customer must receive a timely acknowledgment regarding executed operation.
9	Inquiries to update ratio	5:1	Reasonable rate of inquiries to updates.
10	Distributed workflow	Short	Not a major requirement for this application.

to handle as many customers as required. For the purposes of our prototype application, we used a simple online purchasing service, whose characteristics are listed in Table 4.6.

This application is the model by which most traditional transaction processing applications are designed, with the capability to handle integration with multiple existing system while ensuring data integrity at all times. Ideally, a product for this application will include tools for the integration with existing systems and to effectively handle state management between sessions.

Table 4.5 Indecisive Customer Application Traits

NO.	FEATURE	BUSINESS REQUIREMENTS	TECHNOLOGY IMPLICATIONS
1	Number of concurrent users	Medium	Typically, corporations can reasonably predict and handle an average number of concurrent users.
2	Level of user interaction	High	User may spend a great deal of time accessing the system, so the technology should be able to deal with this prolonged interaction.
3	Average session length	Medium to long	User may spend a significant amount of time working with the application, analyzing results, and resending queries.
4	User population change rate (number of sign-ins/sign-offs)	Medium	Usually, after login, user spends a reasonably predicatable amount of time working with the system before signing off.
5	Number of requests/ responses	Large to very large	System should be able to handle exceptionally large chunks of data that will be sent back to the user (this could include large graphics files).
6	Session and states	Yes	This is a conversation type of application, so the technology should provide a means for maintaining enough state information between user interactions. In case of failure, the system should be able to recover without losing the session data.
7	Number of hits	High	Application should allow the user to run concurrent requests.
8	Response time	Reasonable	Concurrent user requests preclude a specific requirement for rapid response time; however, it should be within a reasonable range.
9	Inquiries to update ratio	10:1	Primarily, the user will be performing inquiries, with few updates. However, the system will probably require access to many data sources.
10	Distributed workflow	Short	As this is mostly an inquiry service, there is no major requirement for combining components.

Table 4.6 Customer with Cash Application Traits

NO.	FEATURE	BUSINESS REQUIREMENTS	TECHNOLOGY IMPLICATIONS
1	Number of concurrent users	Medium	The company usually has a good idea of the number of concurrent users for this system, and the load is typically reasonable because existing systems are handling the load.
2	Level of user interaction	High	Similar to conversation type, with a lot of information going forth and back.
3	Average session length	Long	Session usually spans multiple logins.
4	User population change rate (number of sign-ins/sign-offs)	Medium	Fairly predicatible and does not vary a great deal.
5	Number of requests/responses	Medium/Medium	Average, manageable size.
6	Session and states	Yes	Should be able to save state information, even between sessions, the ultimate requirement for integrity of data.
7	Number of hits	Medium	Reasonable and predicatable number of hits.
8	Response time	Immediate response required only for small number of requests	Technology should be able to provide an immediate response to portions of every request to the system.
9	Inquiries to update ratio	2:1	System requires an almost even number of inquiries to updates. The system will require updates to multiple data sources.
10	Distributed workflow	Very long	May span sessions and include many cooperating components, so the technology should have some way of handling this.

How to Use the Application Patterns

In Part Two of this book, for each of our sample applications, we give an example of how to use the pattern methodology. We also assign percentage ratings for each application to each product. These ratings will give you a quick view of how many application services a particular product can provide to meet the application requirements.

In the preceding tables, we listed 10 variances for each application pattern (which makes calculation much easier!); your own pattern checklists may be much lengthier. And note that though we gave equal weight to each application feature, in practice, needless to say, it makes more sense to apply heavier weight to the more important features. For example, if security is a more important issue for your application than, say, load balancing, security might be assigned 15 percent with load balancing worth only 5 percent, or any percentage in between.

NOTE For the sake of readability and fairness, for the purposes of this book, we used what we'll call an "optimistic" grading policy for our sample patterns. Specifically, we gave each product either 0, 5, or 10 percentage points based on the availability of application services and variances in what the specific application required. For your own charts, we recommend that you more widely vary the number of percentage points. Finally, we do not recommend that you use the percentage points we have assigned as a means of product selection! You must be sure the requirements of your application match your product selection criteria.

Up Next

By now you should have a good understanding of the needs Object Monitors are trying to meet; and perhaps you created your own application pattern to help you to determine which product in this market segment will suit your specific needs. It's time to move on and look at the available products, one of which will hopefully provide the business benefits that address your company's criteria.

Object Monitor Product Comparisons

Part Two introduces the products available in the object monitor market-place. The next six chapters examine the products and companies positioned to provide you with all the benefits discussed in Part One. So though this may be the part many of you have been waiting for, in many ways it is also the most difficult, because you will be confronted with a lot of detailed information that you must evaluate in conjunction with your and your company's specific business needs.

It is important to recognize that this market is in its infancy, and new products will be entering the competition on a regular basis. With that in mind, we chose to review the primary players in the current market. To our knowledge, this is the first time all of these products have been compared in the same setting. And to provide you with the most accurate product information, we have used each of the following products to create a variety of sample applications (as introduced in Chapter 4). Our team of programmers built the same sample applications for the same platforms and made use of the same database technology. Afterward, the products were tested using a variety of custom benchmarks designed to determine not only performance capabilities but also resource utilization. We then tried various configuration schema (dependent on product support) to test the effect these changes had on the overall system. The resulting information gave us more than 100 data points per product.

From the results we judged the way the architecture of each product reacted to various situations, to give you intimate knowledge the products' functionality.

Finally, we also carefully reviewed other attributes of the products that may offer benefits not apparent through performance and resource testing. We asked the following questions:

- What type of development process does the product provide for?
- How easy is it to manipulate the product to account for application differences?
- How does the product provide services (automatically or through custom coding)?
- Does the product provide standard ways to adjust these services (through APIs), or does the product use a proprietary solution?
- What is the best use of the specific technology product?

And keeping in mind the ever-changing face of the market, rather than focus on specific features and functions, we make educated assumptions based on the architecture of the products, architecture that will remain unchanged to a large extent.

The X/Open Distributed Transaction Processing Model

We have already covered the important object architecture standards in conjunction with the products evaluated in this part, but we feel it is necessary to review one more standard. Most of the vendors included in this book (with the exception of Microsoft, as detailed in Chapter 9) agreed to support one standard, X/Open's Distributed Transaction Processing (DTP) standard, which defines a process model and related service interfaces for distributed transaction processing applications. Figure P2.1

shows the various components of a distributed transaction processing application and how these pieces communicate in a standard fashion.

A standard transaction processing system using the X/Open "four-box" model will start the transaction process first by calling the transaction manager (TM) via the X/Open Defined TX interface (TX is an application programming interface defined by X/Open). The transaction manager then notifies resource managers, who will need to participate in the transaction through the X/Open defined XA interface. The application then performs work on the resource managers via native data source interfaces (such as SQL). The application then calls the transaction manager to "commit the transaction" via the TX interface.

At this point, the transaction manager negotiates using the two-phase commit protocol of the transaction processing product with the resources involved; this communication is again done using the XA interface. The transaction manager is in charge of notifying the application of the decision to either commit or abort the transaction.

It is important to note that the X/Open DTP standards are *not* designed to address how different transactional products interoperate with each other; this is vendor-specific. The standards are only designed to provide a common way for products to communicate with the resources of the system and other system sources. (For example, most major databases support XA interfaces and therefore can participate in transaction management.)

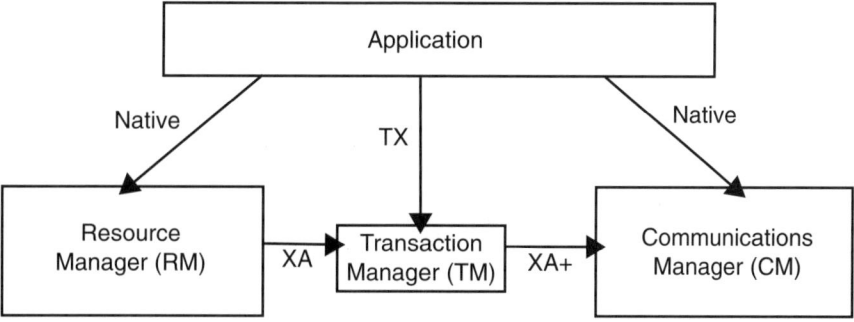

Figure P2.1 X/Open four-box model.
Source: The Open Group

How to Use This Part

Each of the chapters in this part may be treated as a separate entity. You may choose to read only about the products you're most interested in. And to make product comparisons easier, the chapters all follow the same outline. We've also included tables that summarize the major points of each product's capabilities and attributes. Part Two should give you all the information you need to make the right product choice for you and your company.

CHAPTER 5

OrbixOTM from IONA Technologies

IONA Technologies' marketing slogan is "Orbix Everywhere," and considering the strong and loyal following it has found in the CORBA community, particularly among developers, it may prove true.

IONA Technologies, Ltd. was founded in 1991 by researchers at the Department of Computer Science at Trinity College in Dublin, Ireland, where the company is still headquartered. The first beta copy of Orbix was shipped in late 1992, and by mid-1995, IONA opened its first U.S. office in Boston, Massachusetts. Today, though the company offers a variety of software products, its core offering is still the Orbix CORBA Object Request Broker (ORB).

IONA is strongly committed to supporting a standard way for software to work together. To that end, every product the company produces is designed to expand to provide extra services to enhance corporate software interaction. And the company's middleware product is completely independent, meaning it is not tied to a particular operating system, database, or application development software. In addition, IONA is focused on providing a variety of products that address various customer requirements, ranging from small lightweight products for real-time devices to those that offer enterprise application services. OrbixOTM falls into the latter category.

OrbixOTM is IONA's current Object Monitor offering, but it is not the company's first attempt at providing an integrated middleware product.

Previously, the company, in conjunction with BEA Systems, introduced Orbix + TUXEDO, which attempted to deliver an easier way to develop traditional TUXEDO transaction processing applications through object-oriented programming. This short-lived experience led IONA to their current solution.

To develop OrbixOTM, IONA sought a partnership with another TP monitor vendor, and joined with Transarc, producer of the Encina transaction processing monitor, a suite of tools for building distributed transactional applications by leveraging layers of technology, including DCE.

Transarc Corporation

Transarc Corporation, Pittsburgh, Pennsylvania, was founded in 1989 by Dr. Alfred Z. Spector and Dr. Jeffrey L. Eppinger (among others), originally to commercialize the research they had been conducting at Carnegie Mellon University (CMU) in the area of distributed computing. Over the years, Transarc's products have received considerable industry attention, in particular, the Andrew File System (AFS), a distributed file system which was selected as the foundation for the Open Software Foundation's Distributed Computing Environment (DCE).

In addition to its partnership with IONA, Transarc sells its own product for creating object-oriented transactional applications, called Encina++. The Encina++ builds off a DCE foundation, whereas the IONA product does not. If your company is committed to DCE as a distributed object computing foundation, the Encina++ may be ideal for your environment.

The out-of-the-box OrbixOTM solution integrates multiple IONA products, including:

Orbix. IONA's implementation of a CORBA-compliant object request broker.

OrbixOTM. IONA's implementation of the CORBAServices Object Transaction Service (OTS).

OrbixSSL. IONA's implementation of CORBA-level 0 Security, which offers Secure Socket Layer (SSL) security.

OrbixManager. Supports the management of Orbix applications, including the use of SNMP tools.

OrbixNames. IONA's implementation of the CORBAServices Object Naming Service.

OrbixEvents. IONA's implementation of the CORBAServices Event Service, which allows for communication of objects via event channels (allowing for a form of publish-and-subscribe messaging to objects).

> **NOTE** **All of the products in the OrbixOTM suite can be purchased separately, but it's much cheaper to buy them as a suite.**

OrbixOTM Product Architecture

OrbixOTM is implemented as a set of client and server object classes (Figure 5.1 shows its architecture). On the server-side, every OrbixOTM application server contains some portion of user-written server objects, which includes the application-specific code (the business logic) that in-house developers will create. In a separate segment is the standard Orbix ORB libraries, which handle communication with client-side objects.

Also on the server-side is the OTS Server Library, the bulk of which contains the functionality IONA has licensed from Transarc including protection for transactions. Within this portion is the XA Manager, which oversees transactional integrity and provides connections to XA-compliant resources, and the Object Concurrency Control Service, which protects against data corruption. The OTS Server Library's transaction log can be consulted for recovery in case of errors.

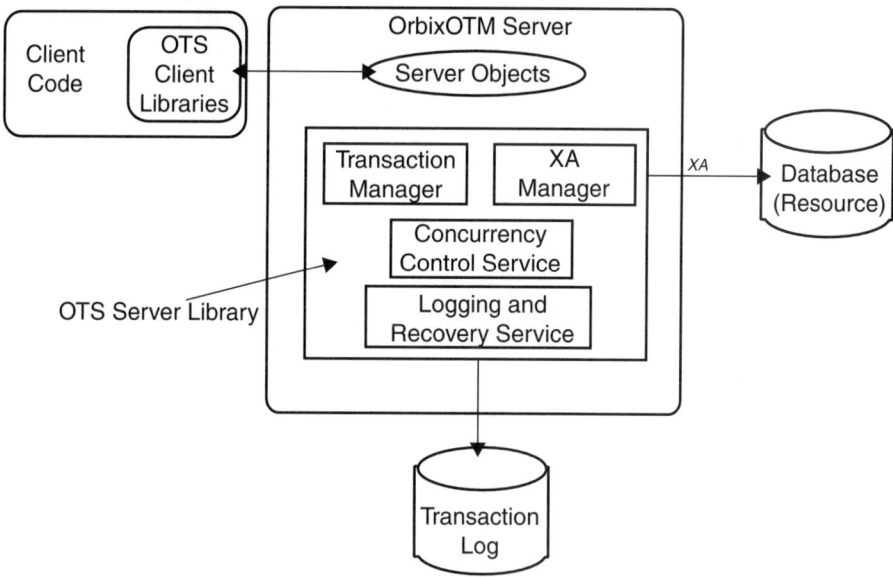

Figure 5.1 OrbixOTM product architecture.

On the client-side are two major elements: the code that implements in-house-created client code, which may be a GUI-based client or just one client-side object; and the IONA-provided OrbixOTM client libraries, which include proxies, or skeletons used to establish communication with server objects.

Figure 5.2 shows how OrbixOTM works at runtime. For transactional applications, the product uses a distributed OTM model, in which each server that is part of an OTM application must contain the OTS server libraries. The figure also shows the relationship between the OTS server libraries and other object services that OTM provides. (Note: The figure does not contain all the services that can be used with OrbixOTM; rather it is designed to show that these operate as external services apart from OTS.)

To bind a client request to a server object, OrbixOTM goes through the following (general, not detailed) steps:

1. Bind request comes to the OrbixOTM ORB.
2. The ORB consults the CORBA implementation repository for the appropriate invocation policy to use and starts the new instance of an object, if necessary returning a pointer to the client object.

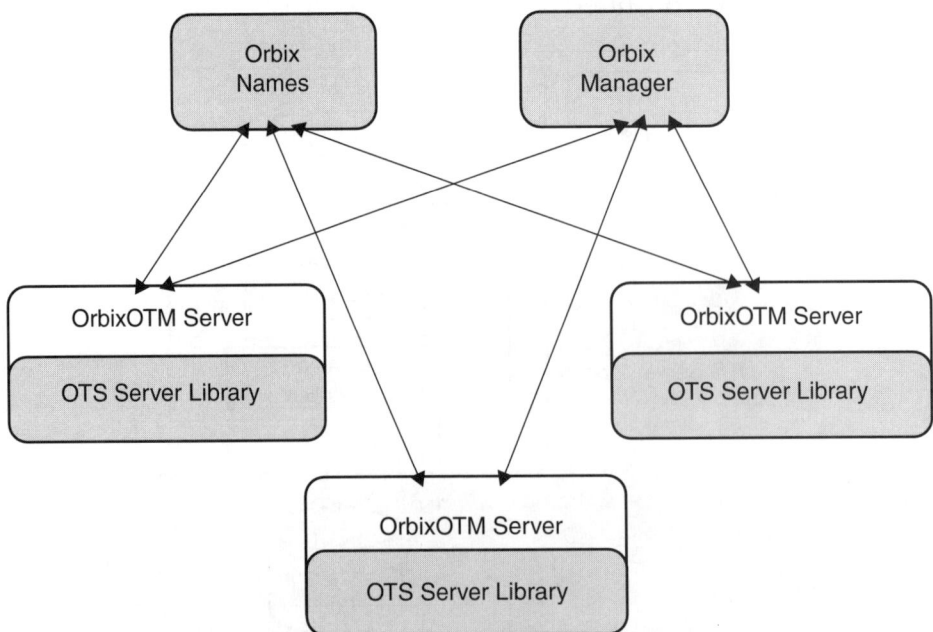

Figure 5.2   OrbixOTM runtime.

3. The server object is notified, then passed the request, thereby receiving full control over the process of initiating a response. It creates a new thread to handle the request.

OrbixOTM has adopted what is called a *distributed transaction management model,* in which the status of each subtransaction (resource involved in the course of the transaction) of a global transaction (entire transaction life cycle) is maintained in the memory of the node that the subtransaction is running. This model is used in most traditional TP monitors, including Transarc's Encina.

The advantages of this model are twofold: It naturally scales, because each node shares the processing of application logic and transaction management; and there is no single point of failure for customers to be concerned with. The drawback to this approach is that it requires the complete transaction manager libraries on each node involved in the course of the transactional application. In addition, centralized management of applications is not as easy as it would be in a more centralized model. Because of these drawbacks, the model can impose an extra administration burden on the user, as the distributed model assumes that each node is independent and complete.

Developing with OrbixOTM

Installing OrbixOTM is fairly straightforward using a command-line interface. Developers do have to take care of configuration files themselves, but this is a manageable job. And all changes are done during the installation, so there is no need to run anything after this process. The entire product suite is very well documented (among the best we've seen) and includes loads of code examples to assist programmers.

IONA's OrbixOTM operates in a pure CORBA environment, therefore applications are created using a traditional CORBA development process. And because the product includes the Orbix ORB, there are language mappings that allow developers to choose which language they would like to use with the product—dependent, of course, on current product availability.

The product does not include a GUI development environment (it's basically just a text editor), but IONA maintains partnerships with various tool vendors to make development easier. (Of course developers can use any product that provides a visual method of creating applications using the language of choice that corresponds to the language mapping that Orbix supports.) The company also offers a product for easy connectivity with Microsoft ActiveX-enabled tools.

IONA and Microsoft COM Technology

As noted, IONA has long been a solid supporter of the CORBA standards, but it has also announced plans to work closely with Microsoft to enable cross-standard support for both the ORB technology and for products in the Object Monitor market. This includes licensing of Microsoft's Component Object Modeling (COM) technology for use in Orbix products.

The goal is to offer interoperability between Microsoft's distributed object and transaction processing technology with IONA's product. If you are considering an environment that will be a mix of MTS and a CORBA-enabled solution, IONA may be a good place to look.

Experience Required

We used C++ for our applications, but we must point out that OrbixOTM is not for inexperienced C++ programmers. To be able to take advantage of the full functionality of the product requires significant knowledge of both C++ and distributed computing. This is not an unusual requirement for products in the CORBA ORB marketplace, but for IONA it is imperative.

For the experienced C++ OO programmer, OrbixOTM is the ultimate playing field, allowing for a great degree of custom manipulation of the product to achieve desired objectives, one reason IONA maintains a very loyal C++ object developer following.

NOTE Our programmers enjoyed working with OrbixOTM. As experienced CORBA and C++ programmers, they appreciated the freedom the product provided, enabling them to extend the functionality as desired. (The well-written product documentation didn't hurt either!)

For example, Orbix lets a programmer specify the execution of additional code before or after that for "normal" operations. IONA provides *filters* (basically, a set of programming interfaces allowing the developer to access and insert application code in the request path between client and server). A filter is not a fully operational program, but a portion of a program. IONA gives developers the source code for this pseudo-program so that they can add code for other services to be executed midstream. This capability lets programmers extend the functionality of OrbixOTM by creating filters for security checks, multithreaded processing, debugging, auditing, and more.

On the client-side, filters may be used to transform proxies in an Orbix environment to *smart proxies*. Smart proxies are created by overriding the default stub code into a new derived class. They allow for the addition of filters to a proxy to customize client behavior; for example, to improve performance by directing filters to cache a request and then to respond locally.

> **NOTE** A *proxy* is a local client representation of a server object. Local calls to proxy objects—located on the client—are intercepted and routed to a remote server. This provides location transparency (clients believe they are conducting a normal local call, when actually the object middleware is passing the request to the appropriate object located anywhere on a network).

Building a sample application in OrbixOTM is very easy, aided by the documentation, which includes detailed instructions. Some server objects, however, must be created by the developer in order for the server to run properly. The localization of error/debugging is a snap, too; all exceptions contain enough information to enable the rapid localization of errors.

Application Architecture Considerations

In this section, we will look at how OrbixOTM handles various application architecture variances, as described in Chapter 4. Before we begin to discuss the following application variances, it is important to note again that the OrbixOTM product is built on a solid CORBA ORB foundation. Because of this, the product offers some solid object-oriented methodologies for development, and includes features designed to benefit a company building a CORBA foundation. With OrbixOTM, such a company will be positioned to add services traditionally found in other middleware products, such as TP monitors and message-oriented middleware.

Number of Concurrent Users

OrbixOTM is based on a traditional CORBA ORB architecture, with scalability gained through the use of multithreaded objects. That said, it is important to point out that no version of Orbix is *automatically* multi-threaded, and using single-threaded objects will quickly limit how many clients the application can support (that is, without the use of extensive hardware). We should point out that IONA states they have changed their strategy and no longer plan to ship a single-threaded version of the product, however for our use this was not the case.

The Orbix capability to provide developers with filters can assist in this regard. Through the use of these filters, developers can implement any threading policy they wish, the use of which can dramatically alter the performance and scalability achieved (but keep in mind, this will be in a separate segment of code). That's the upside; the downside is that because there is nothing inherent to the product, this freedom will cost you.

And remember, to take full advantage of the Orbix product, companies must have the necessary skills in-house to cope with these demands or they will be disappointed with the results.

The use of multithreaded objects can be a nice scalability approach for small to medium system environments, as it does not require a separate object instance for each request. This can be particularly important where back-end resources are scarce. Larger customers might require the addition of custom code for the creation of multiple object instances to handle the load and to prevent crashing the back-end system. (The only alternative would be to have many instances of the same objects available, but this is not advisable as system resources would be wasted outside of peak client loads.) Again, using Orbix filters might help, but necessitates an experienced skill set.

User Session Length

The CORBA ORB foundation is primarily geared for short requests and responses. And because of the default attribute for pure CORBA implementations, OrbixOTM keeps client connections to servers active at all times. For smaller system environments, or those that will primarily involve quick client and server sessions, this approach should not be a problem (the use of multithreading policies should enable the handling of client demands). In fact, the direct connection approach can, in some situations, be ideal, as it can make optimal use of resources.

The downside is that for larger applications that may involve many concurrent clients (beyond the scope of threads) or those that will involve long client sessions, there is no easy way of handling the management of client-to-server connections without some additional custom coding. This would involve the use of filters to instantiate custom code written to automatically create new object instances on demand. Furthermore, this will involve direct connections to these new instances and may require additional hardware. We determined that in larger application or longer session scenarios the direct approach is not ideal, and in fact may have negative effects, which are not easily reparable, on both performance and resource utilization.

User Population Changes

For applications that will not involve rapid population changes, we found that client requests in Orbix can largely be managed through multithreading policies. It is important to remember, however, that the product establishes a direct client-to-server object approach; therefore, the number of clients will be limited to the number of available business object instances.

For applications that must support very rapid population changes, in particular larger environments, it is recommended that customers write their own custom code to handle the creation of new object instances (this is not an easy job). This is an important point, as the use of multithreading alone, without the capability to create new instances, requires some forethought on the part of developers to avoid crashing the system, especially with Internet-based applications where peak levels of users can often be difficult to forecast accurately.

Though this custom code can help to keep an OrbixOTM application running, we must point out that the product does not provide any means for making some objects available in a pool for new clients. For applications with a smaller number of users, this doesn't seem to have any major negative effects, but for applications with many users with frequent sign-on/sign-off variances, this can greatly affect performance because OrbixOTM has to continually locate and instantiate an object for each call.

Data Access

OrbixOTM includes integration with databases via XA connections, therefore any database that supports the XA interface can participate in OrbixOTM transactions. Within its product line, IONA offers optional tools for the integration with object databases via its version of the generic Orbix database adapter framework (ODAF). At the time of this writing, IONA ships adapters for Versant and ObjectStore ODBMSs. Future versions are expected to support OTS integration to provide native ODAF-based object database integration capabilities.

For these databases, OrbixOTM supports a dynamic XA connection, whereby a user does not need to include access information about the data the program has to access at compile time. This allows users to change databases without having to alter the program. This can be very useful for programs that have many data sources, particularly if that data may have to be relocated from one machine to another.

OrbixOTM does not, however, provide any database pool management, which can have a negative effect on performance. It means that each time a request comes to an OrbixOTM server, a new database connection must be made. To help minimize this negative effect, OrbixOTM does provide some primitive load-balancing capabilities through a round-robin policy: A request is passed from one machine to the next in turn to distribute the load. However, at the time of this writing, the product does not offer any other automated options in this area. (Optionally, customers could create their own way of dealing with load balancing through custom coding.)

Legacy System Integration

For integration with legacy applications, IONA offers its version of the Orbix ORB technology that runs on IBM MVS systems (this must be purchased separately). Of course, this implies that a version of the ORB must run in this legacy environment, and this is not always possible. Therefore, IONA also offers two bridges to MVS for CICS and IMS, the OrbixCICS and OrbixIMS adapters. The bridges enable data access in either environment, although for transactional applications they do not allow for support of two-phase commit coordination. (Mainframe resources may be integrated into end-to-end two-phase commit coordination, where they support either an XA or a CORBA interface.)

The product is CORBA-enabled, so customers are able to "wrap" existing applications with a CORBA IDL interface; but this is beyond the scope of OrbixOTM. Customers who require access to these systems must rely on a third-party product.

Response Time

The combination of a standard CORBA architecture and a distributed transaction processing model, without the benefit of multiplexing for either business objects or data access connections, has a negative effect on OrbixOTM performance and resource utilization. This is particularly true as the number of clients and/or servers increases.

To get optimal performance from the product, we recommend using the filters to try various threading policies or to create custom threading policies based on individual application requirements to increase response time. Our tests indicated that using a thread-pooling policy will usually improve performance (as opening a new thread per connection seems to have a significant impact on performance of the system).

For those customers who choose not to manipulate threading policies, OrbixOTM is best suited for small application systems environments, with fewer client requirements. In these situations, the product can sustain good performance.

Application Messaging

Like all CORBA ORB products today, OrbixOTM allows users to create one-way asynchronous calls. This allows you to implement the asynchronous communication paradigm, a standard of the CORBA specifications (though this does require a lot of handwork). And because OrbixOTM allows for smart proxies on a client, it is possible to use this mechanism in combination with implementing a client as both a client and server machine, thereby achieving a level of asynchronous communication. (Again, this is a hand-crafted process, and thus prone to error.)

Fortunately, OrbixOTM has a better way to deal with asynchronous communication. IONA includes a CORBA-compliant event service with OrbixOTM. As shown in Figure 5.3, this service enables asynchronous communication between groups of objects via event channels. Similar to publish-and-subscribe messaging, suppliers of event information push information to consumers, and vice versa.

IONA also offers a separate Orbix product called OrbixTalk, which uses IP multicast for achieving advanced messaging functionality. The company also provides products for integration with existing message-oriented middleware products such as IBM's MQSeries and Peer Logic's PIPES.

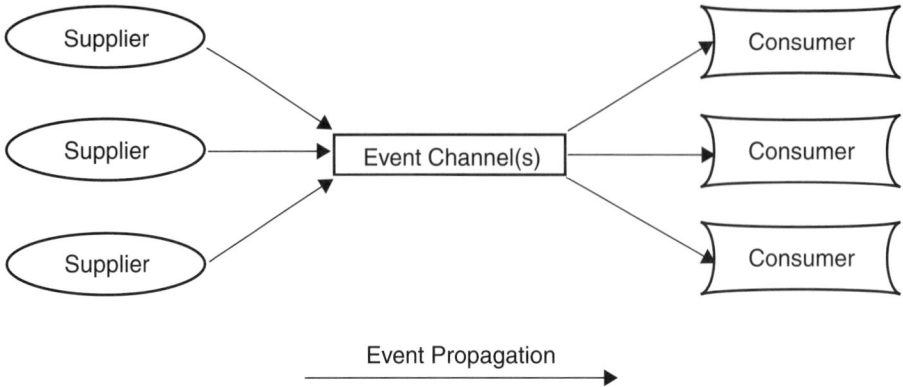

Figure 5.3 OrbixOTM event service.

IONA Technologies is actively working toward advanced messaging functionality for CORBA systems. Further enhancement in this area, including other partnerships with message-oriented middleware vendors, is expected in the near future. So if your application requires asynchronous communication or other advanced messaging functionality, check out IONA's latest product offerings or this book's accompanying Web site for a solution in this area.

State Management

By nature of the CORBA design of OrbixOTM, objects maintain the state of an object between invocations; each object controls when to release the state. (Remember that in a traditional ORB approach, the objects are in control, the ORB only provides a communication mechanism.)

OrbixOTM does not provide any automated services for applications that will require strong state management, so customers will have to create their own state management facilities. This involves the creation of a system in which the user can save the state of the object using Orbix; thereafter, the user can create a system that will find an object and restore it if something goes down.

Orbix does provide a tradition CORBA 2.0 extension to IDL, which allows programmers to define *opaque data types*. In a traditional CORBA implementation, objects are passed to and from each other by way of an object reference (that is, object references are passed to clients rather than copies of the object). Using opaque data types makes it possible to pass objects by value, so that the internal state of the object is included in a return value and a copy of the object is constructed in the receiving process. To take advantage of this, developers must follow some additional configuration and programming procedures.

High Availability/Fault Tolerance

OrbixOTM does not inherently provide high availability or fault-tolerant attributes, but as a CORBA-based product, a degree of high availability can be achieved. To achieve a level of fault resilience, OrbixOTM can be configured to transparently reestablish connections, through resending requests to failed servers. Obviously, this will not correct the problem, but, optionally, the client can remain unaware of the failure (provided the situation is fixed in a reasonable time so that it does not affect the processing of the client's request).

Also because CORBA is, by default, location-independent, it is possible to write some code that will switch calls to another back-up object in the event of a failure. But again, this is hand-crafted fault tolerance, which will require a good deal of coding.

Security

IONA has implemented CORBA-compliant security service level 0, which is included with OrbixOTM. This level of compliance means the product provides an interface for the use of SSL technology to provide security.

To do so, IONA has integrated Secure Socket Layer (SSL) v3.0 security into the basic Orbix product so that the service is very easy to use. Once servers are registered by Orbix as secure, when clients connect they must display their authentication credentials.

Taking advantage of this service is fairly straightforward, and detailed instructions are included in the documentation. Administrators use a single configuration file; then OrbixSSL programmers develop applications that communicate using SSL, with the details completely hidden from the programmer. The only setup involved is to ensure that the applications are linked to an SSL-enabled version of the Orbix library and that X.509 certificates are installed on the server where an OrbixSSL application is running.

This functionality is also supported via IONA's Web client access product, OrbixWeb; therefore, it is possible for IIOP-enabled browsers to communicate securely with OrbixOTM servers.

Secure Socket Layer

SSL is a protocol for data security that includes authentication (verification of the identity of the user), privacy (prevention of data from being understood by an unauthorized third party), and integrity (detection of data modification during transmission) across TCP/IP networks.

In an SSL interaction, a client first identifies to the server which encryption algorithms it supports; the server responds by selecting the appropriate encryption method. At this point, the server also sends a certificate that includes the server's public key to the client. The client checks the authenticity of the certificate and generates a random key to be used for symmetric encryption of the data; it then encrypts the symmetric key with the server's public key and sends the results back to the server. The session is established, and SSL is then used to encrypt and decrypt bytestreams between clients and servers using the random key.

Additional Features

This section briefly discusses other features included in OrbixOTM, some we've mentioned in passing in the preceding discussion, others we've not.

Object Services

IONA has included in OrbixOTM two other object services worth mentioning:

- *The CORBA-defined naming service.* Allows names to be associated with a CORBA object, so that the object can be found by its name (rather than its location) as registered in a names repository (see Figure 5.4). This service eliminates the requirement that a client bind to a specific server; instead, the server institutes a names-to-object mapping through the repository. To use the OrbixOTM naming service, however, takes a good deal of additional work.

- *The CORBA-defined trader service.* Sort of a matchmaking service for client objects looking for server objects. It allows clients to specify conditions for choosing one object from the many server objects of the same type. For example, one criterion could be load, and the trader service would choose the object with the least load. IONA's implementation includes some umbrella interfaces; the criteria selection is left to developers.

Management Features

The OrbixManager, which we've already touched on (Figure 5.5), grants programmers and system administrators direct access to system objects. Essentially, it is a facility for viewing, controlling, and managing Orbix applications. Using it, system administrators can view what is currently running or shut down specified Orbix servers. In addition, they can measure the number of IDL operations processed, the number of exceptions raised, and the number of current connections.

OrbixManager also includes facilities for the notification of unexpected server terminations, of CORBA exceptions from a server, and for viewing the assignment of properties for Orbix applications (e.g., names and version numbers of Orbix apps).

System administrators access these features from an OrbixManager GUI application after system programmers have developed Orbix applications that connect these features through a set of IDL interfaces.

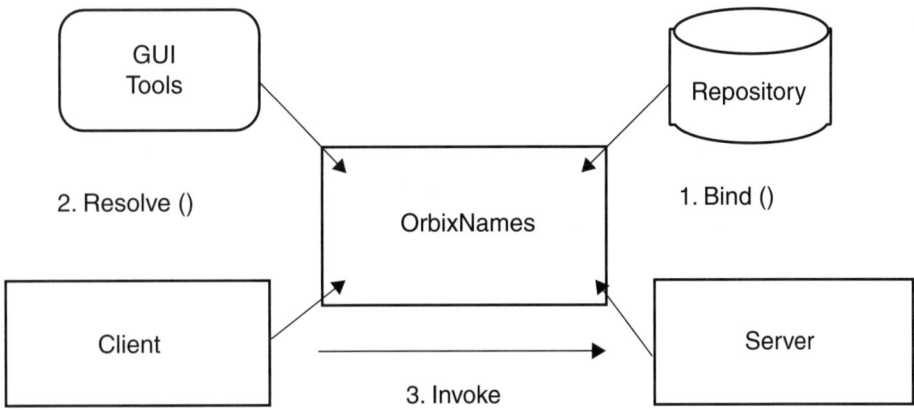

Figure 5.4 OrbixOTM naming service.

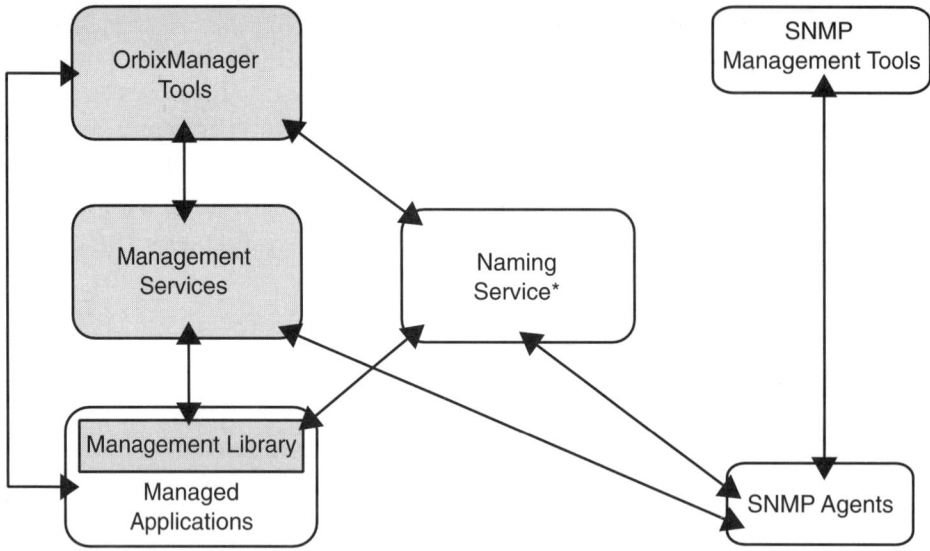

*Use of ObjectManager requires access to an implementation of the CORBA naming service (such as OrbixNames, included with OrbixOTM).

Figure 5.5 OrbixManager.
Source: IONA Technologies

At runtime, Orbix client and server applications are linked with the system management libraries; this link signifies the system is a managed application. Once the executable has been linked, the management library takes care of receiving and monitoring information from the Orbix client and server applications and connecting to the management server.

The management service server manages all servers on a host or number of hosts and controls a management domain. The management service is responsible for interaction with management tools, managing exception forwarding and thresholding, and detecting failures.

Information about a managed Orbix system is obtained via a simple network management protocol (SNMP) module. Therefore, OrbixManager can also operate with any SNMP-based systems management product by translating SNMP operations to equivalent IDL operations.

The Verdict

IONA's OrbixOTM can be used for any type of application because the product can be extended to fit almost any requirements. This is due in part to the CORBA standard approach to the architecture, and in part to the additional development "helpers" bundled with the product.

For the CORBA proponent, IONA offers a solid CORBA environment, including a very pure implementation of CORBA specifications coupled with a number of CORBA-defined interfaces for services. The C++ and CORBA developer will enjoy the product's adherence to distributed object principles and CORBA standard IDL and APIs. IONA also offers more standard CORBA language mappings than any other company covered in this book, allowing for multiple development staffs to take advantage of the benefits of an Orbix architecture.

Thus, when to use OrbixOTM becomes more a question of how much additional coding a customer is willing to add to the product, and how skilled in-house developers are. In addition, for some applications, the product may not allow for minimal resource utilization and will require additional hardware. The applications that will require the most significant investment are those that require a very large number of concurrent users, demand rapid response as a first priority, will use many databases, or need effective state management.

In short, the best type of application for OrbixOTM is one that has a reasonable number of concurrent user requirements, needs to make use of varying messaging policies for object-to-object communication, requires a number of CORBA services, or must integrate well with Microsoft's MTS Object Monitor product.

Table 5.1 summarizes the major application considerations for evaluating OrbixOTM.

Table 5.2 summarizes OrbixOTM application services available for new application development efforts, based on the application patterns (column 1) covered in Chapter 4. Column 2 gives the percentage of application services the product automatically provides; column 3 is additional information that should be considered for this type of application.

Table 5.3 will help you to determine the validity of using IONA's OrbixOTM for your specific application requirements.

IONA's OrbixOTM is a good example of a standard CORBA-compliant ORB-based approach to providing object-oriented application services, including transaction management. IONA did not set out to reinvent the wheel with OrbixOTM, rather to add functionality to its existing ORB

Table 5.1   OrbixOTM Application Considerations

BEST APPLICATION CONFIGURATION	MAJOR APPLICATION CONSIDERATIONS
Small to medium client and server configurations in a heterogeneous environment	For object-oriented applications, particularly those that will run on a range of platforms or access an array of back-end resources. OrbixOTM is also well suited to applications that need to provide asynchronous or advanced communication among client and server objects. OrbixOTM can be used in larger environments or those with a maximum requirement for rapid response, but they will require additional coding and may incur less than optimal response time and resource utilization.

Table 5.2   Results of Testing against Application Patterns

APPLICATION PATTERN	PERCENTAGE OF APPLICATION SERVICES	USE IMPLICATIONS
Customer service direct (Internet-based service)	40%	While IONA does provide good access to OrbixOTM applications from the Web, the product is difficult to use for this type of application, as the primary requirements are the capability to handle large numbers of client requests in a timely manner. In addition, developers will have to add the capability to effectively manage state information and provide strong services for balancing the load across multiple servers.
Customer service indirect (typical customer service)	55%	OrbixOTM can provide important benefits to this type of application because it can connect to many types of back-end data sources running on a variety of platforms.

Table 5.2 *(Continued)*

APPLICATION PATTERN	PERCENTAGE OF APPLICATION SERVICES	USE IMPLICATIONS
Customer service indirect *(Continued)*		Developers will have to add effective state and session management services, as well as a means for dealing with prolonged user interaction to the system. (Please note that response time may not be ideal through the products lack of advanced database connection management.)
Customer on-call (call center)	55%	This application does not typically demand a large array of application services; primarily it requires that requests be handled using an optimal system path. Therefore, OrbixOTM can provide a good environment for the application through its direct connection architecture. Developers will have to add effective state management services. The major problem with this application is that response time may suffer as the number of concurrent users increases. Developers should try a variety of configurations to deflect any performance and scalability problems.
Customer with a vote (online auction or brokerage)	70%	This application represents an ideal use of the product thanks to its capability to guarantee the delivery of messages (publish and subscribe or asynchronous notification).

Continues

Table 5.2 Results of Testing against Application Patterns *(Continued)*

APPLICATION PATTERN	PERCENTAGE OF APPLICATION SERVICES	USE IMPLICATIONS
Customer with a vote *(Continued)*		Developers will have to add effective state and session management services.
Indecisive customer (decision support system)	65%	The fully "objectized" nature of OrbixOTM means it is well suited to this type of application with its typically large files (including graphics). The application has a predictable number of clients and does not require frequent database updating; therefore, performance is in the acceptable range. Developers will have to add effective state and session management services to cope with the prolonged conversation-like application demands.
Customer with cash (online reservation or purchasing)	65%	This application requires only an immediate response for a small portion of requests, so the guaranteed send-and-forget messaging services of OrbixOTM are ideal. The overall environment for the application is fairly predictable with a reasonable population change rate. Developers will have to create effective state and session management services and statically define the workflow requirements of interaction among many components required by this application. (This application does demand multiple updates to databases; therefore response time may not be optimal.)

wheel with OrbixOTM, rather to add functionality to its existing ORB technology (an object-oriented way of thinking!).

The important thing to remember when reviewing OrbixOTM is that the technology remains true to the CORBA design philosophy and provides a wide range of standard APIs for the invocation of services; thus you can be confident that applications are using a widely supported approach for development.

Table 5.3 Evaluation Results

APPLICATION REQUIREMENT	TECHNOLOGY IMPLICATION	PRODUCT SUPPORT
Number of concurrent users: small to medium	Maximize minimal system resources through multi-threading.	**Yes.** through multithreading (developer intervention required).
Number of concurrent users: medium to large	Maximize performance and system utilization through multiplexing of client requests.	**Yes and No.** OrbixOTM can support many clients through multithreading (developer intervention required), provided there are adequate back-end resources to handle the required back-end objects. For large environments, OrbixOTM users may have to add custom code to create objects and maximize server resources.
User session length: short	Support short and quick requests and responses.	**Yes.** OrbixOTM maintains a connection between client and server objects to promptly handle requests.
User session length: long	Manage connections to maximize resource utilization.	**No.** Due to lack of state management and an incapability to optimize resources for long-term client connections.
User population changes: high number of sign-on/ sign off variances	Pool objects to maximize resources.	**No.** OrbixOTM may have a negative effect on resource utilization through a requirement to locate and instantiate new objects for each client request.

Continues

Table 5.3   Evaluation Results *(Continued)*

APPLICATION REQUIREMENT	TECHNOLOGY IMPLICATION	PRODUCT SUPPORT
Number of data sources: small	Maximize performance to a small set of back-end data sources.	**No.** OrbixOTM can support many types of databases through XA interfaces, but it does not provide database connection pooling nor direct connections to these databases.
Number of data sources: large	Effectively distribute the load across many data sources to maximize performance.	**Yes and No.** OrbixOTM provides dynamic XA connections, which will allow companies to move data from one data source to another with minimal impact on the OTM environment. However, the product supports very limited load balancing through a simple round-robin policy.
Object database integration	Provide for interoperating with object database management systems.	**Yes.** ODBMS support is provided through add-on products available from IONA.
Legacy system integration "in the box"	Access legacy system information without the need for an additional product.	**No.** Legacy integration services are not included.
Legacy system integration from additional products, from the same vendor	Purchase an additional legacy systems integration product from the same vendor.	**Yes.** IONA sells both an MVS version of its ORB product as well as individual connection products for CICS and IMS environments.
Average chain of distributed calls: simple	Statically define interaction among components.	**Yes.** Through standard CORBA implementation, customers can statically define component interaction.
Average chain of distributed calls: complex	Support workflow semantics among objects.	**No.** The product currently does not offer an effective state management solution.
Communication among objects: synchronous	Provide request/response communication model.	**Yes.** OrbixOTM provides synchronous communication among objects.
Communication among objects: asynchronous	Guarantee delivery of send-and-forget messages.	**Yes.** OrbixOTM includes an implementation of the CORBA Event Service, which

Table 5.3 *(Continued)*

APPLICATION REQUIREMENT	TECHNOLOGY IMPLICATION	PRODUCT SUPPORT
asynchronous *(Continued)*		can provide a means for asynchronous delivery (not guaranteed delivery) IONA also sells OrbixTalk, which uses IP Multicast for guaranteed reliable asynchronous communication.
Communication among objects: publish and subscribe	Provide services for objects to publish and subscribe event information.	**Yes**. OrbixOTM includes an implementation of the CORBA event service similar to publish/subscribe functionality.
Advanced messaging functionality through interoperability, with additional message-oriented middleware products	Interface to MOM products.	**Yes**. IONA offers separate products for integration with existing MOM products such as IBM's MQSeries and Peer Logic's PIPES.
Automatic maintenance of state between sessions	Support for automated state management facilities.	**No**. OrbixOTM does not provide automated state management facilities. Customers have to write custom code.
Response time: small environment (one server, smaller number of clients)	Ensure rapid response time for small client environments accessing one back-end resource.	**Yes**. OrbixOTM can provide good response for small environments through support of multithreaded objects (but developer intervention is required).
Response time: medium-size environment (four or fewer servers, manageable number of clients)	Ensure reasonable response time for an average size application environment with a manageable number of clients accessing the system concurrently.	**Yes and No**. Through multithreaded objects (but developer intervention is required). Response time will not be optimal but reasonable.
Response time: large to very large environments (more than four servers, hundreds to thousands of clients)	Ensure average response time for a large application environment in which many clients are concurrently accessing many back-end resources.	**No**. Although OrbixOTM can be configured for very large environments, resource utilization and response times may not be acceptable. In addition, the customer may have to write custom code for the multiplexing of objects and to gain effective load-balancing support.

Continues

Table 5.3   Evaluation Results *(Continued)*

APPLICATION REQUIREMENT	TECHNOLOGY IMPLICATION	PRODUCT SUPPORT
High availability/ fault tolerance: objects	Provide failover to back up objects in case of failure.	**No.** No automated services are provided in current release; hand-coding is necessary to achieve a level of fault resilience.
High availability/ fault tolerance: server system	Provide failover to back up resources in case of failure.	**No.** No automated services are provided in current release.
High availability/ fault tolerance: network	Provide mechanisms for switching to back-up network domain in case of network failure.	**No.** No automated services are provided in current release.
Security through authentication	Provide security services to ensure authentication control of objects.	**Yes.** OrbixOTM provides an implementation of CORBA Security Service Level 0 that can be used for authentication control.
Security through access control lists	Provide security services for control of access privileges for specific application components.	**No.** Not supported in current release.
Security through encryption	Provide encryption security for interaction between components.	**No.** Not supported in current release.
Security through integrity of data checking	Provide for detection of data modification during transmission.	**No.** Not supported in current release.

Up Next

In Chapter 6 we take a look at a completely different approach to the IONA design with BEA System's M3 product. As you'll see, the BEA approach builds off an existing transaction processing technology, rather than the ORB model.

M3 from BEA Systems

W ho says you can't buy your way into the enterprise? BEA Systems, located in San Jose, California, was founded in 1995 as a start-up in the OLTP market. Since then, the company has built up a nice collection of middleware products through acquisition and merger, including the following:

BEA TAP (formerly called BEA CICx). Acquired from VISystems, Inc. An IBM CICS-compatible transaction system environment that enables IBM mainframe TP applications to be distributed open systems easily.

BEA MessageQ. Acquired from Digital Equipment Corporation. A message-oriented middleware product.

BEA ObjectBroker. Acquired from Digital Equipment Corporation. A CORBA-compliant ORB.

BEA Top End. Acquired from NCR. An open systems-based distributed TP monitor.

BEA TUXEDO. Licensed from Novell, TUXEDO. An open systems-based distributed TP monitor.

BEA WebLogic Application Server (formerly known as Tengah). Acquired through merger with Web Logic Incorporated, A Web/Java application server that provides a platform for running server-side Java components and Java-to-database access tools for Internet-based applications.

And in 1996, BEA also acquired sole licensing and distribution rights on non-NetWare platforms to the TUXEDO transaction processing monitor from Novell Corporation. This move has proved to be a cornerstone to BEA's success in this marketplace.

TUXEDO, originally developed around 1984 by AT&T's UNIX Systems Laboratories (USL) for internal UNIX-based network-switching and directory assistance applications, Novell acquired USL in 1993 and, by default, TUXEDO. Since its creation, TUXEDO has undergone numerous changes and today has captured a majority share of the open systems OLTP market. According to data from The Standish Group, in 1998 BEA held 49% of this market and 12% of the overall middleware market.

Two of BEA Systems' middleware products named in the preceding list, ObjectBroker ORB and MessageQ were developed by Digital Equipment Corporation. BEA's current Object Monitor product, M3, in essence combines the ObjectBroker ORB with the TUXEDO TPM. In the future, the company plans to incorporate the MessageQ MOM. The company also plans to integrate key functionality from the recently acquired Top End TPM within the TUXEDO base portion of the M3 product architecture.

Finally, BEA Systems' 1998 merger with WebLogic Corporation, a provider of Web application services for Java applications, will provide a front end for both TUXEDO and M3 for Internet-based applications.

M3 Architecture

M3 is implemented as a framework built off BEA's TUXEDO TPM. This framework makes the product look a bit different from the previous product (OrbixOTM) evaluated in this book. M3 uses major portions of TUXEDO to implement application services and communication which is now referred to as the BEA Engine. On top of this base sits a CORBA-compliant ORB, based on BEA's ObjectBroker, known as the M3 ORB.

NOTE   A *framework* offers a complete architecture in which a collection of objects can work together. Rather than explicitily defining the flow of an application (how one object calls another, the order they should be called in, etc.), the framework defines both the execution flow and how objects that are part of the framework perform their functions. Using framework for development allows a product to automate server tasks, in turn making the programmer's life easier.

As indicated in Figure 6.1, there are two parts to the M3 environment: the first portion contains libraries, which are downloaded to each client machine in an M3 systems architecture, and the objects necessary to connect to the M3 server; the second part is the TP framework, indicated in the figure as a server application. Each application object in an M3 environment resides within this M3 server process; and within each process is the TP framework (actually the TUXEDO executable) which must be resident on each server in an M3 managed environment.

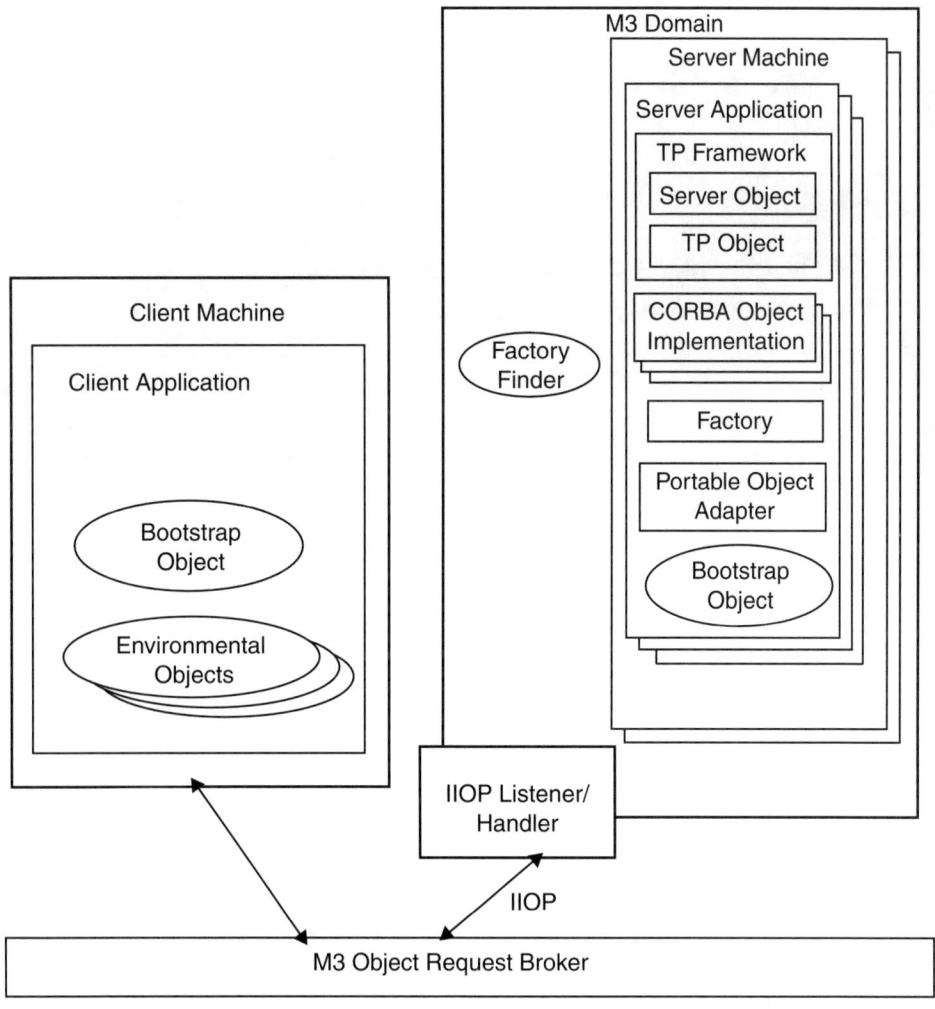

Figure 6.1   BEA product architecture.

Source: BEA Systems Inc.

Unlike a traditional CORBA implementation, in M3, the client objects communicate with *listeners*, and these assign IIOP *handlers* during the client's bootstrap process. At bootstrap time the listener assigns a handler which is responsible for subsequent communications with the client. Thereafter, all messages between client and server objects are passed over this single communications link, even when multiple server objects reside on different machines. The handler is the communication concentrator which uses the CORBA-defined Internet Inter-ORB Protocol (IIOP) for communication with the M3 server framework. The framework is responsible for managing the state associated with server-side objects including managing XA resources.

Figure 6.2 shows how the M3 system works at runtime. Clients do not go directly to a server object but to the M3 communication *concentrator*. This communication concentrator consists of the listeners, which find an appropriate instance of an object to invoke. The communication concentrator then uses the handlers to set up a communication model for client and server objects, which use the M3 runtime services. Every application object that the system will use resides within the M3 TP framework, which provides the flow of execution for invoking M3 services, thereby allowing these objects to take advantage of M3 services. From a client perspective, it appears there is a direct connection between the client and server objects, while behind the scenes, it is actually M3 that is in charge of routing the connections for each client request.

Like OrbixOTM, BEA has adopted a distributed transaction management model for M3. To review, this means that the status of each subtransaction (the resource involved in the course of the transaction) of a global transaction (entire transaction life cycle) is maintained in the memory of the node in which the subtransaction is running.

The advantage of this model is that it scales naturally, because each node shares the processing of application logic and transaction management. In addition, there is no single point of failure; if one node fails, the others can take over the load. The drawback to this approach is that it requires that the complete M3 server framework system on each server node be involved in the course of the transactional application. This assumes sufficient resources are available for both the installation and runtime requirements of both the M3 framework and the application objects. Plus, the centralized management of applications is more difficult than

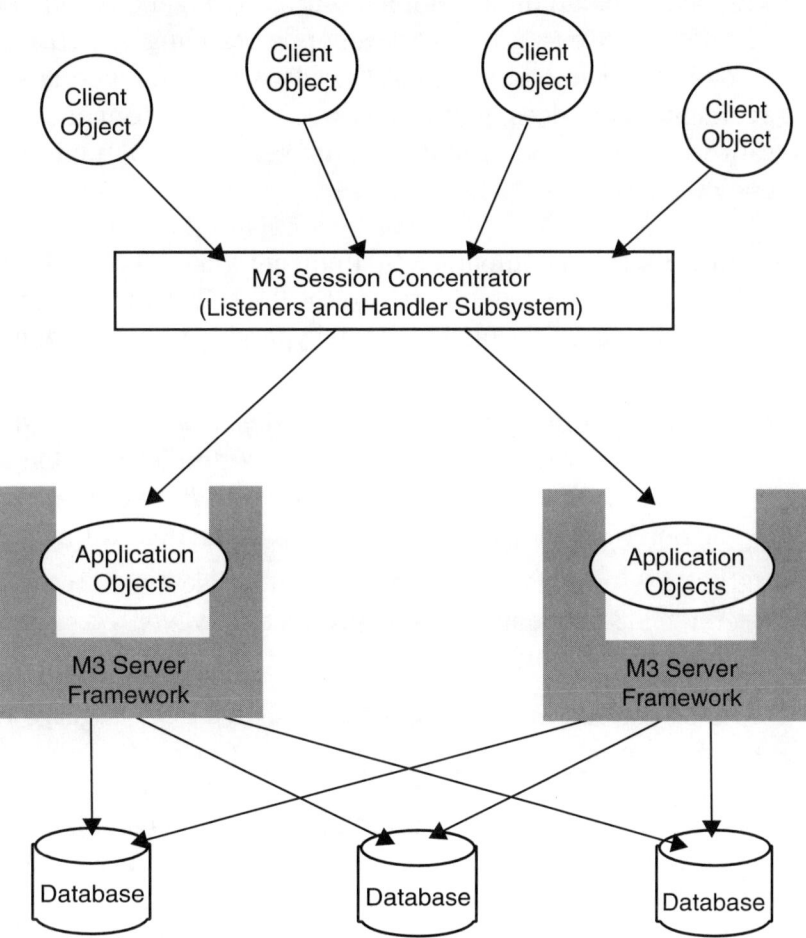

Figure 6.2   BEA runtime.

in a more centralized transaction model, because the distributed model assumes that each node is independent and complete.

Developing with M3

M3 includes a GUI-based installer that makes installation a snap. In addition the M3 documentation is superb, written in easy-to-understand language and highlighted by good examples. The M3 architecture makes liberal use of the TUXEDO TPM, so if you're familiar with TUXEDO, you will have a leg up on developing with M3. In general, however, working with M3 requires a good working understanding of CORBA and distributed object technology, though because the product comes bundled with a number of services, you won't have to add custom code to most applications. Here are other major parameters to keep in mind for M3 development:

- Developers in companies that currently have TUXEDO applications can use M3 to write directly to the TUXEDO Application to Transaction Manager Interface (ATMI), bypassing the ORB technology altogether.

- At the time of this writing M3 provides for C++ server development only. Java, C++, and ActiveX are supported for client side development only. BEA plans to provide for Java development and support for Enterprise JavaBeans interfaces in the near future.

- BEA Systems also has an agreement to use Symantec's VisualCafé to create M3 applications. This product, however, was not yet available at the time of this writing.

> **NOTE** **For the purposes of our review of M3, we used the C++ language on both client and server objects.**

The process of developing an M3 application is similar to a traditional CORBA process; it differs in the way to find objects and uses slightly different APIs and terminology. Because you are using a framework approach in M3, you do not write directly to traditional CORBA APIs, but to "M3-style CORBA APIs," which are specific to the M3 product.

Figure 6.3 shows the three main elements of the M3 TP framework: the main program, the service objects, and the portable object adapter (POA), defined as follows:

- The main program is primarily responsible for starting a server application, connecting the ORB and POA to the server application, and invoking an initialization method on the server object. It is also responsible for notifying objects in the event of a failure and for shutting down server applications.

- The service objects (which BEA refers to as "convenience" objects) provides methods that the main program will invoke to create and release server objects. It also supplies objects for the creation of object references, for registering and unregistering factories, and for other miscellaneous operations.

- The portable object adapter (POA) locates an available instance of a class of object as requested by the client. (Currently, M3 is the only CORBA-enabled product on the market that supports the use of the

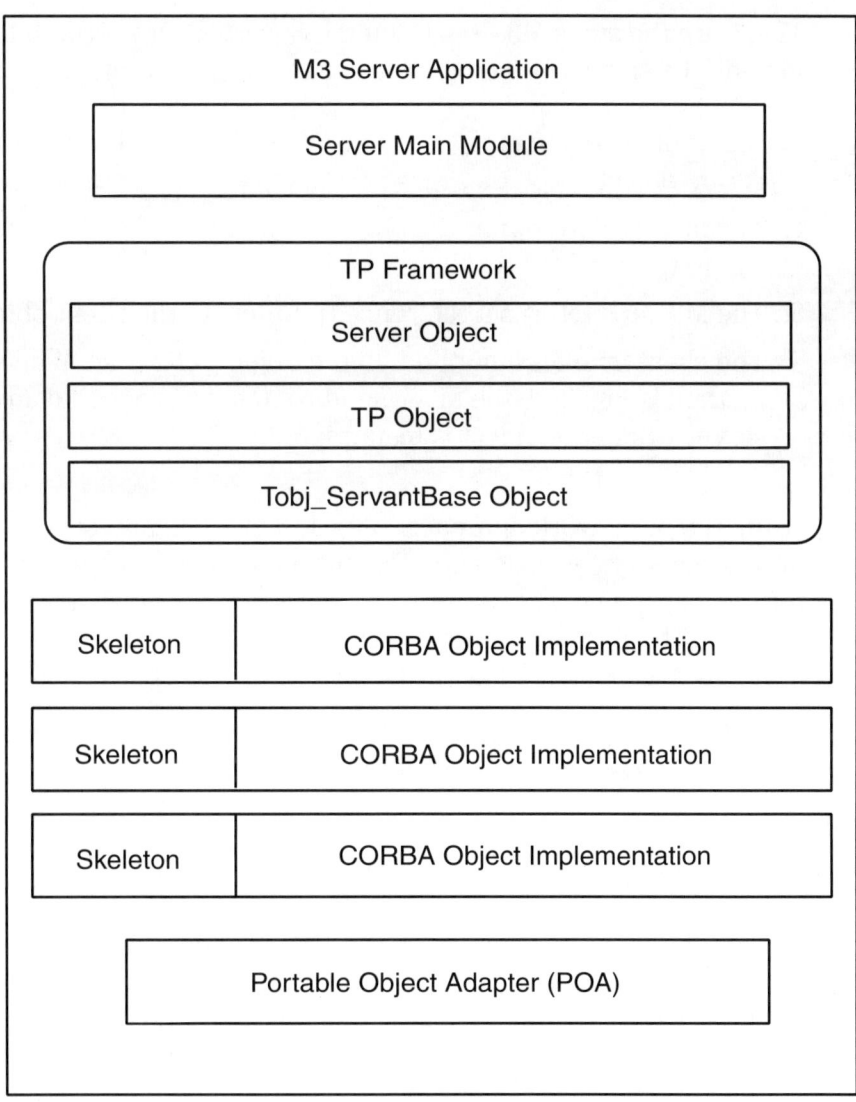

Figure 6.3 BEA's M3 framework.

Source: BEA Systems Inc.

CORBA-defined POA.) It does not need the same level of detailed information that the more traditional basic object adapter (BOA) requires; it only needs information on the class of the object requested. The POA takes this high-level information and finds an available instance of the class. This results in a more flexible and portable system.

These are the steps M3 uses to bind to a server object (note they do not include the steps involved for the use of security or other services):

1. Client binds to a factory and asks it to create a reference to an application object.
2. The factory determines the type of object to create, then makes a call to the M3 ORB for the reference.
3. The M3 ORB returns a reference (pointer) to the client object.
4. The client invokes a method on the object reference. When the method is invoked, the M3 system routes the request to an available server where the object is instantiated.

Using the framework approach, M3 can automatically provide a number of runtime services, made possible through the inheritance of M3 classes for the management of user-created objects. These management services enable M3 to discover information about the objects using the system, and it therefore can manipulate the behavior of these objects automatically.

For COM-based systems, M3 provides creation and runtime support for allowing ActiveX clients to access M3 CORBA objects.

Application Architecture Considerations

Though M3's heavy reliance on the BEA Engine (TUXEDO) somewhat limits its flexibility, using proven services can mean the difference between having to add a great deal of custom code for large application environments and taking advantage of the strong application service technology of a traditional transactional product. The following sections dissect the pros and cons of this approach across the application pattern requirements introduced in Chapter 4.

Number of Concurrent Users

M3 implements a slightly different way of handling multiple concurrent users from that of the traditional CORBA approach to scalability. For starters, it does not support multithreaded objects, probably because the execution environment for M3 is still the TUXEDO system (TUXEDO was not built as an object-oriented product, therefore it never required such).

This implies there is a limit to the number of clients that can access the same object. Instead, M3 offers what is referred to as *multiplexing*. When a client makes a request to the M3 system, M3 finds an instance (an object) that can perform the requested operation and takes care of connecting the client to that instance. The result is that, rather than limiting the number of concurrent clients to the availability of threads, M3 clients are limited by the number of instances that back-end resources can support to perform the requested operation. Thus, M3 can create new instances of objects on demand. Therefore, scalability need not be statically defined; M3 is in charge of managing the number of server objects required. Consequently, in general, there is no limit to the scalability that M3 can offer, provided you have the hardware to run the number of instances to meet your application needs (Figure 6.4).

What does this mean for your applications? First, M3 can scale *up* very nicely. If your application requires that a large number of users be able

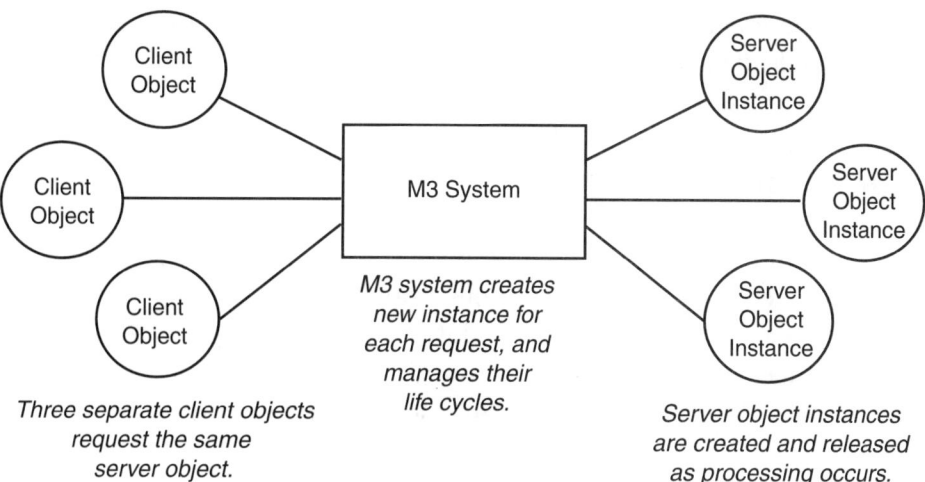

Figure 6.4 BEA's M3 approach to scalability.

to access the application concurrently, you'll find the product has an almost limitless capability to handle the load. And, importantly, this is dynamic and does not require a great deal of forethought on the part of developers (except to ensure server memory resources are sufficient to handle peak loads).

The downside to multiplexing (versus multithreading) is that M3 cannot effectively scale *down*. So, for those applications that do not have a significant concurrent client access requirement, or for those in a smaller execution environment, M3 will not be able to utilize minimal system resources for concurrent access to the same object.

User Session Length

In a typical CORBA architecture, the ORB maintains the connection between a client and a server at all times, even when the client machine is doing nothing, and the only way to deal with this is through custom-coding. But thanks to M3's concentrator and handlers, there is a built-in method to eliminate this waste of resources. Through the TP framework, M3 automatically manages these connections; they are only established for the execution of a request, and are immediately released upon response.

This is very useful for applications that may have long-term connections to the system that may not always be active (such as in a customer service or call center application). In this regard, we found that M3 shows a clear advantage over more traditional direct client-to-server object connection approaches for both performance and resource utilization.

User Population Changes

Handling rapid population changes is also improved thanks to M3's session concentrator. Clients need not connect directly to a server object; instead they can take advantage of the M3 framework multiplexer, which can create new instances dynamically (without user intervention). Thus, the product can effectively maintain an environment even during rapid climbs and drops in the client population. M3 also provides for the automated management of "pools of objects," which allows M3 to keep some popular objects resident to handle very large numbers of users. The downside is that because the product does not provide for multithreaded objects, it must create an entirely new instance of an object for each client (rather than just create a new thread).

Prior to testing, we were concerned that the indirect approach might have some performance disadvantages for applications with short user sessions, but this is not the case, probably due to the fact that M3 relies on the TUXEDO engine, which has been optimized throughout the years. M3 will manage a pool of business objects so that new client requests are given an optimal route to a recently available or new object instance. The more important effect of this may be on resource utilization, as server machines must have enough memory to handle the creation of multiple instances during peak periods.

Data Access

M3 allows for connections both through XA as well as directly to many relational database management systems. In fact, M3 currently boasts the richest set of connections to databases today. In the course of our investigation of the product, we switched from Oracle version 7.3 to Oracle 8 and the transition was very smooth; we just recompiled— nothing more. We found only one drawback: A requirement to reestablish a new database connection for each request. Consequently, performance to a database is not, by default, optimal (but not reduced enough to warrant any concern).

M3 offers a number of database pool management facilities to assist in balancing the load across back-end systems. To do so, the product makes use of the advanced load-balancing capabilities of the TUXEDO system. When M3 receives a request for an object, and no current transaction exists, it will analyze load conditions of possible server processes to find the one that is least busy, then automatically route the request to that system. Where there is a transaction running, M3 will attempt to route the new instance to the same machine for performance optimization.

In addition, M3 allows administrative control of M3 factories. Administrators can assign data-routing rules defined by an administrator, and perform what BEA calls "factory-based routing." This enables the object factories to influence on which system the new instance runs, based on object references. For large environments involving many clients this can be essential for keeping an application in operation (no need to worry about crashing a server system, provided you have a big enough pool for M3 to utilize).

> **NOTE** M3 does not have any automated tools for integration with object database management systems, nor is the company currently in partnership with object-to-relational mapping vendors. For those applications that may require this, a third-party product is the only option.

Legacy System Integration

BEA Systems currently markets BEA Connect for connecting to legacy systems (it must be purchased separately). BEA Connect contains a set of libraries that allow developers to connect to CICS and IMS systems. The product does not allow for two-phase commit coordination between legacy and relational systems for transactional applications, but it does allow companies to access existing information. Currently, the product is very programming-intensive, requiring developers to do quite a bit of handwork. As an option, BEA offers consulting services, which can provide integration to many legacy systems on a per-project basis.

A company could alternatively provide IDL wrappers for existing applications to take advantage of the M3 CORBA architecture, but this would have to be done in-house or in combination with a consulting organization. To address this deficiency in the future, BEA plans to integrate its MessageQ product, which should grant easier access to many legacy systems and to packaged applications.

Response Time

The M3 system is optimized for the addition of clients and servers to the environment with minimal impact. In addition response time is further increased through the listener/handler subsystem of the M3 environment which limits network utilization to outstanding invocations. To optimize performance, handlers can be distributed across multiple machines. For very large environments, entire machines may even be designated as listener or handler servers; in which case, these machines can be fine-tuned for communications and to minimize performance degradation even further.

As mentioned briefly in the previous section, M3 also allows for transaction processing performance through transaction clustering. In this case, M3 can route requests that are part of the same transaction to the same server systems; this optimizes performance by grouping objects that are working together on the same machine.

The incorporation of the TUXEDO technology, which has been continually optimized for performance over the years, plays a crucial role in allowing M3 to perform well even with very large client and server configurations. It is important to note that on large applications, M3 will maximize the load and connections so all users have a good, average response time for every query, with a reasonable rate of increase as new clients and/or servers are added to the system.

In contrast, in environments that require very rapid response time for a small number of clients, M3 may not be able to optimize system resources. In these smaller environments we note that an alternative product which utilizes a multithreaded object design may provide better performance and the ability to take advantage of limited hardware.

Messaging

Like all CORBA ORB products today, M3 allows users to initiate one-way asynchronous calls, a form of asynchronous communication that is CORBA-compliant. That said, this does require a lot of custom configuration and coding, and message delivery is not guaranteed. Also note that M3 does not presently support the TUXEDO transactional messaging features, although this support should be forthcoming.

As noted earlier, BEA Systems plans to incorporate its MOM, MessageQ, with M3 to provide advanced messaging functionality for objects that use the M3 environment. Currently, MessageQ offers message queuing, guaranteed and assured delivery, and asynchronous and broadcast messaging services. (Check with BEA Systems or this book's Web site for updates on this integration.)

State Management

The architecture for M3 requires a reliable state management facility, so it's no surprise that the product offers a great deal here. In building M3 applications, developers are required to build two extra methods for each class of server object that will use the M3 system, to describe how to save state and how to restore state. However, unlike a traditional

CORBA implementation, developers do not need to provide any additional state management; M3 fully automates this task.

M3 introduces a layer between the client and server objects through the server-side framework, which enables the M3 framework to automatically invoke these methods. When a client object makes a call to a server object, the M3 system will find an instance of the required object and restore its state based on the object's restore method. After the procedure has finished, M3 will save the state of the object in a persistent store, typically a database, which has been defined within the save method of the object.

High Availability/Fault Tolerance

M3 includes high availability/fault tolerance attributes for a variety of potential failures:

Client Failures. In a normal CORBA environment, each time clients connect to a server object, they are connected to the server the object is running on, whereas in the M3 environment, clients access the system first by connecting to the session concentrator. It is the session concentrator that takes care of connecting the client to an appropriate instance of an object. Then when a user disconnects from the system and reconnects he or she may be connected to a different instance on a different server. If a client is connected to a server or process that fails, M3 automatically reconnects the client to another instance of that object on a different machine.

Server Failures. The M3 system allows users to define replicated server processes that can take over in case of a server failure. In the event of a failure, M3 will automatically roll back any in-process requests and redirect them to the replicated server. System administrators may also configure the M3 system to retry the downed server process.

Planned Maintenance Outages. The M3 administration tools provide facilities for the migration of server processes to a backup machine without impacting the production application.

Network Failures. During network failures, M3 can be configured to partition the network into two domains, one on either side of the failure. M3 will continue to manage the domains separately; and when the network is fixed, M3 can reintegrate the environment.

Security

M3 provides both level 1 and level 2 CORBA-compliant security services using SSL-based security mechanisms. This allows the product to provide authentication of clients as well as the encryption of passwords for access control. M3 also protects against data corruption through a proprietary security mechanism within the M3 domain; this offers link-level encryption between bridge links (in the future, BEA plans to offer SSL as a means for integrity).

Systems Management

M3 has many automated management features for objects through its capability to automatically create object instances and manage their life cycle and to automatically manage failures and load-balancing. M3 administration tools can also be used to specify load-balancing or failure scenarios as well as to monitor the status of M3 operations. These services can be centrally managed through a Java-based management console.

The M3 management console offers initial configuration information, operation statistics, events and alerts, and both a global and local view of M3 domains; it also has the capability to monitor and change a running system. Optionally, M3 users can use a traditional local command-line management interface.

The same tool used for M3 application administration can also be used for new and existing TUXEDO programs, providing a logical view of both object transaction and traditional transactional applications, of particular benefit to TUXEDO users. Finally, BEA offers additional tools to integrate the M3 console with existing systems management tools from third parties through SNMP agents.

The Verdict

M3 is ideal for applications that must support a large number of customers or that need to share resources. The product is primarily geared toward medium to large configurations of server machines that contain adequate memory to run the M3 server framework and sustain the ongoing creation of multiple object instances. M3 is also clearly a winner for mission-critical applications that require no-fault transaction processing, very good response time, the ability to scale to very large environments, and a systems infrastructure consisting of many types of databases. It is also recommended for current TUXEDO users, as it continues to leverage both technologies, on the development end as well is in the administration of both environments.

M3 is less ideal for smaller environments that could benefit from multithreaded object support and database connection pooling for fast performance. And in its current form, M3 is not well suited to applications primarily geared toward offering a Web-based front end to existing applications or that require the mixing and matching of objects written in different languages (remember, the current product supports only C++ for server-side objects).

Object purists may find M3 a bit too structured and inflexible, because it relies heavily on a traditional transaction processing product. And CORBA proponents should be aware that applications created with M3 make use of a number of proprietary services that make moving M3 applications to another CORBA environment very difficult. However, experienced developers probably could quickly overcome these limitations thanks to M3's application services that can be implemented easily, without additional coding.

Table 6.1 lists the factors to consider when evaluating M3 for your application requirements.

New applications can take advantage of M3's proven set of application services. Table 6.2 breaks down these services, and Table 6.3 lists the results of our testing.

BEA's M3 uses the novel approach of adding object interfaces to a proven technology base. At times this means that the technology is not as "objectized" as other products in the market, but it also means that the technology can offer a number of application services, in particular,

Table 6.1 M3 Application Considerations

BEST APPLICATION CONFIGURATION	MAJOR APPLICATION CONSIDERATIONS
Medium to very large client and server configurations in heterogeneous environments	Ideally suited to transaction-intensive applications with many users accessing many back-end systems.

for new applications. Likewise, for applications that require a lot of powerful application services, M3, like its counterpart TUXEDO, has a lot to offer. In summary, we believe that most application scenarios could benefit from M3's functionality.

Table 6.2 Results of Testing against Application Patterns

APPLICATION PATTERN	PERCENTAGE OF APPLICATION SERVICES	USE IMPLICATIONS
Customer service direct (Internet-based service)	85%	Has the capability to handle many clients and many back-end resources and to manage these connections. The product could benefit from database connection pooling and multithreaded object support, but overall is still a good choice.
Customer service indirect (typical customer service)	85%	Through the capability to manage connections for a large number of users and provide effective state management M3 is very useful for this type of application. It does, however, suffer from the incapability to share databases connections and provide support for distributed workflow.
Customer on-call (call center)	95%	A wide array of services can assist in this type of application: complete management of state information, client and server object communication, and good response time. Only applications that require additional support for component combinations will require extra service development.
Customer with a vote (online auction or brokerage)	90%	A wide array of application services are available for this application type, plus very good response time. Developers may need to add the capability to guarantee message delivery between various components through some form of reliable messaging transport.
Indecisive customer (decision support system)	100%	
Customer with cash (online reservation or purchasing)	100%	

Table 6.3 Evaluation Results

APPLICATION REQUIREMENT	TECHNOLOGY IMPLICATION	PRODUCT SUPPORT
Number of concurrent users: small to medium	Maximize minimal system resources through multithreading.	**No.** M3 does not support multithreading; may be overkill for small environments.
Number of concurrent users: medium to large	Maximize performance and system utilization through multiplexing of client requests.	**Yes.** M3 provides multiplexing, and has been optimized for maximum performance and minimal resource utilization for medium to large environments.
User session length: short	Support short requests and responses.	**Yes.** M3 is optimized and has been proven reliable for multiple short requests and responses, even in very large environments.
User session length: long	Manage connections to maximize resource utilization.	**Yes.** Connections between client and server objects are fully managed by M3, and are only required during the actual processing of requests.
User population changes: high number of sign-on/ sign-off variances	Pool objects to maximize resources.	**Yes.** M3 manages a pool of objects and is able to sustain very good response rates and minimal resource utilization even during rapid population changes.
Number of data sources: small	Maximize performance to a small set of back-end data sources.	**Yes and No.** M3 offers options for direct connections to many databases, which can increase performance; however it does not provide for database connection multiplexing, which could increase performance, particularly to smaller database configurations.
Number of data sources: large	Effectively distribute the load across many data sources to maximize performance.	**Yes.** M3 provides a variety of load-balancing options, which are fully managed by the product to assist with the use of many data sources.
Object database integration	Provide for interoperating with object database management systems.	**No.** M3 does not provide any automated tools for connections to ODBMSs.

Table 6.3 *(Continued)*

APPLICATION REQUIREMENT	TECHNOLOGY IMPLICATION	PRODUCT SUPPORT
Legacy system integration "in the box"	Access legacy system information without the need for an additional product.	**Yes.** Legacy access is through add-on BEA products.
Legacy system integration from additional products: from the same vendor	Purchase an additional legacy systems integration product from the same vendor.	**Yes.** BEA Connect enables connections to CICS and IMS environments (but resources cannot participate in 2PC coordination).
Average chain of distributed call: simple	Statically define interaction among components.	**Yes.** Through CORBA technology, developers can define static interaction among components.
Average chain of a distributed call: complex	Support workflow semantics among objects.	**No.** Current implementation does not support any workflow features for communicating objects.
Communication among objects: synchronous	Provide request/response communication model.	**Yes.** M3 natively supports synchronous communication through both CORBA ORB and TUXEDO portions of the product.
Communication among objects: asynchronous	Guarantee delivery of send-and-forget messages.	**No.** Current implementation only allows users to create one-way asynchronous calls (due to CORBA structure).
Communication among objects: publish and subscribe	Provide services for objects to publish and subscribe event information.	**No.** Current implementation has no support for publish and subscribe.
Advanced messaging functionality through interoperability with additional message-oriented middleware products	Interface to MOM products.	**No.** Current implementation does not provide interfaces to any MOM products (though integration with BEA MessageQ product is planned).
Automatic maintenance of session state	Support automated state management facilities.	**Yes.** M3 fully automates state management of objects.
Response time: small environment (one server, smaller number of clients)	Ensure rapid response time for small client environments accessing one back-end resource	**Yes and No.** M3 can provide very rapid response for small configurations, but the product may use unnecessary amounts of resources, as it is not optimized for this type of environment.

Continues

Table 6.3 Evaluation Results *(Continued)*

APPLICATION REQUIREMENT	TECHNOLOGY IMPLICATION	PRODUCT SUPPORT
Response time: medium-size environment (four or fewer servers, manageable number of clients)	Ensure reasonable response time for an average size application environment with a manageable number of clients accessing the system concurrently.	**Yes.** M3 has been optimized for rapid response rates from medium to large environments.
Response time: large to very large environments (more than four servers, hundreds to thousands of clients)	Ensure average response time for a large application environment in which many clients are concurrently accessing many back-end resources.	**Yes.** M3 is ideally suited to large and very large environments; it is adept and ensures very good response times even during significant increases in the number of clients and/or servers.
High availability/fault tolerance: objects	Provide failover to back up objects in case of failure.	**Yes.** In the event of client object failure, the M3 session concentrator can take control of reconnecting to an alternative back-up object.
High availability/fault tolerance: server system	Provide failover to back up resource in case of failure.	**Yes.** M3 allows for user-defined replicated server processes that automatically take over in case of server failure.
High availability/fault tolerance: network	Provide mechanisms for switching to back-up network domain in case of network failure.	**Yes.** M3 can be configured to partition a network into two domains and provide failover and recovery services.
Security through authentication	Provide security services to ensure authentication control of objects.	**Yes.** M3 provides SSL-based authentication security.
Security through access control lists	Provide security services for control of access privileges for specific application components.	**No.** M3 does not use access control lists for security.
Security through encryption	Provide encryption security for interaction between components.	**Yes.** M3 provides a proprietary security service for link-level encryption.
Security through integrity of data checking	Provide for detection of data modification during transmission.	**No.** M3 does not use security mechanisms for data integrity checking.

Up Next

Chapter 7 introduces a product that is different from both OrbixOTM and M3, in that it does not combine two distinct middleware products, but has been built from the ground up as an object-oriented transaction system. Read on to see how Inprise Corporation has developed its Integrated Transaction Service (ITS) product.

Integrated Transaction Service from Inprise Corporation

Inprise Corporation's Integrated Transaction Service (ITS) was established as an amalgam of different product backgrounds. The base architecture of the product, the object request broker (ORB) was initially developed by a small Silicon Valley startup by the name of PostModern Computing. This company entered into an agreement with Hitachi Software for the development of an Object Monitor product called TPBroker.

PostModern Computing was purchased in 1996 by Visigenic Corporation, a database connectivity vendor that primarily distributed its products through OEM agreements. It was under this company's direction that the base ORB technology garnered substantial notice due to licensing agreements with the likes of such companies as Netscape Communications, Inc., Novell Corporation, Oracle Corporation, and Sybase Incorporated. Also during this time, Visigenic changed direction with respect to object-oriented transactional capabilities and began development of the Integrated Transaction Service (ITS) with less of a focus on the original TPBroker technology.

NOTE **If your company is partial to the Inprise implementation of a CORBA ORB, you have two choices in this market. Hitachi Software has continued to develop the TPBroker product line (covered in Chapter 8). The ITS product detailed here and the Hitachi implementation of an object monitor can both be used to extend your existing VisiBroker environment with transactional capabilities.**

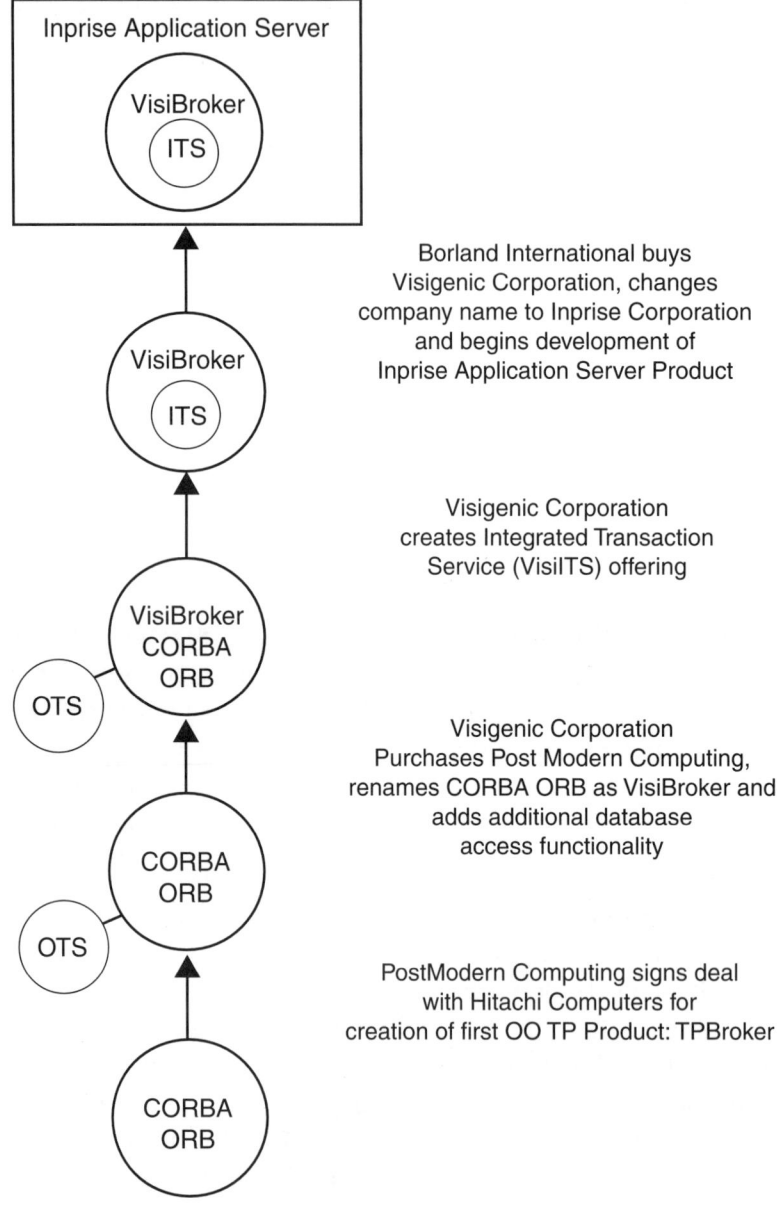

Inprise Application Server

VisiBroker

ITS

Borland International buys
Visigenic Corporation, changes
company name to Inprise Corporation
and begins development of
Inprise Application Server Product

VisiBroker

ITS

Visigenic Corporation
creates Integrated Transaction
Service (VisiITS) offering

VisiBroker
CORBA
ORB

OTS

Visigenic Corporation
Purchases Post Modern Computing,
renames CORBA ORB as VisiBroker and
adds additional database
access functionality

CORBA
ORB

OTS

PostModern Computing signs deal
with Hitachi Computers for
creation of first OO TP Product: TPBroker

CORBA
ORB

PostModern Computing Creates
CORBA ORB Product called Orbeline

Figure 7.1 Evolution of the ITS technology.

In 1998, Borland International, the well-known development tool company, surprised the market with its acquisition of Visigenic. Shortly thereafter, Borland changed its company name to Inprise, an acronym for *In*tegrating the Enter*prise*, to reflect its new direction: To create a completely integrated environment for both the development and execution of enterprise-level applications.

Inprise Corporation plans to incorporate the ITS technology with a product called the Inprise Application Server (expected to be available by the time this book is published). The Inprise Application Server product will combine the ITS technology with Inprise development and management tools. The goal is to hide much of the complexity of building object-oriented distributed applications within an easy-to-use development and management suite.

ITS has been built from the ground up as an object-oriented transactional product. We want to stress this point, because the architecture of the product is very flexible and can be confusing to anyone accustomed to a typical transaction processing monitor product. So hold onto your hats as we examine all the options.

Fortunately, though the base ITS technology can be very difficult to grasp, the complexity promises to largely be hidden from developers following the introduction of the aforementioned Inprise Application Server.

ITS Product Architecture

ITS is implemented as a set of class libraries and executables. As indicated in Figure 7.2, the product is completely object-oriented, with each portion of the architecture performing a specific task. All elements of the transaction services communicate through the base VisiBroker ORB. The actual transaction management portion of the product, called the ITS Transaction Service, includes logging, recovery, and coordination of two-phase commit for transactional integrity. The ITS Session Manager is responsible for communication with database resources, and can be used for either direct connections with databases or for ITS XA connections. In the latter case, the ITS Session Manager uses the ITS XA Resource Director for managing XA protocol interactions.

In contrast to a traditional transaction processing model, the transaction management portion of the product, ITS Transaction Service, is a separate process; it is not tied to any resource manager. In essence, this means that the product is very flexible, allowing for an infinite array of possibilities for users configuring their ITS systems, dependent on specific systems or application requirements.

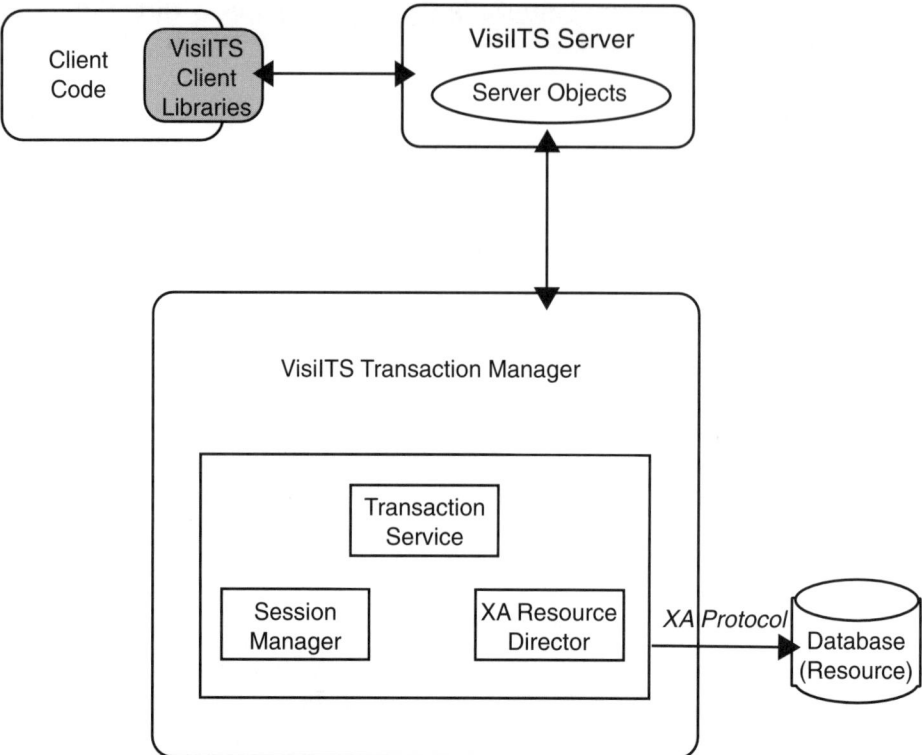

Figure 7.2 ITS product architecture.

There are two ways to use the transaction management features: in-process in combination with application objects, or as a separate external service (also indicated in Figure 7.2). When using ITS as an in-process transaction service, transaction management performance can be improved thanks to access via a virtual function call within the specific application.

Inprise uses a centralized model for transaction processing, meaning that each time clients make a request, they go through the same logical transaction server process. Thus, ITS maintains the status of a global transaction (the resource is involved in the course of the transaction) within the memory of the ITS server running somewhere in the network. All transaction requests, such as *begin* and *commit*, are sent to the ITS server through a stub. It is possible to run multiple copies of ITS servers on the network, in which case load balancing can be achieved on a per-transaction basis, but the global transaction belongs to one ITS server only.

The advantage of this model is that it is simple to administrate and uses fewer resources; when one node is configured to run a server, all other nodes require just a client library. Using this model, entire servers can be dedicated to transaction management, with individual data sources managing data access on the resource machine. The disadvantage is that if it is not configured properly, ITS can become a single point of failure and performance bottleneck. However, the transaction service machine can be replicated to avoid single-point-of-failure concerns. The centralized model assumes interdependent network computing, so using services on the other node is easy and cheap.

Because the product is completely object-oriented, and therefore very flexible, users have the option of using the transaction service as a centralized service on one machine (or set of replicated machines) for centralized management. Or the service may be distributed within multiple applications or across multiple server machines (for performance and scalability). Environments can even use any combination of the two; with ITS, it is fairly easy to switch between modes simply by changing configuration files.

 The distributed transaction management features of ITS are not based on an existing transaction processing technology product and have not undergone rigorous production experience. For this reason, we recommend that companies *carefully* and *thoroughly* perform reference checks before using ITS for mission-critical applications that require absolute transaction integrity via two-phase commit coordination.

Figure 7.3 shows how the various elements of ITS work at runtime, along with the relationship between these services. Note that all transactions go through the same logical central transaction server, which can be replicated to run on multiple database instances (though the product will still use one logical transaction server system).

There are two options for binding client requests to server objects with ITS. Using a traditional CORBA approach, the product goes through the following steps:

1. Bind request comes to ITS ORB.
2. The ORB consults the CORBA implementation repository for the appropriate invocation policy to use, and starts the new instance of an object, if necessary, returning a pointer to the client object.
3. The server object is notified and passed the request, thereby receiving full control over the execution of initiating a response and creating a new thread to handle the request.

ITS also provides a proprietary way of binding to a server object, but users must be aware that this approach is not CORBA standard and therefore will make moving applications to another CORBA product more difficult. The proprietary ITS option uses an *OSAgent* to locate an instance of the server object and an *Activation Daemon* to invoke this object.

Choosing the model to use depends on whether you would like your application to include additional functionality provided through the proprietary OSAgent in combination with the Activation Daemon. This chapter provides information on both approaches in the Application Architecture section, next.

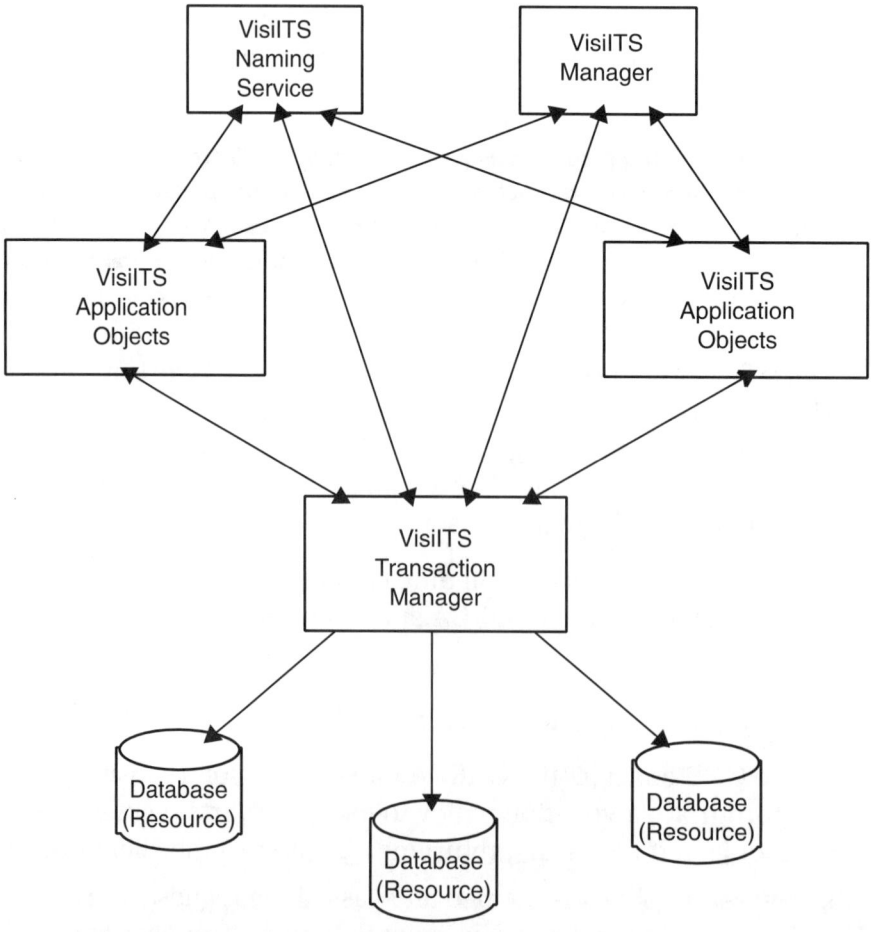

Figure 7.3   ITS runtime environment.

Developing with ITS

Installing ITS is fairly easy using a GUI-based installation interface. While the "Borland effect" is not yet apparent for development in the current version of the product, it is forthcoming. And Inprise plans to allow for the creation of ITS applications through virtually all of its development tool offerings. An early demonstration of the integration between ITS and Inprise's JBuilder development tool were impressive. If your company currently makes use of Inprise development tools, this will greatly ease the creation of ITS applications.

Currently, though, ITS has no integrated development environment. We used a C++ version of the product, but Inprise also has a complete Java version of both its ORB product and ITS, which implements the standard Java Transaction Service (JTS). If Java development is important for your company, ITS is worth a closer look.

Netscape has extended its API with the Web Application Interface (WAI) for Internet-enabled applications. WAI uses a licensed version of the Inprise VisiBroker ORB, thereby allowing CORBA (and therefore ITS) applications to be easily accessed from Netscape browsers or Netscape servers; both options are shown in Figure 7.4.

NOTE **Netscape has extended its API with WAI (Web Application Interface) for Internet-enabled applications. WAI uses a licensed version of the Inprise VisiBroker ORB, which in turn allows TPBroker applications to be easily accessed from Netscape browsers (see Chapter 7 for details on this approach).**

To take full advantage of ITS, significant CORBA skills are required, as well as experience with distributed systems. In some cases a high-level skill set in object-oriented programming might also be necessary to create application services, depending on application requirements. And beware, the flexibility of the architecture introduces a catch-22: Though object application designers have an almost limitless choice for how to use the product, if they don't consider all their options up front, the result could be less than optimal.

Application Architecture Considerations

The ITS products application services, including transaction services, are built on a CORBA ORB foundation. As an enhanced ORB-based product, it is positioned to offer services for both mission-critical and nonmission-critical applications. In the following sections you will discover how ITS works in relation to various application considerations.

> NOTE **As you read, keep in mind that ITS is a developing product, and that the information given here is current only as of the time of this writing.**

Number of Concurrent Users

Scalability with ITS is achieved through standard CORBA multithreaded object policies: thread pool and thread per call. There is no single-threaded version of the product. ITS makes it easy to switch threading policies simply by adjusting parameters. This can come in handy, enabling

Option 1: Using HTML

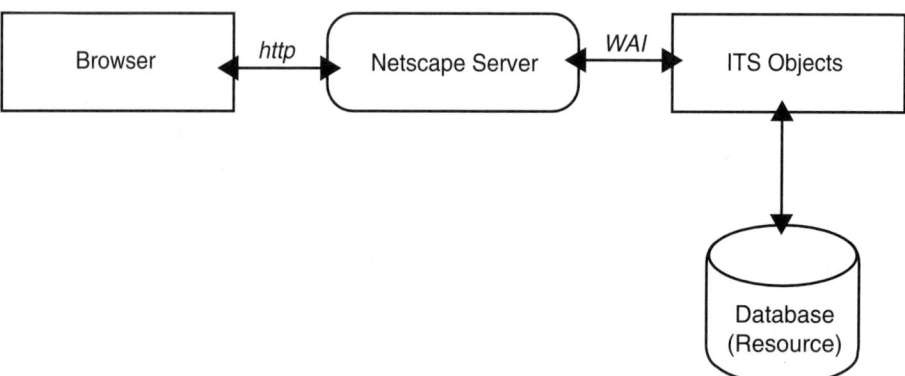

Option 2: Using Java applets

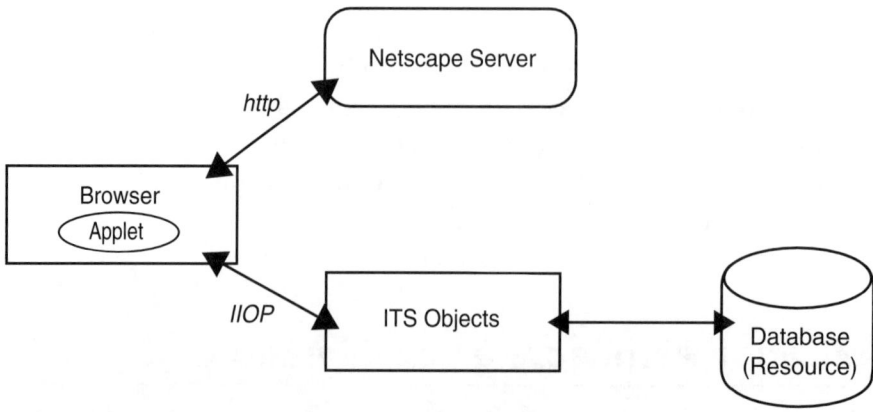

Figure 7.4 Internet access to ITS applications: two options.

a company to try different threading policies according to application requirements for optimum performance. The multithreading approach also means ITS can be configured to handle many users in both large and small environments with minimal resource requirements.

That said, ITS is limited to available server objects therefore larger environments might require custom-coding to create the multiple object instances necessary to handle the load and to prevent crashing the back-end system. (The only alternative would be to have many instances of the same objects available, but this is not advisable, because system resources would go to waste during off-peak periods.)

It is noteworthy that due to the product's flexibility, ITS can be enhanced as an application's user requirements increase. Though as just mentioned large environments will need additional custom-coding, the ITS base architecture makes it possible to be used for a range of applications from small to large population configurations.

But note, as an application increases in size, and therefore application requirements, the ITS systems architecture can quickly become very complex, and customers may want to switch from using ITS as a centralized product to a more distributed model for the sake of performance and scalability. While this will help it in turn means that using the ITS services in a distributed model can cause a major configuration headache, as the design must be carefully managed to avoid single-point-of-failure scenarios and performance bottlenecks.

User Session Length

True to its CORBA nature, ITS keeps client connections to servers active at all times. For quick requests and replies, the direct connection approach is not a problem, and can in fact offer some performance advantages. Conversely, there is no easy way of handling the management of these client-to-server connections without some additional custom coding. In terms of resource utilization, the continuous connection approach may impact applications whose users access the system for long periods of time (which may not always be active). For applications that require long-term connections, this translates to a need for sufficient resources to handle peak demands.

To help with this, ITS lets users configure the system to perform load balancing across machines on a per-transaction basis. This makes it possible to allocate specific machines for transactional applications that may involve many users. In this case, full servers or server configurations can be designed as transaction management servers even for specific types of applications.

User Population Changes

ITS establishes a direct client-to-server object approach. Therefore, the number of clients is always limited to the number of available object instances. For applications that will not involve rapid population changes, client requests in ITS can largely be managed through the use of multithreading policies. In the case of very rapid population changes, in particular for larger environments, it is advisable that customers create their own custom code to handle the creation of new object instances. This is important, as the use of multithreading alone, without the ability to create new instances, requires some forethought on the part of developers to avoid overloading and then crashing the system. (This can be quite difficult for Internet-based applications.)

ITS does not provide for automated object pool management for rapid changes in the number of requests. In smaller environments this probably won't be an issue, but in applications with numerous users who are constantly signing on or off, performance may degrade noticeably as ITS locates and instantiates an object for each call.

Data Access

A copy of the ITS Session Manager must be installed on each resident database in an ITS system to provide connection management. The ITS Session Manager has a unique way of handling connections to databases, which can optimize both performance and resource utilization. ITS automatically stocks a pool of database connections, to provide multiplexing of data access to databases.

This pooling feature is available through either direct connections to database resources or through XA access. Officially, the product supports traditional XA. But ITS adds a layer on top of XA to provide connection pooling. This additional layer is required for these services, because traditional XA will open connections for database access and close them as soon as the access is complete. In an ITS environment, traditional XA is used only for the initial database access; ITS then creates a kind of sub-connection, which ITS can keep open for an indefinite amount of time.

 Currently, the ITS way of providing XA connections does not allow for the use of embedded SQL statements, because the XA connection is not the traditional XA implemented with databases. The product's DirectConnection option does, however, allow customers to use other means of database calls, though currently it only supports Oracle and Sybase.

ITS automatically manages the database access pool to find the best possible connection. This capability results in very good response rates for making database connections, which in turn improves performance. We found that it is primarily this feature that enables ITS applications to maintain very good response times, especially for applications involving large numbers of database updates.

The downside to this approach is that customers must wait for database access support from Inprise (rather than just use any database that supports the XA interface). At the time of this writing, the product supports only Oracle and Sybase. To deal with access to multiple back-end systems, the VisiBroker ORB technology has some primitive load-balancing capabilities through a round-robin policy (request is passed from one machine to the next in line to distribute the load). In addition, ITS can be configured to balance load across machines on a per-transaction basis.

Legacy System Integration

ITS has licensed, and bundles, a third-party product for legacy integration from InSession Corporation. The product consists of two parts:

- TransFuse, used for ECI access to CICS, MQSeries, IMS, and TUXEDO (Figure 7.5). Data from these environments can participate fully in transactions coordinated by ITS (with the exception of IMS). This enables a uniform way of access across all legacy systems information.

- CodeSync, which takes source code from mainframe transactions and generates CORBA IDL files. Basically, CodeSync generates something similar to a data object that includes methods and attributes necessary to access the legacy transaction information.

Response Time

The combination of multithreaded objects and close database integration enables the ITS product to achieve very good response rates for client requests, particularly for smaller numbers of clients and/or servers. Performance for transaction applications can be further improved by implementing the ITS transaction service in-process, so that the service can be accessed by a virtual function call.

In larger environments, too, ITS responds well, though resource use increases significantly and may require additional hardware. For larger client/server configurations, where applications will be transactional, we recommend using the ITS Service separately so it can be dedicated to transaction servers in the system architecture (nontransaction applications can access servers running just the VisiBroker ORB). In this case, it is important to replicate the service across several machines to prevent a single point or failure, as well as to improve performance (certain transaction applications can access specific transaction servers).

In general, ITS can be configured for small or large configurations and sustain above average response times thanks to the flexibility of the architecture, which offers a number of configuration options to achieve desired application effects. But we remind you that this flexibility can

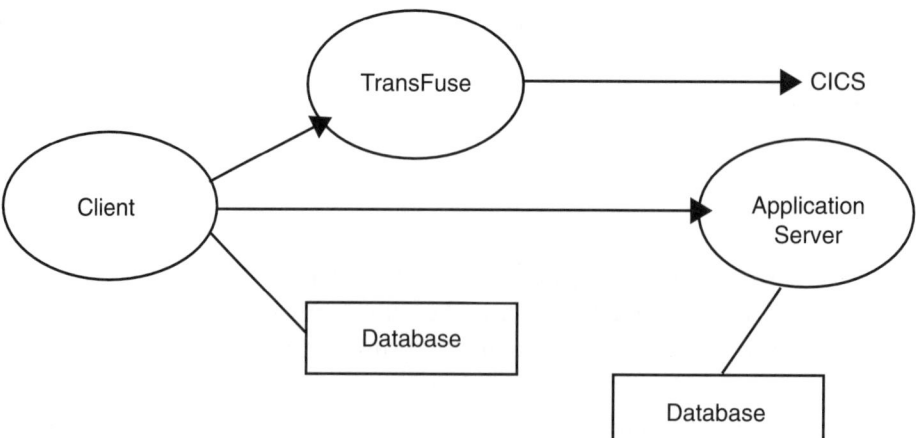

Figure 7.5 The TransFuse environment.

Source: Inprise Corporation

cause problems if its use is not carefully planned. Especially for applications with large numbers of clients, forethought must be given to the handling of peak loads to avoid performance degradation and the potential of crashing server systems. This requires a solid understanding of distributed systems and object-oriented architecture considerations.

Messaging

Like all CORBA ORB products today, ITS allows users to create one-way calls. This allows you to implement the asynchronous communication paradigm, a standard of the CORBA specifications, but it also requires a lot handwork. And it's important to note that there is no guaranteed message delivery. Furthermore, the ITS approach to asynchronous communication with a CORBA model is not very elegant.

For those customers that want a stronger solution, Inprise offers an implementation of a CORBA-compliant event service to enable asynchronous communication among groups of objects using event channels (this is sold separately). Similar to publish and subscribe, suppliers of event information push information to consumers, or vice versa. Other than accessing IBM's MQSeries information through the InSession technology, Inprise offers no other options in this area and has not announced plans to do so in the future.

State Management

By nature of the CORBA design of ITS, objects maintain state between invocations; each object controls when to release the state so that another client can use the same instance. As in a traditional ORB approach, the objects are in control; the ORB is only a communication mechanism.

ITS does not provide any automated functionality for applications that require state management. Users of such apps will have to add this functionality by hand in a complex process, which involves the creation of a system that enables the user to save the state of the object in a persistent store. Then, using ITS, the user would have to create another system to find the object and restore it, if something goes down. Using the proprietary OSAgent and Activation Daemon, which can provide failover for downed objects, can help with the latter.

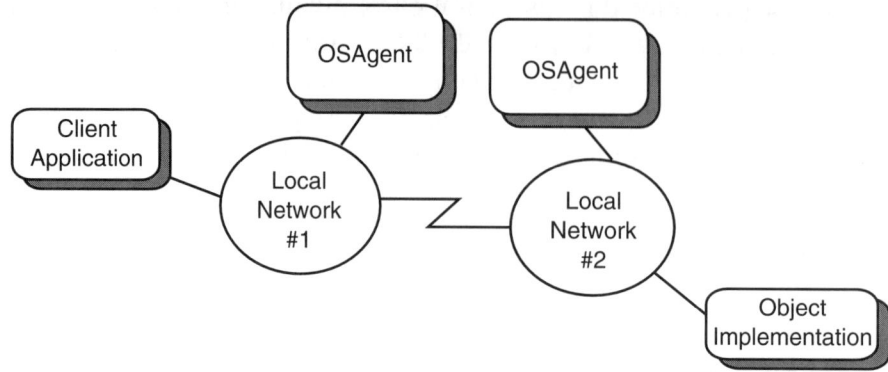

Figure 7.6 OSAgent and Activation Daemon.
Source: Inprise Corporation

High Availability/Fault Tolerance

ITS can be configured to transparently reestablish downed connections by resending requests to failed servers. This does not correct the problem for long-term failures, but the client may remain unaware of a problem if it is quickly fixed.

In addition, the aforementioned ITS OSAgent and Activation Daemon can provide another level of assurance (Figure 7.6). The OSAgent takes charge of binding client objects to a server instance and automatically takes care of finding an instance of the appropriate class. In the event a client object fails, the OSAgent can locate another instance of this class, and using the Activation Daemon, reconnect the client to this new instance. This requires a bit of handwork to configure but can be used when necessary to provide some level of high availability and fault resilience.

Configuring for full server or network failures, on the other hand, requires a great deal of careful custom-coding and manipulation of the systems environment. This must be preceded by careful planning to ensure that back-up objects are available on remote back-up servers or networks. For mandatory high-availability or fault-tolerant applications, this type of software failover scenario is very tricky to create, and in certain situations could cause more failures than solutions.

And keep in mind that if transaction applications are not configured properly, the central approach to transaction management can introduce a single point of failure. Therefore, central transaction management machines should be replicated for failover.

Security

ITS does not bundle any security services; instead, Inprise offers a product called VisiBroker SSL Packs for Java and C++. SSL Packs provide full Secure Socket Layer services across TCP/IP networks, including authentication (verification of the identity of the user), privacy through encryption of messages (assurance that the data cannot be accessed by an unauthorized third party) and integrity (detection of data modification during transmission). What is most interesting about this product is that by virtue of its Internet capabilities, Java applets in a Web browser are able to communicate securely with server objects using either IIOP or HTTP.

Additional Object Services

To date, Inprise has implemented the CORBA-defined event service and naming service. In the case of ITS, for applications that will run on more than one machine, these supplemental object services can provide some much needed functionality.

As a reminder, the naming service makes it possible to associate names with a CORBA object, which are then registered in the names repository. Use of the service precludes the need for a client to bind to a specific server. The server instead institutes a name-to-object mapping through the repository. This institutes an additional layer of location transparency.

Systems Management

As of this writing, ITS offers only very basic management features, though future plans include implementation of an extensive application management solution. The ITS Application Server will introduce a fully "Borland-style" GUI management product called AppCenter, whose tools are designed to look and feel like the Inprise development tools for a complete integrated application development and deployment environment.

Our prerelease evaluation of AppCenter indicates it will allow for management within the same environment as development, so that developers can forecast various configuration effects. Figure 7.7 shows a beta version look at AppCenter.

The Verdict

The application best suited to ITS is one with a stable number of clients (whether in large or small numbers); that is a client base that can be accurately forecast. In particular, the product has a lot to offer Internet-based applications, through the Java version, coupled with the easy communication with browsers (even securely).

The object purist will find ITS to be fully object-oriented, and very flexible. The transaction services were created from the ground up to work in a pure object world, and our tests indicated that ITS achieved no-fail transactional integrity. These facts alone make ITS A major development feat

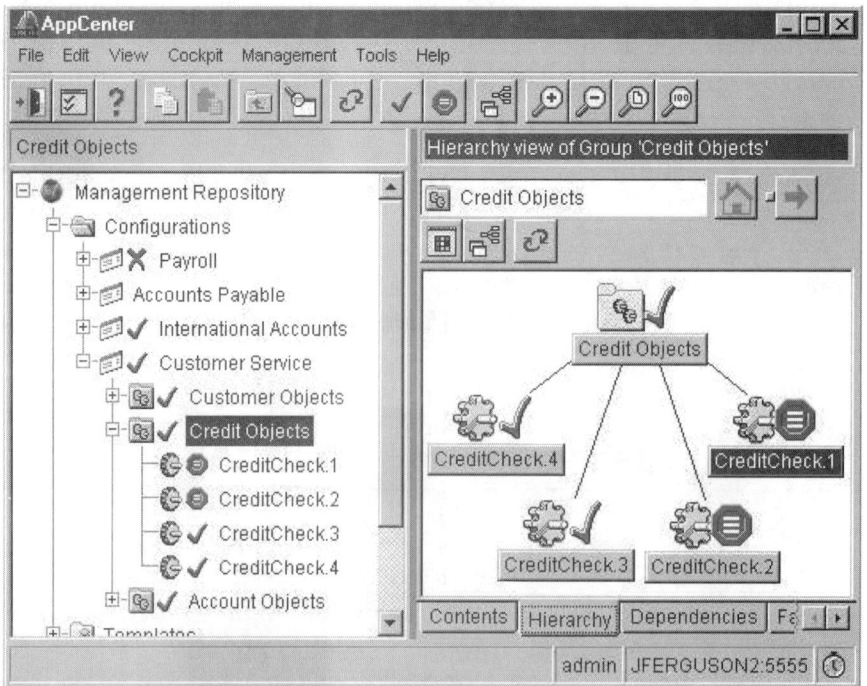

Figure 7.7 Inprise AppCenter.

worthy of great admiration. The benefit of the product's flexibility is the capability to customize the behavior of the product to specific systems and application needs. (Taking advantage of this, will, however, require adequate planning.)

CORBA fans will appreciate the product's clean implementation of the CORBA specifications for communication among objects, and for the invocation of services—although some may be tempted to use the proprietary services of the product, depending on their application requirements. And note, in certain situations, ITS may require custom coding.

For those more familiar with traditional transaction processing concepts, ITS can be hard to grasp. Though it can be manipulated to perform a number of important application services, if it is not configured properly, the result may be less than optimal performance and difficult-to-resolve failure scenarios.

As in previous product chapter, the first table, Table 7.1, lists the major application considerations for reviewing ITS.

Table 7.2 itemizes the application services ITS can provide new application development efforts, based on the application patterns covered in Chapter 4.

Table 7.3 reviews ITS with respect to a variety of application requirements that have various technology implications.

Inprise's ITS approach to object-oriented application services takes full advantage of object technology. Though a diversion from the more tried and true design of traditional transaction products, our testing indicated it is a viable option for many types of applications.

Table 7.1   ITS Application Considerations

BEST APPLICATION CONFIGURATION	MAJOR APPLICATION CONSIDERATION
Small to large client and server configurations in heterogeneous environments	Best suited for new object-oriented applications and for existing applications being modified for Web access. ITS provides a premiere environment for pure object-oriented implementations, in particular for Java-based applications that will operate in a heterogeneous environment.

Table 7.2 Results of Testing against Application Patterns

APPLICATION PATTERN	PERCENTAGE OF APPLICATION SERVICES	USE IMPLICATIONS
Customer service direct (Internet-based service)	65%	Solid performance services through multithreading capabilities and database connection pooling.
		Additional coding may be needed to handle state management and management of a pool of objects for optimal resource utilization. ITS has to be correctly configured to handle load balancing across many servers.
Customer service indirect (typical customer service)	65%	Significant performance enhancements for the database-intensive requirements. ITS needs additional resources to handle lengthy sessions, and will require state management services. ITS does not provide an automated way of dealing with the complicated workflow requirements this application type will demand.
Customer on-call (call center)	70%	Good performance attributes for this application type. ITS can handle the large number of concurrent user requirements through its inherent multithreading capabilities (though this may require additional copies of objects during peak periods).
		Developers will have to add powerful session and state management functionality.
Customer with a vote (online auction or brokerage)	70%	Good services for this application, in particular the capability to optimize connections to database resources.
		Developers will have to add services for state and session management. Developers may also have to provide a way to deal with the reliable message transport requirements of the application (perhaps through interfacing to an existing product such as IBM's MQSeries).
Indecisive customer (decision support system)	60%	The fully objectized nature of ITS is well suited to handle the large files (sometimes including graphics) of this application.

Table 7.2   *(Continued)*

APPLICATION PATTERN	PERCENTAGE OF APPLICATION SERVICES	USE IMPLICATIONS
Indecisive customer *(Continued)*		Developers will have to add solid state and session management services. Additional resources may also be required to deal with peak loads and the prolonged interaction between client and server objects (which may not always be active). In addition, this application often demands access to many types of databases, which will be difficult for ITS to handle.
Customer with cash (online reservation or purchasing)	70%	Overall, ITS can handle a large number of clients and provide good response time through database connection pooling. Developers will have to add state management services, as well as a way to cope with distributed workflow requirements.

Table 7.3   Evaluation Results

APPLICATION REQUIREMENT	TECHNOLOGY IMPLICATION	PRODUCT SUPPORT
Number of concurrent users: small to medium	Maximize minimal system resources through multithreading.	**Yes.** Through multithreaded object policies, ITS is automatically multithreaded and supports two policies (which are easy to switch between), thread per call and pool of threads.
Number of concurrent users: medium to large	Maximize performance and system utilization through multithreading and multiplexing of client requests.	**Yes and No.** ITS can support many clients through multithreading provided there are adequate back-end resources to handle the number of back-end objects required. It is fairly straightforward to add new back-end objects by notifying the product's basic object adapter. Customers in very large environments may have to add custom code to create new objects on demand, and to maximize server resources to handle large volumes of requests.

Continues

Table 7.3 Evaluation Results *(Continued)*

APPLICATION REQUIREMENT	TECHNOLOGY IMPLICATION	PRODUCT SUPPORT
User session length: short	Support short requests and responses.	**Yes.** ITS handles quick requests and responses by keeping a specific connection to handle client and server requests in a timely manner.
User session length: long	Manage connections to maximize resource utilization.	**No.** Due to a lack of state management and an incapability to optimize resources for memory- and CPU-intensive applications (product will maintain connection even when client is inactive).
User population changes: large number of sign-on/sign-off variances	Pool objects to maximize resources.	**No.** ITS must locate and instantiate a new object for each client request, which may impact resource utilization when there are major sign-on/sign-off variances. Customers would have to add custom code to handle a pool of objects.
Number of data sources: small	Maximize performance to a small set of back-end data sources.	**Yes.** ITS is optimized for database connection pooling through product-specific layering over XA interface. ITS also supports an optional direct connection to some databases.
Number of data sources: large	Effectively distribute load across many data sources to maximize performance.	**Yes.** The product's database connection pooling can assist in maximizing performance to many databases and can be configured to distribute the load on a per transaction basis.
Object database integration	Provide for interoperating with object database management systems.	**No.** Inprise currently offers no services for supporting object database systems.
Legacy system integration "in the box"	Access legacy system information without the need for an additional product.	**Yes.** ITS includes a third-party product from InSession Corporation for legacy access to CICS, IMS, MQSeries, and TUXEDO systems.
Legacy system integration available from addition product from the same vendor	Purchase an additional legacy systems integration product from the same vendor.	Not applicable.

Table 7.3   *(Continued)*

APPLICATION REQUIREMENT	TECHNOLOGY IMPLICATION	PRODUCT SUPPORT
Average chain of distributed calls: simple	Statically define interaction among components.	**Yes.** Through standard CORBA implementation customers can statically define component interaction (which can improve performance).
Average chain of distributed calls: complex	Support workflow semantics among objects.	**No.** ITS currently does not offer effective state management.
Communication among objects: synchronous	Provide request/response communication model.	**Yes.** ITS inherently supports synchronous communication among objects through CORBA support.
Communication among objects: asynchronous	Guarantee delivery of send and forget messages.	**Yes and No.** Through custom-coding standard CORBA "one-way calls" ITS can be configured to send-and-forget messages, but delivery cannot be guaranteed. Use of the separately sold Inprise CORBA Event Service implementation can be used as an alternative.
Communication among objects: publish and subscribe	Provide services for objects to publish and subscribe event information	**Yes and No.** ITS does not bundle publish-and-subscribe capability, but customers may purchase a product to implement the CORBA-defined event service.
Advanced messaging functionality through interoperability with additional message-oriented middleware products	Interface to MOM products.	**Yes.** ITS can interface to IBM's MQSeries.
Automatic maintenance of state between sessions	Support automated state management facilities.	**No.** ITS does not provide automated state management facilities; customers must custom-code.
Response time: small environment (one server, number of clients)	Ensure rapid response time for small client environments accessing one back-end resource.	**Yes.** ITS is optimized through multithreading and database connection pooling to provide very good response for smaller environments.

Continues

Table 7.3 Evaluation Results *(Continued)*

APPLICATION REQUIREMENT	TECHNOLOGY IMPLICATION	PRODUCT SUPPORT
Response time: medium-size environment (four or fewer servers, manageable number of clients)	Ensure reasonable response time for an average size application environment with a manageable number of clients accessing the system concurrently.	**Yes.** ITS responds well in medium-size environments.
Response time: large to very large environments (more than four servers, hundreds to thousands of clients)	Ensure average response time for a large application environment in which many clients are concurrently accessing many back-end resources.	**Yes and No.** ITS can be configured for very large environments, though resource utilization may not be optimal. Customers may have to custom-code to multiplex objects.
High availability/fault tolerance: objects	Provide failover to back up objects in case of failure.	**Yes.** Through OSAgent and Activation Daemon, ITS can be configured to redirect requests to back-up objects.
High availability/fault tolerance: server system	Provide failover to back up resources in case of failure.	**No.** Possible, but not recommended in ITS environment, as this requires substantial use of OSAgent and Activation Daemons, and may not be foolproof.
High availability/fault tolerance: network	Provide mechanisms for switching to back-up network domain in case of network failure.	**No.** Possible, but not recommended (see the previous entry).
Security through authentication	Provide security services to ensure authentication control of objects.	**Yes.** Not bundled with ITS, but Inprise provides authentication security through SSL Packs for JAVA and C++.
Security through access control lists	Provide security services for control of access privileges for specific application components.	**No.** ITS does not use access control lists for security.
Security through encryption	Provide encryption security for interaction between components.	**Yes.** Through SSL Packs, ITS can provide encryption security.
Security through integrity of data checking	Provide for detection of of data modification during transmission.	**Yes.** Through SSL Packs, ITS can provide for integrity checking security.

Up Next

For those who like Inprise's implementation of object request broker technology, but who may not yet be ready to take the risk that a completely new transaction processing design implies, the Hitachi technology examined in Chapter 8 may be the answer. Remember, the early designers of the Inprise ORB product worked with Hitachi to deliver the first release of an object-oriented transaction product called TPBroker. Though the VisiORB developers eventually took an alternative path from the Hitachi engineers, the next chapter follows the progress of this base technology in a more traditional transaction design, and takes a close look at the difference between these two products and its additional functionality.

CHAPTER 8

TPBroker from Hitachi

Hitachi Ltd., founded in 1910, became in 1969 one of the first companies in the world to gain a significant presence in the software industry when it launched the Hitachi Software Development Center (SDC) for the production of software for Hitachi's mainframe computers. It was this group that developed Hitachi's open online transaction processing monitor product, OpenTP1, which continues to hold a significant portion of the Japanese middleware market.

In 1994, Hitachi established the Advanced Software Center with a vision for promoting, supporting, and encouraging the market for Hitachi's line of open middleware products in North America. Shortly thereafter, the center entered into a partnership agreement with a small startup, Post-Modern Computing (now absorbed by Inprise, as detailed in Chapter 7) becoming the first OEM vendor for the Orbeline ORB. The goal was to create the first object-oriented transaction processing system that would support the emerging CORBA standards. This was realized in 1995 when PostModern Computing and Hitachi Software jointly announced the release of TPBroker.

Today, Hitachi is committed to continuing this development; to that end, it has embarked on an effort to enhance the basic CORBA model to become a complete execution environment for enterprise systems.

TPBroker does not alter the base VisiBroker ORB technology, but extends it through the addition of CORBA-supported services.

Initial releases of TPBroker used a transaction manager from the company's more traditional transaction processing monitor, Open/TP1, but since that time this functionality has been completely rewritten for cleaner integration. The newest version is built in C++ and JAVA. This chapter explores the major architecture considerations of TPBroker to give you insight into the differences between Inprise's ITS technology and Hitachi's TPBroker.

TPBroker Product Architecture

TPBroker is implemented as a set of client and server object classes; Figure 8.1 shows its architectural structure. On the server-side, every TPBroker application server contains some portion of user-written server objects. Included in this segment of the architecture is the application-specific code (the business logic) developed in house. In a separate segment are the standard VisiORB libraries, which handle communication with client-side objects.

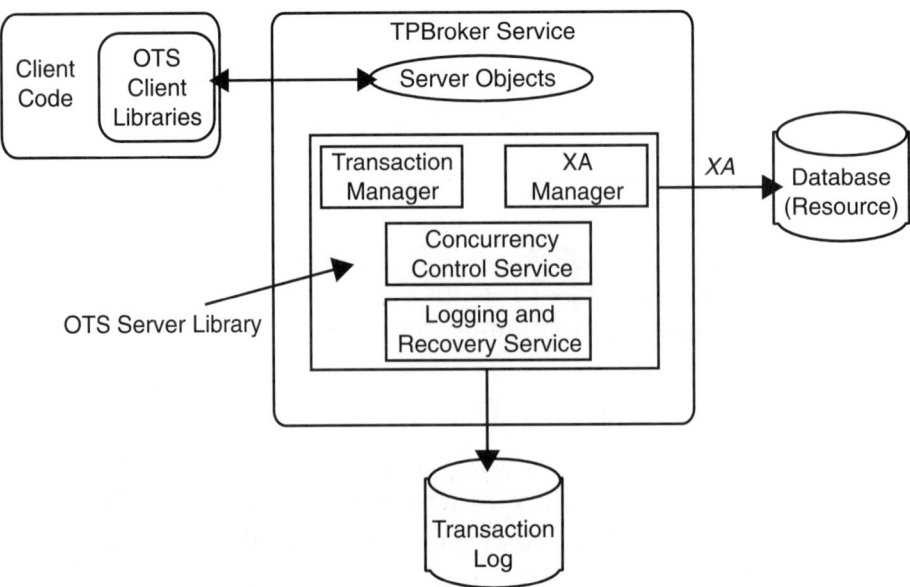

Figure 8.1   TPBroker product architecture.

Also on the server-side is the TPBroker OTS Server Library, based on Hitachi's OpenTP1, which includes transaction protections via: the transaction manager, which oversees transactional integrity; the XA Manager, which provides connections to XA-compliant resources; and the Object Concurrency Control Service, which protects against data corruption. The OTS Server Library uses the transaction log files, which can be consulted for recovery in case of errors.

On the client-side are two sections: the client code that implements in-house code; and the VisiBroker ORB client libraries, which include proxies or skeletons of interfaces used to establish communication with server objects.

Figure 8.2 shows how TPBroker works at runtime. For transaction applications, it uses a distributed transaction management model (used by most traditional TP monitors, including OpenTPI), whereby each server that is part of a TPBroker application must contain the OTS server libraries. The status of each subtransaction (resource involved in the course of the transaction) of a global transaction (entire transaction life cycle) is maintained in the memory of the node that the subtransaction is running. The advantage of this model is that it scales naturally,

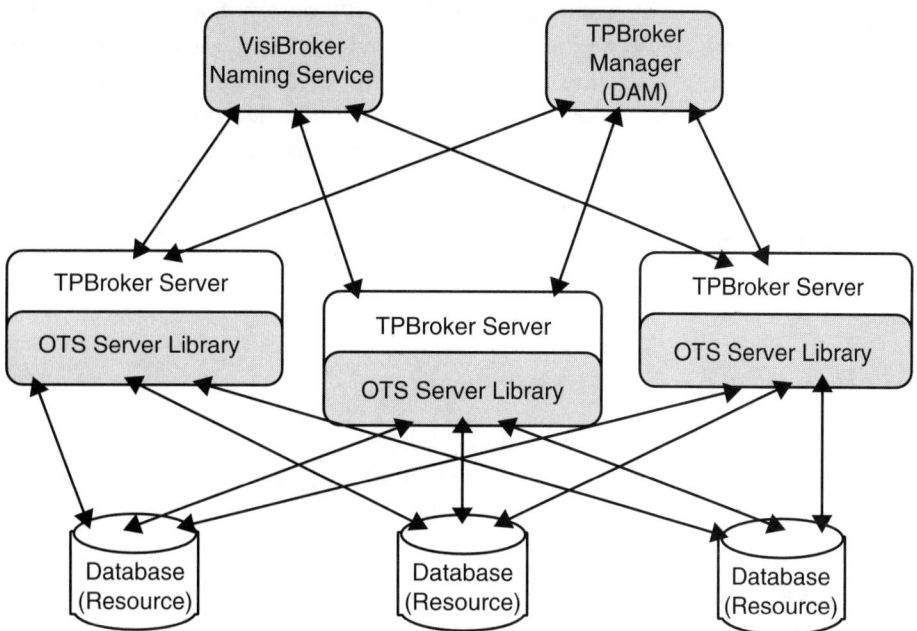

Figure 8.2 TPBroker runtime.

because each node shares the processing of application logic and transaction management. In addition, there is no single point of failure.

The disadvantages to this approach are that it requires the complete transaction server libraries on each node involved in the course of the transaction application, and centralized application management is more difficult. Consequently, the model can require additional administration.

TPBroker operates in a pure CORBA environment. To bind a client request to a server object, TPBroker goes through the following steps:

1. Bind request comes to the TPBroker ORB.

2. The ORB consults the CORBA implementation repository for the appropriate invocation policy to use, and starts the new instance of an object, if necessary returning a pointer to the client object.

3. The server object is notified and passed the request, thereby receiving full control over the execution of a response, then creates a new thread to handle the request.

NOTE   **It is important to reiterate that TPBroker uses the Inprise CORBA ORB both as its base architecture (after quality assurance testing and slight modifications) and for communication among objects in the TPBroker system. The primary architecture difference between Hitachi's TPBroker and Inprise's ITS is distributed versus centralized. Hitachi has opted for the distributed transaction model because it has been proven to be scalable and reliable in production systems; the centralized model does not have the benefit of that experience.**

Those interested in or partial to the Inprise VisiORB can choose between the Inprise ITS (detailed in Chapter 7), which uses a centralized transaction model, and TPBroker, which uses a distributed transaction model.

Developing with TPBroker

For UNIX versions TPBroker is delivered as a large file. Therefore, the first step to installing it is to unpack this file and run the supplied install script. You will then have to modify some configuration files and run two executables. The NT version of the product uses installshield, a JAVA installshield is proposed for UNIX platforms but was not available for our purposes. By default, TPBroker is delivered in both C++ and Java versions, which is convenient for companies that use both programming languages.

The current version of the product has no integrated development environment. But because of the product's implementation of the Inprise ORB, it is anticipated that customers will be able to use Inprise development tools with TPBroker in the future—depending, of course, on delivery of CORBA support to the Inprise product line. Developers may also, of course, use any development product that supports C++ or Java applications.

To optimize TPBroker, customers must have high-level object-oriented programming skills (although this varies according to specific requirements), along with a good working knowledge of CORBA and distributed systems.

Application Architecture Considerations

As noted, TPBroker uses the VisiBroker ORB as the base of its architecture, then has added Hitachi technology that is specific to the transaction management portion, plus add-on object services and management tools. In contrast to Inprise's use of this base ORB technology, Hitachi has taken an alternate path, which means TPBroker reacts differently from Inprise to a variety of application services. The following sections explain how the TPBroker architecture tackles a variety of application requirements.

Number of Concurrent Users

Scalability with TPBroker is achieved through VisiBroker's CORBA multithreaded object policies: thread pool and thread per call. Hitachi has not added anything in this regard. The product relies on its distributed transaction model to make scalability easier to configure for transaction applications, which guards against performance bottlenecks.

The VisiBroker ORB enables developers to easily switch between threading policies simply by adjusting parameters. As a result, a company can try different threading policies according to application requirements to get the best performance possible.

Designing applications with multithreaded objects can generate good scalability, in particular for small to medium systems environments. This approach can also save precious system resources because it does not require a separate object instance for each request (this is particularly important where back-end server resources are minimal).

Scalability is still limited to the availability of threads on available objects in larger environments; TPBroker does not automatically create new instances. It is possible to have many instances of the same object available for peak loads, but these system resources would be wasted during slower use periods. Therefore, when using TPBroker in larger systems environments, we recommend adding custom code to create multiple object instances to prevent crashing the back-end system.

User Session Length

With respect to managing user sessions, TPBroker's capabilities are based on the VisiBroker ORB. TPBroker keeps client connections to servers active at all times, a default attribute of CORBA implementations, which are primarily geared to handle quick requests and responses.

In smaller systems environments, or in those that will primarily involve short client and server sessions, the use of multithreading policies should be sufficient to handle client demands. In fact, the direct connection approach can, in some situations, be ideal since it can make optimal use of resources.

In contrast, for larger applications that may involve many clients accessing the system concurrently (beyond the scope of threads) or those that will involve long client sessions, there is no easy way of managing client-to-server connections without custom coding to automatically create new object instances on demand. (And note, direct connections to these new instances is required and may imply additional hardware.)

In our sample application testing scenarios, the direct approach is not ideal in these larger system configurations or longer session scenarios, and can cause negative effects on both performance and resource utilization, which are not easy to mitigate. There is also the negative impact on resource utilization, because a connection is maintained even when no processing is taking place. In short, TPBroker can be used for this type of application, but it will require additional hardware and may incur some performance degradation.

User Population Changes

TPBroker's capability to handle rapid population changes is based on the VisiBroker ORB only; Hitachi has not added features in this regard. Applications with fairly stable population rates can rely on threading policies, though developers will have to plan for this to avoid overloading the system—remember, TPBroker does not automatically create new object instances.

For rapidly changing populations, we recommend that TPBroker users add custom code to create new object instances, because the number of clients will be limited to the number of available objects. A word of warning: This is not an easy job, but it may be critical, because multithreading alone, in particular for Internet-based applications where peak levels can be very difficult to predict, will not be enough.

By adding custom code, TPBroker can handle rapidly changing populations of clients, although it may incur some performance degradation because it does not provide automated management for new requests to a pool of available objects. With a smaller number of users, this doesn't seem to be a problem, but where many users are involved, this can significantly affect performance because TPBroker has to locate and instantiate an object for each call.

Data Access

TPBroker uses a traditional distributed transaction processing model to connect to databases, and provides access via XA connections. Therefore any database that supports the XA interface can participate in TPBroker transactions. TPBroker supports a static XA connection, which means a developer must include specific access information about the data the program needs to access at compile time. Thus, if a user later wants to go to different databases, the TPBroker application will have to be modified. This can be a burden for programs that have many data sources, particularly if that data may need to be relocated from one machine to another.

TPBroker does not have additional database pool management capabilities. Each time a request comes to a TPBroker server, a new XA connection must be made. For applications that do not involve many database updates, this is a nonissue, but in cases of frequent updating, our testing showed performance degradation when using TPBroker.

To efficiently deal with requests to numerous back-end sources, TPBroker provides some primitive load-balancing capabilities through a round-robin policy (a request is passed from one machine to the next to distribute the load). However, at the time of this writing, it does not offer other automated options in this area.

Legacy System Integration

TPBroker does not provide for legacy system access "out of the box;" instead, Hitachi resells a product from InSession Corporation to gain access to CICS, MQSeries, IMS, and TUXEDO. (This product includes two pieces: TransFuse and CodeSync which are also covered in Chapter 7 under the same section name.) Data from these environments can completely participate in transactions coordinated by TPBroker.

This product also makes it possible to take source code from mainframe transactions and generate CORBA IDL files, and to generate a data object that includes the methods and attributes necessary to access the legacy transaction information.

Response Time

By virtue of its standard CORBA architecture with a distributed transaction processing model, without multiplexing for business objects or data access connections, performance and resource utilization can be less than optimal using TPBroker. To improve the odds, we recommend the use of a variety of threading policies—depending on the application design.

Transaction applications can use the transaction management functionality of the ORB architecture to avoid performance degradation. Hitachi has done a good job of optimizing transaction management performance.

TPBroker is best suited for small to medium application systems environments; and in larger environments, it can be manipulated through additional code to provide adequate performance. (Without custom code, we found that performance can become a problem as the number of clients and servers increases, in particular in those applications that involve multiple database updates).

Messaging

TPBroker includes the VisiBroker implementation of a CORBA-compliant event service, which can enable asynchronous communication between groups of objects using event channels. Similar to publish and subscribe, suppliers of event information push information to consumers, or vice versa.

Hitachi has also developed an implementation of the CORBA-defined Notification Service. It supports additional data types, filtering, and enhanced quality of service through event reliability, connection reliability, and the prioritization of events. Though the Notification Service is a bit difficult to master, it provides benefits similar to a message queuing product (such as IBM's MQSeries or Microsoft MSMQ).

Hitachi's implementation of the CORBA Notification Service that is completely independent from the VisiBroker Event Service. The service guarantees the delivery of messages, in order of receipt, and that they are delivered only once. The product can make use of any database as a message queue resource, and can access IBM's MessageQ through a gateway interface. As shown in Figure 8.3, the Notification Service makes use of the capabilities of the CORBA Event Service to transmit structured CORBA event information.

The Notification Service adds these capabilities: to filter event information, to define whether messages should be received one at a time or in

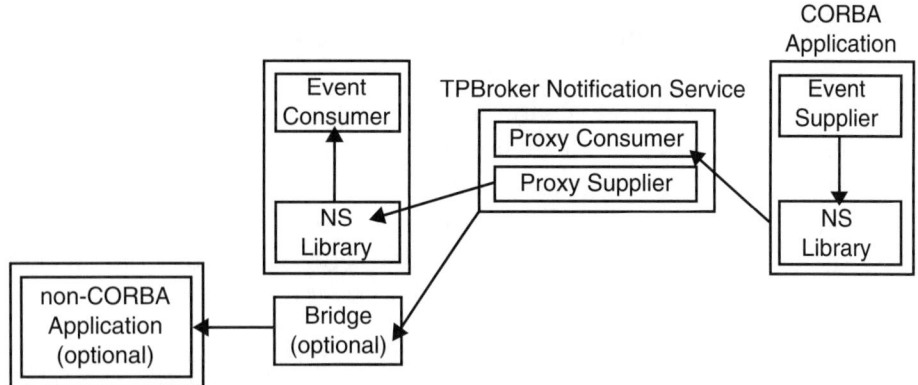

Figure 8.3 TPBroker's CORBA Notification Service.

Source: Hitachi

Note: This diagram does not show the control flow, which generally travels in the opposite direction from that of events.

batch mode, to prioritize messages, to time stamp, and to log messages. In addition, the Notification Service can provide queuing facilities, when a resource is unavailable or busy.

State Management

As in a traditional CORBA ORB model, objects in a TPBroker environment maintain the state of an object between invocations. Each individual class of objects is then responsible for controlling when to release the state so that another client can use the same instance. (Remember, in a traditional ORB approach, the objects are in control; the ORB is only providing a communication mechanism.)

TPBroker does not provide automated services for state management, which would be a problem for applications that will require such a solution. Those apps would have to have their own state management facilities. Developers would also have to create a system to find and restore an object if something goes down (VisiBroker ORB's OSAgent and Activation Daemon could help with the latter).

High Availability/Fault Tolerance

TPBroker can be configured to transparently reestablish downed connections by resending requests to failed servers. Though this will not correct the problem for long-term failures, the client may remain unaware of a problem if it is quickly fixed.

TPBroker customers can also make use of the VisiBroker proprietary OSAgent and Activation Daemon for another level of assurance. The OSAgent is in charge of binding client objects to a server instance and automatically takes care of finding an instance of the appropriate class. In the event of a client object failure, the OSAgent locates another instance of this class, and using the Activation Daemon, reconnects the client to this new instance. This requires a bit of work to configure, but when necessary can achieve a level of high availability and fault resilience.

Using the OSAgent and Activation Daemon for full server or network failures is another story, requiring a great deal of careful custom-coding and manipulation of the system environment. Planning would have to include the assurance that back-up objects were available on remote back-up servers or networks. This type of software failover scenario is very tricky to create, and could cause more failures than solutions, especially for mandatory high availability or fault tolerant applications.

TPBroker also provides an Operation Support Function. The function provides for automatic start, stop, and restart of the ORB Daemon, transaction service daemon, application process, and other daemons (like the DBMS daemon).

Security

The current TPBroker version does not have any security features, but users can purchase the Inprise VisiBroker SSL Packs for both Java and C++ versions of TPBroker to provide encryption and authentication security services. This product is resold by Hitachi and can be purchased directly through them or through Inprise.

> NOTE Hitachi plans to provide to provide an OMG Level 2 CORBA Security Service in the near future. This component was originally developed by a company called Concept 5 under a joint development contract with Hitachi. While the service was unavailable for our purposes, Hitachi tells us it is now under final productization.

Systems Management

Currently, TPBroker offers only some very basic administration services through a command-line systems utility. Hitachi is, however, planning to release a product which is positioned to provide additional systems and application management services. The product is implemented as a framework comprising four main components, shown in Figure 8.4, and offering the following functions:

Management API. Defines the interfaces CORBA objects use to access the management framework. These will include interfaces for event, performance, and configuration services.

Graphical User Interface. A centralized tool for the administration and management of the framework. Provides a graphical representation of management metrics, namespace, and configuration information.

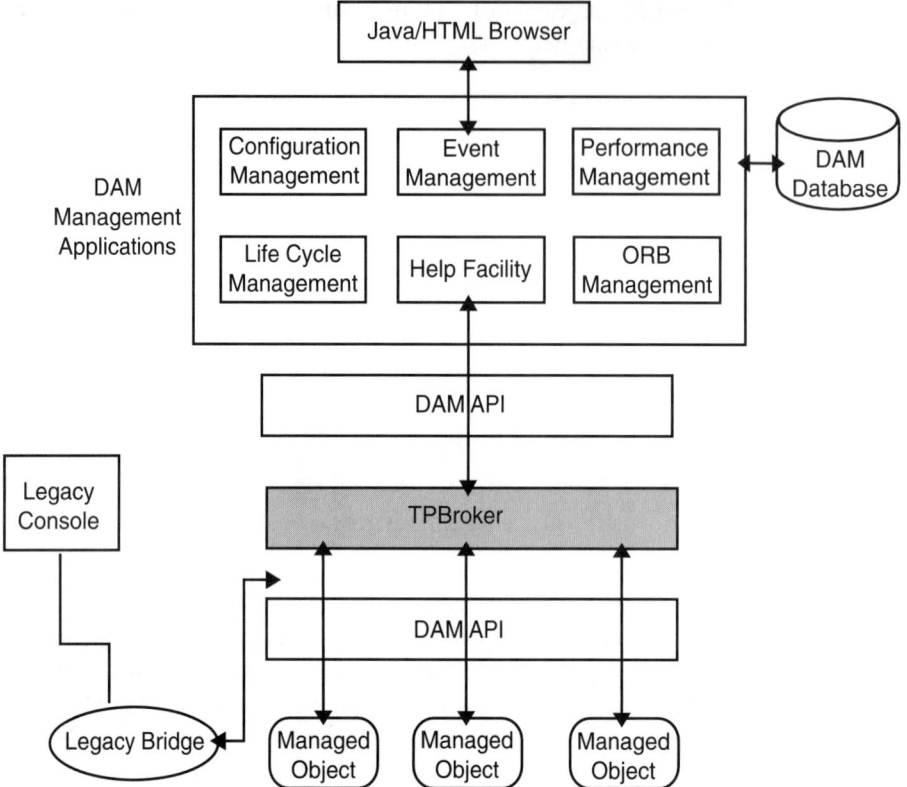

Figure 8.4 Hitachi's distributed application management framework for CORBA systems.

Management Database Interface. Used by a persistent storage system (typically, a database) to hold metrics, namespace information, and metric templates.

Legacy Bridges. Bidirectional data sharing with existing management systems (JP1, SNMP, and Tivoli) and the framework.

The Verdict

Hitachi's TPBroker is ideally suited to those companies that can take advantage of the Inprise VisiBroker ORB for object-oriented transaction applications and that need the comfort level that comes with a proven reputation for providing transaction processing capabilities. The product is uniquely positioned to provide a distributed transaction management model to allow for the use of the VisiBroker ORB technology free

Table 8.1 TPBroker Application Considerations

BEST APPLICATION CONFIGURATION	MAJOR APPLICATION CONSIDERATIONS
Small to medium client and server configurations in heterogeneous environments	For new object-oriented applications that will benefit from a distributed transaction management model. TPBroker provides a good environment for CORBA applications, in particular Java-based applications that will operate in a heterogeneous environment.

of the configuration worries that the more "objectized" Inprise ITS product can impose. TPBroker is, on the downside, unable to implement some of the performance optimizations Inprise has built into ITS, such as close database interaction.

Hitachi also offers numerous consulting and support services to which only a similarly large company can compare. The TPBroker technology is used as the base for a wide variety of Hitachi technology products, so customers can feel confident that the product will stand the test of time.

The best type of application for TPBroker is one that has a reasonable number of concurrent user requirements and needs a variety of messaging policies for object-to-object communication or that will interoperate with existing MOM products such as IBM's MQSeries. For larger applications or applications for which the number of concurrent clients is difficult to predict, TPBroker may require some additional coding. Table 8.1 is a snapshot of the best application configurations and overall major application considerations for using Hitachi's TPBroker.

Table 8.2 itemizes the application services that TPBroker can offer new application development efforts, based on the application patterns covered in Chapter 4.

Hitachi's commitment to maintaining the integrity of OMG's CORBA specifications is evident in TPBroker, a fully CORBA-compliant implementation of CORBA services on the Inprise ORB technology. The company's experience with transaction processing has enabled it to mimic the proven distributed transaction processing paradigm with an objectized twist in this product. As summarized in Table 8.3, TPBroker offers some enticing functionality, in particular for transactional applications that involve advanced event coordination through implementation of the CORBA Notification Service.

Table 8.2   Results of Testing against Application Patterns

APPLICATION PATTERN	PERCENTAGE OF APPLICATION SERVICES	USE IMPLICATIONS
Customer service direct (Internet-based service)	40%	Access to TPBroker applications from the Web is possible, but difficult to use, as the primary requirement of this application pattern is the capability to handle a large number of client requests in a timely manner. In addition, developers have to custom-code for effective management of state information and to provide powerful services for load balancing across multiple servers. This application could benefit from database connection pooling.
Customer service indirect (typical customer service)	55%	TPBroker is well suited to provide access to many types of back-end data sources. Developers have to add effective state and session management services, as well as a means for dealing with prolonged user interaction with the system. Response time may not be ideal because TPBroker has to reconnect to databases for each new request.
Customer on-call (call center)	55%	Because this application does not typically demand a large array of application services, but primarily requires that requests be handled using an optimal system path, TPBroker can provide a good environment through its direct connection architecture. Developers will have to add state management services. Response time may suffer as the number of concurrent users increases and developers should try a variety of configurations to deflect any performance and scalability problems.
Customer with a vote (online auction or brokerage)	70%	This application represents an ideal use of the product. TPBroker can guarantee the delivery of messages between objects using the event and notification services. Developers have to add state and session management services.

Table 8.2 *(Continued)*

APPLICATION PATTERN	PERCENTAGE OF APPLICATION SERVICES	USE IMPLICATIONS
Indecisive customer (decision support system)	65%	The object nature of TPBroker is well suited to handle the large files (that may contain graphics) of this application type. The application has a predictable number of clients and does not require numerous database updates, so performance should be in the acceptable range. Developers have to add state and session management services to cope with prolonged client interactions.
Customer with cash (online reservation or purchasing)	65%	TPBroker offers good benefits for this application since an immediate response is only required for a small number of requests. In addition, the application can benefit from TPBroker's messaging services, which can guarantee send-and-forget messages. The overall environment for the application is fairly predictable with a reasonable population change rate. Developers have to create state and session management services and statically define the workflow requirements of interaction among many components. And because the application demands multiple updates to databases; response time may not be optimal.

Table 8.3 Overall Evaluation Results

APPLICATION REQUIREMENT	TECHNOLOGY IMPLICATION	PRODUCT SUPPORT
Number of concurrent users: small to medium	Maximize minimal system resources through multithreading.	**Yes.** Through incorporation of the Inprise VisiBroker ORB, TPBroker supports multithreaded object policies. TPBroker is automatically multithreaded and supports two policies (which are easy to switch between), thread per call and pool of threads. *Continues*

Table 8.3 Overall Evaluation Results *(Continued)*

APPLICATION REQUIREMENT	TECHNOLOGY IMPLICATION	PRODUCT SUPPORT
Number of concurrent users: medium to large	Maximize performance and system utilization through multiplexing of client requests.	**Yes and No.** TPBroker can support many clients through multithreading, provided there are adequate back-end resources to handle the number of back-end objects required. Customers in large environments may have to add custom code to create new objects on demand and to maximize server resources to handle large volumes of requests.
User session length: short	Support short requests and responses.	**Yes.** TPBroker handles quick requests and responses by keeping a specific connection to handle client and server requests in a timely manner.
User session length: long	Manage connections to maximize resource utilization.	**No.** Due to a lack of state management and an incapability to optimize resources for memory- and CPU-intensive applications (TPBroker maintains connection even when client is inactive).
User population changes: high number of sign-on/sign-off variances	Pool objects to maximize resources.	**No.** TPBroker has to locate and instantiate a new object for each client request, which may have an impact resource utilization for high sign-on/sign-off variances. Customers have to add custom code to handle a pool of objects.
Number of data sources involved: small	Maximize performance to a small set of back-end data sources.	**No.** TPBroker can support many types of databases through support of XA interfaces, but it does not provide database connection pooling or direct connections to these databases.
Number of data sources: large	Effectively distribute the load across many data sources to maximize performance.	**No.** TPBroker supports static XA connections, which require the inclusion of specific access information for programs at compile time. This can be a burden when data is moved to other machines. Furthermore, TPBroker offers very limited support for load balancing, through a simple round-robin policy.

Table 8.3 *(Continued)*

APPLICATION REQUIREMENT	TECHNOLOGY IMPLICATION	PRODUCT SUPPORT
Object database integration	Provide for interoperating with object database management systems.	**No.** Not supported in current release.
Legacy system integration "in the box"	Access legacy system information without the need for an additional product.	**No.** Legacy integration is possible through add-on product sold by Hitachi.
Legacy system integration available from addition product: from the same vendor	Purchase an additional legacy systems integration product from the same vendor.	**Yes.** Hitachi resells a a third-party tool for legacy access from InSession Corporation. It provides access to CICS, IMS, MQSeries, and TUXEDO systems, all of which can participate in transactions coordinated by TPBroker.
Average chain of distributed calls: simple	Statically define interaction among components.	**Yes.** Through standard CORBA implementation, customers can statically define component interaction (which can improve performance).
Average chain of distributed calls: complicated	Support workflow semantics among objects.	Not currently offered.
Communication among objects: synchronous	Provide request/response communication model.	**Yes.** TPBroker inherently supports synchronous communication among objects through CORBA support.
Communication among objects: asynchronous	Guarantee delivery of send-and-forget messages.	**Yes.** TPBroker provides only for standard CORBA one-way calls, but Hitachi sells an add-on CORBA notification service product that can be used for guaranteed asynchronous communication.
Communication among objects: publish and subscribe	Provide services for objects to publish and subscribe event information.	**Yes.** TPBroker does not bundle publish/subscribe model, but customers may purchase a product for the implementation of CORBA-defined event and notification services.
Advanced messaging functionality through interoperability with additional message-oriented middleware products	Interface to MOM products.	**Yes.** TPBroker does not bundle the capability to interface to MOM products, but companies can do so via the purchase of InSession's product or Hitachi's implementation of the notification service, both of which support IBM's MQSeries.

Continues

Table 8.3 Overall Evaluation Results *(Continued)*

APPLICATION REQUIREMENT	TECHNOLOGY IMPLICATION	PRODUCT SUPPORT
Automatic maintenance of state between sessions	Support automated state management facilities.	**No.** TPBroker does not provide automated state management facilities; customers must custom-code.
Response time: small environment (one server, smaller amounts of clients)	Ensure rapid response time for small client environments accessing one back-end resource.	**Yes.** TPBroker offers good response for small environments through support for multithreading.
Response time: medium-size environment (four or fewer servers, manageable number of clients)	Ensure reasonable response time for an average size application environment with a manageable number of clients accessing the system concurrently.	**Yes and No.** TPBroker supports this capability through multi-threaded object support, though response may be only reasonable.
Response time: large to very large environments (more than four servers, hundreds to thousands of clients)	Ensure average response time for a large application environment in which many clients are concurrently accessing many back-end resources.	**No.** Though TPBroker can be configured for very large environments, resource utilization and response times may not be acceptable. In addition, the customer may have to custom-code for the multiplexing of objects and effective load-balancing support.
High availability/ fault tolerance: objects	Provide failover to back up objects in case of failure.	**Yes.** Through the use of the VisiBroker ORB's OSAgent and Activation Daemon, TPBroker may be configured to redirect requests to back-up objects.
High availability/ fault tolerance: server system	Provide failover to back up resources in case of failure.	**Yes and No.** Possible but not recommended in the TPBroker environment as this requires substantial use of OSAgent and Activation Daemons and may not be foolproof. TPBroker provides Operation Support Function to restart daemons upon system crash and failover.
High availability/ fault tolerance: network	Provide mechanisms for switching to back-up network domain in case of network failure.	**Yes and No.** Possible but not recommended (see preceding entry).

Table 8.3 *(Continued)*

APPLICATION REQUIREMENT	TECHNOLOGY IMPLICATION	PRODUCT SUPPORT
Security through authentication	Provide security services to ensure authentication control of objects.	**Yes.** Not bundled with TPBroker, but Hitachi resells Inprise's SSL Packs for Java and C++ for security.
Security through access control lists	Provide security services for control of access privileges for specific application components.	**No.** TPBroker does not use access control lists for security.
Security through encryption	Provide encryption security for interaction between components.	**Yes.** Through the addition of Inprise's SSL Packs, TPBroker can support encryption security.
Security through integrity of data checking	Provide for detection of data modification during transmission.	**Yes.** Through the addition of Inprise's SSL Packs, TPBroker can use SSL for integrity checking.

Up Next

Chapter 9 moves away from the CORBA world to introduce Microsoft's version of an Object Monitor: the Microsoft Transaction Server (MTS). Like the Inprise ITS covered in Chapter 7, Microsoft uses a less traditional transaction design model, as a feature of its NT Server operating system.

MTS from Microsoft

The "king of the desktop" is now out to conquer the server market as well, via the integration approach. One aspect of Microsoft's vision for an integrated server-side offering is the Microsoft Transaction Server (MTS). Microsoft intends to combine operating system services with database technology and mission-critical application services within one server product. Unlike other products in this market, it is impossible to discuss MTS without considering its surrounding technology.

Microsoft's plan for delivering application services for the distributed environment focuses on the seamless integration of multiple Microsoft products, which include COM/DCOM, Microsoft Transaction Server (MTS), Microsoft Message Queue (MSMQ), Microsoft's SQL Server database, and the NT operating system, among others. Figure 9.1 shows the current product integration road map. The company believes that this tight coupling of application services with the operating system will maximize performance as well as make these services completely transparent to both users and developers.

MTS is intended to work within this environment to provide object-oriented services for transactional applications. Microsoft's goal is to make transaction processing "for the masses," through easy-to-use development and management tools. And it hardly need be stated that because much of the functionality offered by MTS relies on the company's other products, MTS is primarily suited for Microsoft environments. In fact, it is fair to say that MTS is not currently for heterogeneous computing environments. Although it can, in certain situations, take advantage of other systems, doing so degrades the product's potential and is often only supported through third-party offerings. In addition, the MTS core functionality is only offered for the Microsoft NT server.

> **NOTE** Due to this tight integration, Microsoft uses its own terminology for functionality otherwise referred to in CORBA terms.

This chapter introduces you to Microsoft's plans for MTS and the role it will play in the future of NT Servers. As for the other products described in this part of the book, we describe how MTS handles application architecture considerations and help you to evaluate MTS for specific application requirements and systems architecture environments.

MTS Product Architecture

MTS uses a centralized transaction processing model; everything goes through what Microsoft calls the Distributed Transaction Coordinator

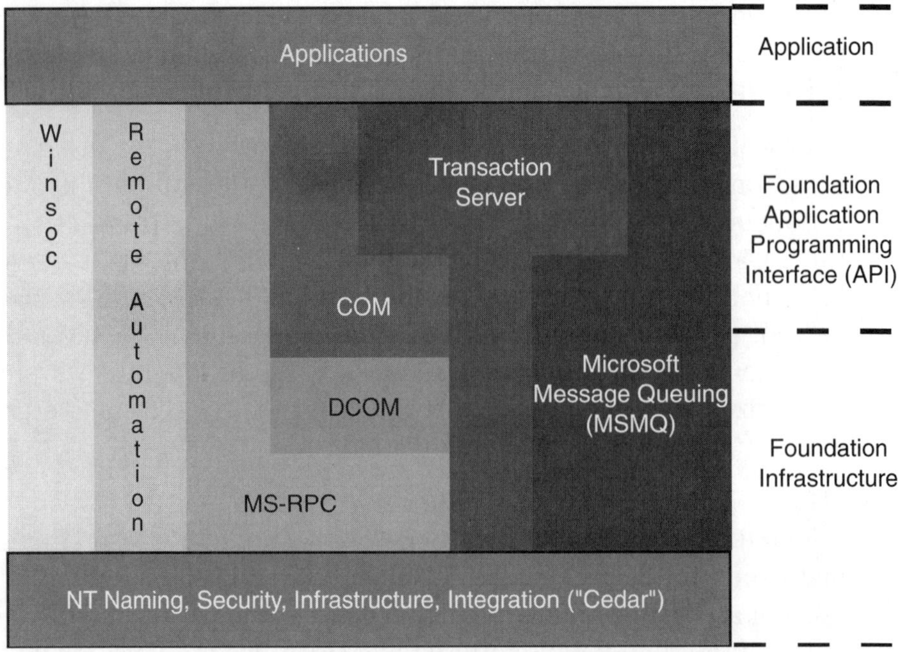

Figure 9.1 Microsoft's server-side integration strategy road map.

(DTC). DTC, which originally shipped with Microsoft's SQL Server 6.5 database, is in charge of transaction coordination in the MTS system, and is responsible for managing the two-phase commit coordination of resources. Each MTS server is required to run a copy of DTC as a separate process on every machine that participates in an MTS transaction. Each copy of DTC acts as a centralized transaction coordinator in charge of its single-server environment only. If that server goes down, the MTS transaction will be lost. And DTC is only available in NT, so though other systems may eventually support MTS (through third-party offerings), transaction coordination is always maintained on a Microsoft NT Server system.

This centralized transaction model means that the DTC maintains the status of a global transaction (resource involved in the course of the transaction) within the memory of the MTS server running somewhere in the network. All transactional requests are sent to the MTS server as properties of the DCOM object that makes the request.

As shown in Figure 9.2 clients in an MTS environment can be either Windows or browser-based. In the case of Internet Explorer browsers, clients may directly access DCOM server objects through ActiveX controls.

For other browsers, an HTTP connection can be used to link to the Microsoft Internet Information Server (IIS), in which case IIS acts as a client to MTS. This is possible through the use of Active Server Pages (ASP) for the creation of HTML pages. (Developers use ASP to create programs that run on IIS using VisualBasic or JavaScript. Active Server Pages are made up of ActiveX components.)

NOTE   **If you plan to purchase MTS as an add-on, be aware that DTC is not bundled with the MTS package. It is available separately or as part of other Microsoft products (like SQL server).**

Unlike the other products covered in this book, Microsoft does not support the X/Open distributed transaction processing model. Instead, the company uses its own model, called OLE Transactions. As shown in Figure 9.3, OLE Transaction interfaces replace both X/Open TX and XA interfaces. The transaction manager can, however, support XA interfaces to communicate with resource managers (typically, a database), though this is not advised.

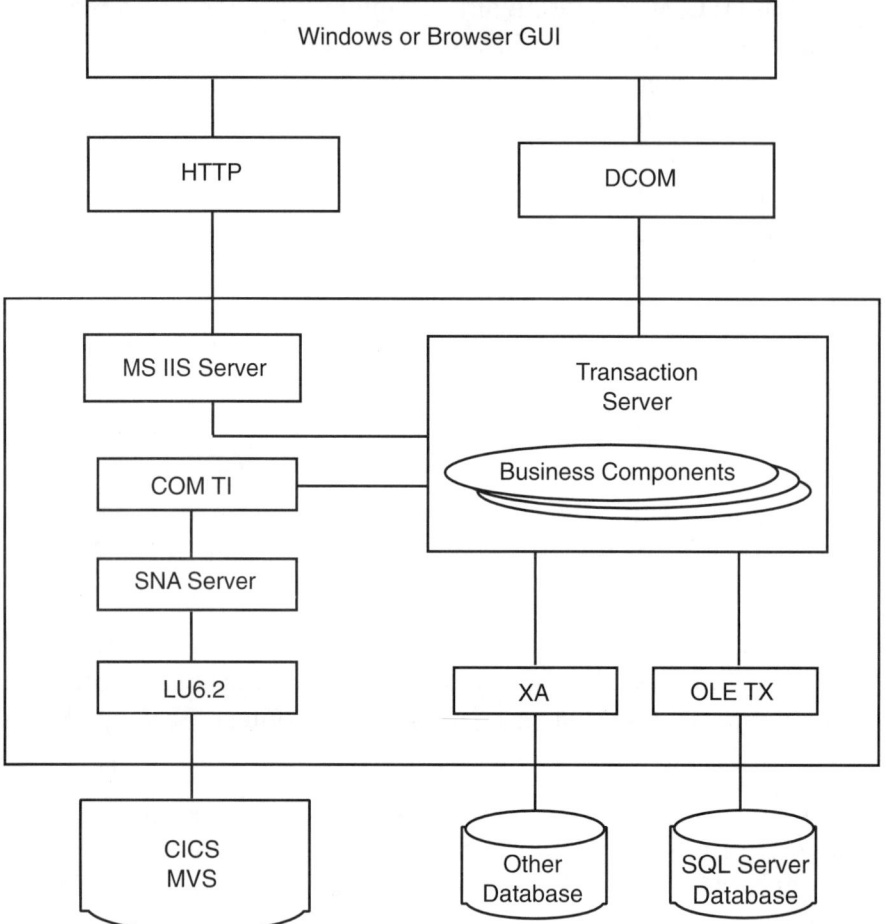

Figure 9.2 MTS runtime architecture.

Furthermore, MTS does not support so-called clean XA; an XA-compliant resource must be enhanced to work with MTS, to accept OLE transaction calls in place of XA calls. The client library must then translate OLE Transaction calls into an XA version that will translate the OLE Transaction Identifier (TRID) into an XA Transaction Identifier (XID). To do so, the client library calls an MTS-provided DTC helper procedure for the conversion.

MTS relies on other pieces of the Microsoft server-side "puzzle" to work: OLT TI is automatically supported by Microsoft's SQL server database, Microsoft's Message Queuing product, and future Microsoft-enabled

Microsoft's OLE Transaction Model

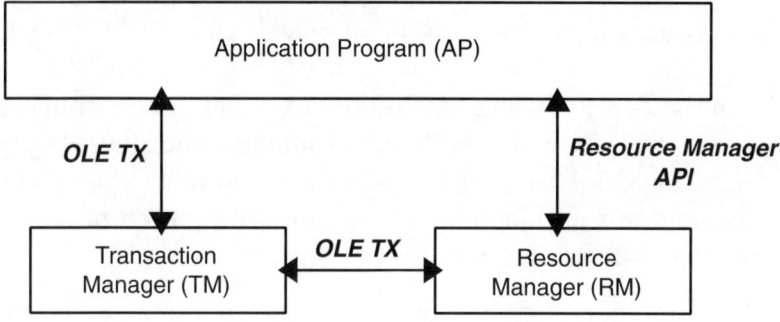

X/Open's Distributed Transaction Processing Model

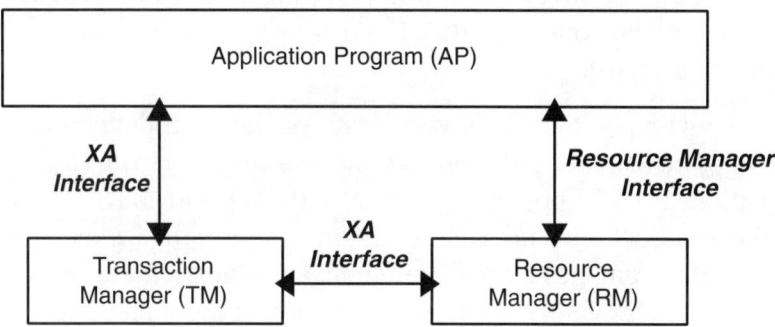

Figure 9.3   Microsoft's OLE transaction model versus the X/Open DTP model.

resources. By bypassing XA, using a more direct connection to the database, OLE TI can offer better service. This direct connection also enables the product to take full advantage of SQL server database services. That's the good news; the bad news is that MTS does not "automatically" support a lot of back-end resources. Customers are expected to create their own OLE TI interfaces; but at present, this is quite difficult and requires the direct assistance of Microsoft. (The resources MTS does support are detailed throughout this chapter.)

 The distributed transaction management features of Microsoft Transaction Server are based on a proprietary—and therefore not time-tested—technology. For this reason, we recommend that anyone considering implementing MTS *carefully* and *thoroughly* perform reference checks before using it for mission-critical applications that require absolute transaction integrity via two-phase commit coordination.

Developing with MTS

Microsoft Transaction Server integrates with the COM/DCOM object architecture from Microsoft. Consequently, any COM/DCOM object (which can be created using any Microsoft development tool) can be a transactional object in the MTS environment. The advantage of this approach is that COM is naturally and completely language-independent; developers can mix and match components from different languages in the same executable program.

The MTS development environment is easy to understand, because any COM or DCOM object can automatically be made transactional simply by changing its properties in the MTS management tool (MTS Explorer). The same is true for turning a COM object into a DCOM object. This is quite useful because not only can that COM object become a DCOM component, but it can participate in a transaction.

What this means is that life is very easy for the MTS developer, because any development tool (and there are many to choose from) that supports the creation of COM objects can inherently support MTS. To the developer, these models are no different from one another, except that they support a different property—the client and server code is exactly the same. Thus, if a developer builds a COM object for a client machine and finds it works well, he or she can move it to the server, changing nothing but the registry.

But DCOM is not location-independent; client objects must know the exact location of server objects. The information for connecting client objects to server objects is defined in the client machine's registry. What this means is that if you move an object from one machine to another, the client's registry must be updated. (Microsoft plans to fix this inefficiency with the release of the Microsoft Active Directory).

In an MTS environment, all components involved in a transaction are grouped within "packages," one executable process. The easiest way to generate these packages is using the Transaction Server Explorer interface (which is very similar to a traditional Windows Explorer program). The objects representing resources (or COM objects) are grouped into a package and are represented by typical Windows-style icons. From within this package, MTS provides access to data sources or other COM/DCOM objects.

No specific skill sets are required for developing MTS applications—other than the ability to use a development tool to create COM objects. But custom-coding and experience in distributed systems and the COM/DCOM architecture are still required to meet specific application requirements. This is particularly essential for large applications or those that will make use of many client or server machines.

Application Architecture Considerations

MTS is a new product that introduces new ways of delivering transaction processing technology through integration with a variety of products, not all of which have fully come of age. As with any new model, this early release has some faults, as you'll see in the following application architecture considerations. But MTS is a key product for Microsoft, and the company plans to provide this functionality as part of one neat, easy-to-use package.

Number of Concurrent Users

MTS fully automates the use of multithreaded COM/DCOM components through the NT operating system. The product uses a "pool of threads" model, enabling MTS to maximize performance through reuse of existing threads. This then enables developers to write single-threaded components, because MTS takes care of assigning threads and eliminating threads as needed.

However, the DCOM architecture makes it very hard for MTS to support a large number of concurrent users. In the current implementation, the client has to register with a specific server object; consequently, for each client object, a user has to register that object to its specific machine. If the object is moved to another machine, it must be registered again in the new machine. This limits scalability, as the addition of a new machine to handle the load will force developers to update all the client registries to reflect any changes.

The only option is to make sure the server has sufficient memory to handle a peak number of clients. But, as you'll see throughout this chapter, this requires careful forecasting on the part of developers.

Scalability is not MTS's only failing. It is also difficult to use with Internet applications where the number of concurrent users is often unpredictable and often surpasses "guesstimations." (MTS does offer good performance and resource utilization in applications with a small and stable number of users.)

User Session Length

MTS has extended the COM object model with Microsoft's *just-in-time (JIT) activation.* JIT activation allows MTS to manage the lifetime of components so that server resources are maximized. After the completion of work, MTS deactivates the component and uses system resources for other processes until such time that the component is recalled.

JIT activation, along with the other MTS services, are primarily geared to handle quick requests and replies, which will not require state management, will not require a lot of memory, or CPU use, and so on. Other application types will not fare as well using MTS; they will require custom-coding, but in any cases will probably suffer from performance degradation and inefficient resource utilization.

User Population Changes

The current DCOM architecture requires that each client must have precise information about the specific server object to which the client will connect. Therefore, on deployment, a DCOM server object must account for the maximum number of clients. This limitation means that MTS has to have multiple copies of the same objects to handle peak loads, which in turn impacts resource use. The restriction, is, however, mitigated somewhat by the product's stateless paradigm and JIT activation.

A more problematic issue is whether a company can accurately forecast how many components will be needed to handle peak population changes. For some applications this may be easy; for others this could be more difficult and thus require ongoing "finessing" of the architecture to meet the demand. Internet applications, for example, are notoriously difficult to predict the number of users. Certainly other Object Monitors are limited in this regard, but in MTS the problem is magnified by the more static nature of the current DCOM architecture. And the solution—adding new objects to handle the demand or moving objects to another machine—is an involved process that requires the updating of client registries.

Data Access

To access back-end resources, MTS has *resource dispensers*, which are used to manage a pool of connections and to enable resources to participate in MTS transactions. Microsoft currently offers three resource dispensers: an open database connectivity driver (ODBC) manager (for database connections), an MSMQ driver (for messages from a queue), and COMTI (for legacy access). The latter two are covered later in this chapter.

For database connectivity, MTS uses database connection pooling, which is implemented by an ODBC driver manager. It maintains a pool of available ODBC connections and draws from this pool through SQL calls as an application demands. The connections are returned to the pool through another SQL call; thereafter, the connection can be reused.

> **NOTE** There is currently no way to control the number of ODBC connections in a pool through limits or preallocated connections. Therefore, requests to a resource are limited by the availability of memory in the server system. Developers will have to plan carefully to avoid "crashing" the system.

This type of connection pooling is implemented as a standard feature of ODBC 3.0 and ODBC 3.5. Driver managers and can be used with any 32-bit ODBC driver that is thread-safe. It is extended to the MTS environment by configuring the ODBC driver and the MTS application to make the appropriate ODBC calls. The ODBC resource dispenser inserts a layer of Microsoft code that is implemented over an ODBC driver manager. The application makes what appears to be a standard ODBC call, but the MTS resource dispenser intercepts this call to provide MTS with connection pool management and to coordinate transactions to the resource.

Database pooling results in faster performance by eliminating the need to continually establish new connections for each request. Its disadvantage is that MTS should only be used with resources that offer a Microsoft resource dispenser. Currently, that means Microsoft SQL Server and newer versions of Oracle.

> **NOTE** Though MTS customers may choose not to use connection pooling, not doing so will cause MTS performance to suffer. MTS components are designed to be short-lived; that is, they are only available for the life the transaction they were created for. By not using connection pooling, MTS is forced to establish new connections, thereby degrading performance and resource utlization.

Legacy System Integration

Microsoft has also created a resource dispenser for accessing legacy environments called *COM Transaction Integrator* (COMTI). The current product allows MTS to execute CICS and IMS applications running on IBM's MVS Systems. COMTI ships with SNA, enabling it to communicate with MVS through a standard LU6.2 connection.

COMTI has three main elements:

COMTI ComponentBuilder. A graphical tool that makes it possible to automatically translate COBOL copybooks from mainframe transaction processing into COM-type libraries for use in the MTS environment.

COMTI Runtime Proxy. When a COMTI component's methods are invoked, the COMTI Runtime Proxy translates these messages from COM to the mainframe application. Likewise, when the mainframe application returns data to the COMTI Proxy, these messages are translated into a format the COMTI component can understand.

COMTI Management Console. A feature that provides administration functions for COMTI environments. It can be incorporated into Microsoft's systems management product, the Microsoft Management Console (MMC).

For CICS, COMTI components can be set with the same transactional properties as any COM object. The Microsoft Distributed Transaction Coordinator maintains transactional integrity through two-phase commit coordination.

For applications that require access to IBM MVS systems, the COMTI option is an easy-to-use option. In the future, Microsoft plans to support transactions for IMS and to roll out more access options to other legacy environments.

Response Time

Because MTS is fully integrated with other Microsoft server-side products, such as the NT operating system and Microsoft's SQL Server database, not surprisingly, it sustains very good performance for this systems environment.

NOTE For the purposes of this book, the Microsoft-only integration of MTS makes it difficult to compare to other products in the market.

Messaging

To date, Microsoft's DCOM (and therefore MTS) does not inherently provide the means to communicate between objects other than in a synchronous (request/reply) mode. Microsoft offers instead a resource dispenser called the MSMQ driver for accessing messages from Microsoft's message queuing product, MSMQ.

MSMQ is delivered with NT 4.0 Enterprise Edition Server, and provides for message passing, message queuing (including dynamic queue creation and location), and guaranteed message delivery. MTS applications can include MSMQ operations within transactional units of work. When used with a transaction, MSMQ will not complete send operations until the transaction is committed; this protects against sending messages from transactions that may be aborted.

MSMQ enables DCOM, and therefore MTS, to provide asynchronous object invocation to applications that require asynchronous or advanced messaging functionality. Future improvements include plans to implement a publish and subscribe service for MSMQ; and through closer integration between MTS and MSMQ, Microsoft intends to offer built-in COM/DCOM support for queued components.

MTS and MSMQ interoperate cleanly and easily. And though Microsoft does not currently enable interoperability with other messaging products, such as IBM's MQSeries, this is planned for a future release.

State Management

MTS supports a stateless object concept (the object releases the state as soon as it is outside transaction boundaries). This allows MTS to conserve system resources in applications that do have to maintain state outside of a transaction context. This not only helps to save on system resources, but can lead to faster performance as well.

But for applications that require state management, MTS is less than ideal, as it does not have an automated way of handling this. Therefore, developers of these apps have to supply their own state management functionality; and for this, they should be highly skilled in COM/DCOM. Custom-code will have to save the state of each object in persistent storage, allocate a storage mechanism, and restore this state through a server component method upon a new invocation request. Each server object that requires state management will have to include these customized method calls.

Using the Shared Property Manager

To assist with creating state management facilities, MTS provides a mechanism called the *Shared Property Manager* (SPM), which enables developers to program properties so that they are available to all objects in the same server process. Objects that have access to these properties are contained in a logical "package." SPM can be used in applications that need to maintain state for all objects within the same server process. But this also means that the sharability unit will be in a process on the same server system, which in turn means that if not implemented properly, SPM could cause major problems: for example, mixing account objects from different customers—that is, "sharing" the funds between two unrelated accounts!

High Availability/Fault Tolerance

The generic MTS environment does not have automated high-availability/fault-tolerant features. And custom-coding a solution to this problem in a DCOM environment is a challenge because the client object always knows the exact location of the server object. If the server goes down, the client has no way of dealing with this.

Microsoft does, however, offer Microsoft Cluster Software (MSCS), built into the Windows NT Server Enterprise Edition. Using MSCS, NT will create a virtual address for accessing SQL Server (in contrast to the traditional static communication with standard DCOM). By using a virtual address, which is managed by MTS, MSCS can reroute requests to a backup clustered server in the event of a failure. MSCS also includes a graphical management tool for monitoring the status of servers, and makes it possible to reallocate workload between nodes for load balancing. Unfortunately, the current release is limited to two node configurations; therefore it is still necessary to ensure that client requests do not exceed the memory of these two machines, to prevent a system failure.

The bottom line is, though you do not have to use MSCS with MTS, the alternative requires a great deal of custom-coding and could significantly impact resource utilization. Developers would have to create a couple of different instances of the same object on different servers, provide a custom state management service, and provide a custom solution to initiate failover to another object. So for applications that require high-availability or fault-tolerant services for MTS, we recommend that you make use of MSCS, and make sure that the nodes in the cluster are able to meet peak user requirements.

Security

MTS objects use NT for security through the LAN Manager portion of the NT Server operating system. This segment of the OS currently uses Kerberos for access control list (ACL) authentication. Using ACL authentication, developers can design security into components without knowing how the component will be deployed, simply by assigning names to access privileges. Administrators can then take these names and assign "roles" to the users who will call the MTS components. Using ACL security is very easy; because MTS is running on the NT Server, these objects automatically can take advantage of the operating system's security features simply by defining these objects as secure.

MTS also provides for *declarative security*, which requires no developer intervention. Using this model, administrators declare which users (or groups of users) have access to a group of objects through the MTS management service console.

MTS does not currently provide encryption-level security for the communication of messages between COM/DCOM components.

NOTE **Kerberos is a security technology orginally developed at the Massachusetts Institute of Technology (MIT). In a Kerberos secure interaction, a user connects to the security server, is authenticated, and obtains authorization "tickets" use to access server resources and encrypt session information. In a Kerberos system, there is a time limit authorization ticket; upon expiration, the user must repeat the authentication procedure.**

Systems Management

Microsoft integrates a systems management tool with NT called the Microsoft Management Console (MMC). All NT servers and all COM/DCOM objects (and therefore MTS objects) fall under this umbrella. For specific MTS management, the company offers a plug-in interface for MMC called the MTS Explorer, which is completely graphical, and offers the following: Drag-and-drop installation of components into the MTS environment and operational features such as the ability to lock groups of components to prevent changes, to view the status of MTS executions, and to change security or transaction roles for all components in the NT environment.

Microsoft also offers management plug-ins for a variety of other products including IIS, COMTI, and the Microsoft Cluster Server. This "one stop" approach is very convenient from an administrator's perspective because all Microsoft NT Enterprise Server products have the same look and feel and follow the same design methodologies of traditional Microsoft client software products, which makes them easy to learn and use.

The Verdict

Microsoft Transaction Server is still in its infancy, and thus lacks some application functionality, which may be a problem depending on specific application requirements. The product overall is unsuitable for applications with large numbers of users or that will need to access numerous back-end resources, primarily because it cannot operate in a heterogeneous environment; it is a Microsoft-only systems architecture.

That said, for NT-based applications, MTServer offers a very user-friendly approach to the often rocky terrain of transaction processing functionality. In addition, NT workgroup environments can take advantage of the performance attributes that the operating system feature design can provide. Table 9.1 lists the basic information to consider when considering MTS for existing and new applications.

In Table 9.2, we look at the availability of application services for MTS based on the sample application patterns we considered in Chapter 4. In Table 9.3, we summarize MTS functionality.

Table 9.1 MTS Application Considerations

BEST APPLICATION CONFIGURATION	MAJOR APPLICATION CONSIDERATIONS
Small numbers of clients and servers that primarily operate in a Microsoft systems environment	MTS offers numerous performance enhancements, and makes good use of existing Microsoft technology. MTS works well with applications that use a combination of NT and legacy systems; in particular, it can provide easy access to Web services for Microsoft-based intranet applications.

Table 9.2 Results of Testing against Application Patterns

APPLICATION PATTERN	PERCENTAGE OF APPLICATION SERVICES	USE IMPLICATIONS
Customer service direct (Internet-based Service)	45%	The static nature of the DCOM environment makes this a difficult application for MTS, although the creation of Internet-based applications is very easy when combined with Microsoft Web products. New applications of this type will require a lot of custom-coding to handle dynamic changes in user populations (which are difficult to forecast), state management, and load balancing.
Customer service indirect (typical customer service)	55%	This application's stable environment makes using MTS feasible. MTS can provide some good performance enhancements, in particular for updates to SQL Server databases. Developers have to add custom code for state management and to hand code possibly complicated workflow requirements.
Customer on-call (call center)	65%	MTS can be useful for this type of application if the number of users can be accurately predicted, because it can respond efficiently to "quick hits" on the system. If peak loads cannot be predicted, MTS is not a good choice. And developers have to hand-code for required state management.
Customer with a vote (online auction or brokerage)	60%	MTS is good for this type of application, as it is ideally suited to quick responses for short interactions. And coupled with MSMQ, MTS has a nice way of handling guaranteed delivery of messages and transactional integrity. Unfortunately, the user population for this type of application is very unpredictable, which as noted is a problem for MTS. And for this type of application, too, state management functionality had to be hand-coded.
Indecisive customer (decision support system)	40%	MTS is not well suited for this type of application, which must have solid state management facilities. And MTS

Continues

Table 9.2 *(Continued)*

APPLICATION PATTERN	PERCENTAGE OF APPLICATION SERVICES	USE IMPLICATIONS
Indecisive customer *(Continued)*		cannot maximize system resources during lengthy sessions typical of this type of application, nor does it provide support for accessing many types of back-end data sources.
Customer with cash (online reservation or purchasing)	70%	This application may be the best suited to MTS capabilities. The number of users is fairly predictable, with a requirement for rapid response (which MTS can certainly offer) and data integrity. Customers will have to add state management code. Note: This application should take advantage of the MSCS services, as the transaction management will be controlled on a single system.

Table 9.3 Evaluation Results

APPLICATION REQUIREMENT	TECHNOLOGY IMPLICATION	PRODUCT SUPPORT
Number of concurrent users: small to medium	Maximize minimal system resources through multithreading.	**Yes.** Through multithreading support on NT.
Number of concurrent users: medium to large	Maximize performance and system utilization through multiplexing of client requests.	**Yes and No.** Yes, if machine has sufficient memory and the application allows for accurate forecasting of peak number of requests; no, if peak loads are difficult to forecast or may change due to the static nature of client and server object binding.
User session length: short	Support short requests and responses.	**Yes.** Product is optimized for quick requests and responses through just-in-time activation.
User session: long	Manage connections to maximize resource utilization.	**No.** due to a lack of state management and incapability to optimize resources for memory- and CPU-intensive applications.

Table 9.3 *(Continued)*

APPLICATION REQUIREMENT	TECHNOLOGY IMPLICATION	PRODUCT SUPPORT
User population changes: high number of sign-on/sign-off variances	Pool objects to maximize resources.	**Yes and No.** Through just-in-time activation, MTS can handle a predefined number of users who are rapidly accessing the system; however, due to static nature of DCOM, peak must carefully be predefined otherwise MTS may be unable to maximize resources.
Number of data sources involved: small	Maximize performance to a small set of back-end data sources.	**Yes.** Through database connection pooling to Microsoft SQL Server and Oracle.
Number of data sources involved: large	Effectively distribute the load across many data sources to maximize performance.	**No.** Load balancing is only available across two server processes through MSCS, and it must be statically defined.
Object database integration	Provide for interoperating with object database management systems.	**No.** Not supported in current version.
Legacy system integration "in the box"	Access legacy system information without the need for an additional product.	**Yes.** Through COMTI Resource Dispenser for CICS and IMS on MVS Systems (CICS can participate in transactions; not IMS).
Legacy system integration available from addition product: from the same vendor	Purchase an additional legacy systems integration product from the same vendor.	Not applicable.
Average chain of distributed calls: simple	Statically define interaction among components.	**Yes.** MTS is ideally suited for quick requests and responses.
Average chain of a distributed call: complex	Support workflow semantics among objects.	**No.** MTS's stateless model means long sessions with workflow semantics are a difficult challenge to manage.

Continues

Table 9.3 Evaluation Results *(Continued)*

APPLICATION REQUIREMENT	TECHNOLOGY IMPLICATION	PRODUCT SUPPORT
Communication among objects: synchronous	Provide request/response communication model.	**Yes.** Product inherently supports synchronous communication among objects.
Communication among objects: asynchronous	Guarantee delivery of send-and-forget messages.	**Yes.** Standard MTS and COM environment does not offer automated asynchronous communication; however, this is easy to configure with MSMQ.
Communication among objects: "publish and subscribe"	Provide services for objects to publish and subscribe event information.	Not supported in current release.
Advanced messaging functionality through interoperability with additional message-oriented middleware products	Interface to MOM products.	**Yes.** MTS provides easy interoperability with MSMQ.
Ability to automatically keep state of sessions between sessions	Support automated state management facilities.	**No.** MTS works with a stateless model, so significant additional custom-coding is required for applications that require state management.
Response time: small environment (one server, smaller numbers of clients)	Ensure rapid response time for small client environments accessing one back-end resource.	**Yes.** In a "pure" Microsoft systems environment, very rapid response is possible.
Response time: medium-size environment (four or fewer servers, manageable number of clients)	Ensure reasonable response time for an average size application environment with a manageable number of clients accessing the system concurrently.	**Yes.** Possible if number of clients is stable and runs in a pure Microsoft environment.
Response time: large to very large environments (more than four servers, hundreds to thousands of clients)	Ensure average response time for a large application environment in which many clients are concurrently accessing many back-end resources.	**No.** MTS is not recommended due to the static nature of the DCOM environment and its incapability to load-balance and multiplex requests, etc.

Table 9.3 *(Continued)*

APPLICATION REQUIREMENT	TECHNOLOGY IMPLICATION	PRODUCT SUPPORT
High availability/fault tolerance: objects	Ability to provide failover to back up objects in case of failure.	**Yes and No.** Data Objects only (through Microsoft Cluster Software).
High availability/fault tolerance: server system	Provide failover to back up resource in case of failure.	**Yes.** Through the use of Microsoft cluster software (two node configurations only).
High availability/fault tolerance: network	Provide mechanisms for switching to back up network domain in case of network failure.	Not supported in current release.
Security through authentication	Provide security services to ensure authentication control of objects.	Not supported in current release.
Security through access use control lists	Provide security services for control of access privileges for specific application components.	**Yes.** MTS supports the of ACL security defined both explicitly and implicitly.
Security through encryption	Provide encryption security for interaction between components.	Not supported in current release.
Security through integrity of data checking	Provide for the detection of data modification during transmission.	Not supported in current release.

Microsoft Transaction Server is a good solution for smaller NT workgroup environments courtesy of its application services, which are features of the Microsoft operating system. In the future, it should become easier to use MTS in combination with other Object Monitor offerings, thereby providing a transition path for these Microsoft applications. The base Microsoft transaction technology is a solid approach, which will improve as the other features of the NT operating system continue to evolve.

Up Next

In the final chapter in Part Two, we look at the other major computer industry force: IBM. Chapter 10 rounds out the Object Monitor product discovery by introducing you to the ComponentBroker, which plays an active role in IBM's enterprise offerings. Like much of IBM's technology, the product is rich with functionality.

ComponentBroker from IBM

At the time IBM was incorporated in 1911, its product line featured the day's state-of-the-art technology: scales, time clocks, and punch card tabulators. Later, it gained a virtual monopoly on mainframe operating systems and mainframe-based transaction processing technology. IBM was also early to offer open versions of its application service products through OpenCICS, and was at the forefront in enterprise messaging, with its MQSeries. According to Standish Group International, Inc., this product is the leader in the messaging market, capturing 43% of market share in 1998.

IBM's history in enterprise-level technology plays a key role in the company's entry into the Object Monitor market, called ComponentBroker. ComponentBroker is positioned as one of IBM's key offerings in the enterprise application services market, which also includes the aforementioned OpenCICS, Encina, and MQSeries. Also in this group is a Web service product by the name of WebSphere, which offers Web development and Internet standards support. WebSphere can be used in conjunction with ComponentBroker for Web-based applications.

As part of their new recently announced integration strategy, IBM will be rolling out new product introductions which combine the benefits of the WebSphere product line with their enterprise products including ComponentBroker. All of the products in this group are now referred to under the brand name WebSphere Application Server Family. The full range of products included in the WebSphere Application Server Family are:

- *Standard Edition.* Includes an HTTP Web server, Java servlet engine, Web page content authoring and management tools, Java server page support and more.
- *Advanced Edition.* Includes full Standard Edition offering plus Enterprise Java Server (EJS) support, selected resource connectors to data stores and TP Monitors, Enterprise Java Platform service support, moderate scalability, etc.
- *Enterprise Edition.* Full Advanced Edition offering plus ComponentBroker extended to be a full function EJS.

We expect some of the above products to be generally available by time of publication, while others will be rolled out over the next year.

ComponentBroker Product Architecture

ComponentBroker is implemented within a large-scale framework, shown in Figure 10.1, which is really a series of frameworks that work together from a common base. It uses a logical three-tier architecture that separates presentation objects, application (and business) objects, and data objects. We detail the first two tiers here, and cover the third in the development subsection next. ComponentBroker is designed to offer services for each of these domains. The framework approach is intended to provide a complete environment for the development and execution of object-oriented applications. All of these product elements (including the development framework) can be managed with ComponentBroker services.

The first tier of the architecture contains the presentation-level services, which are for creating, testing, and managing access to different types of presentation devices. As shown, the product supports Java or traditional CORBA clients, as well as Windows clients through an ActiveX-to-CORBA bridge. These presentation objects take advantage of ComponentBroker services by calling user-defined application and business objects through the ComponentBroker development environment. The client objects do not bind to server objects themselves; ComponentBroker manages this process.

The second tier of the architecture defines how application objects call ComponentBroker services. It is important to realize that although application objects may consist of many different business objects (such as a checking account and customer object, etc.), the relation between the application objects and business objects enables the developer to work with applications at a high level. The developer calling a ComponentBroker application does not see all of the individual objects; he or she sees everything in the environment as a higher-level application component.

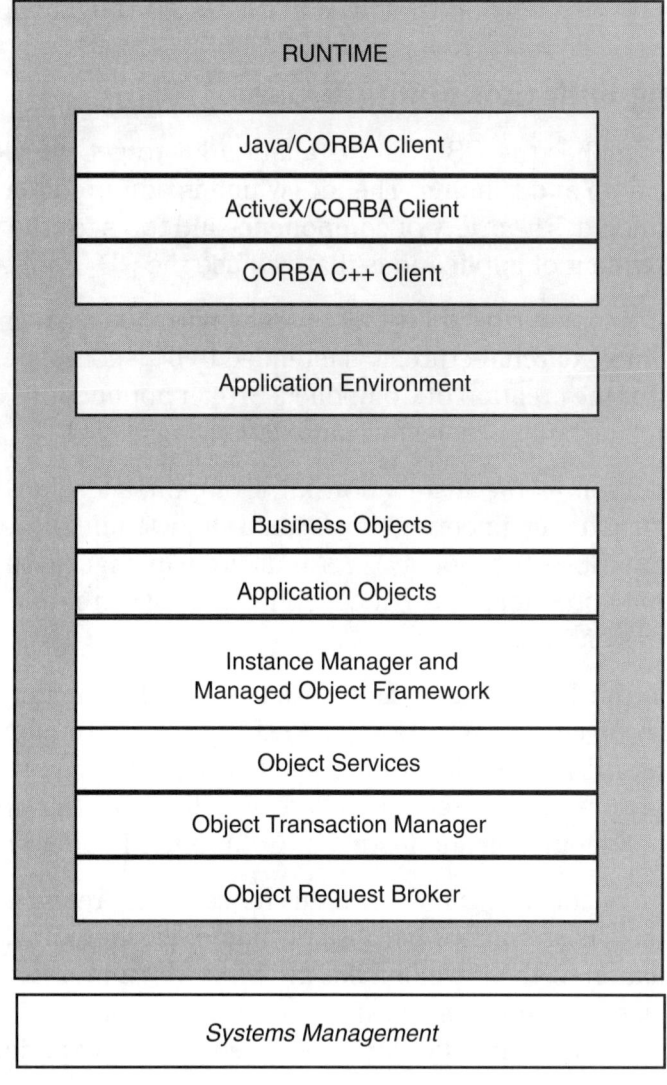

Figure 10.1   ComponentBroker services framework.

As mentioned, ComponentBroker has adopted a distributed transaction management model that uses IBM's OpenCICS Open Transaction Processing Monitor and Transarc's Encina for transactional applications. As described for other products that use this model, the status of each subtransaction (the resource involved in the course of the transaction) of a global transaction (the entire transaction life cycle) is maintained in the memory of the node that the subtransaction is running. Its great advantages are natural scalability and no single point of failure. Its disadvantage is that it requires a complete ComponentBroker server framework must be on each node involved in the transactional application.

Developing with ComponentBroker

IBM supplies the CBC/SM installation kit to get the ComponentBroker system up and running. The kit (which is admittedly a little complex to use) includes a variety of components and tools for the management and deployment of applications that will use the CB framework.

The ComponentBroker development environment takes full advantage of its complex architecture; it is intended to be a complete environment not only for the creation of ComponentBroker applications but for designing, testing, installing, managing, and debugging as well.

In addition to the installation kit, ComponentBroker includes a set of design and reengineering tools called ObjectBuilder (an incorporation of RationalRose technology). As indicated in Figure 10.2, ObjectBuilder offers bidirectional design capabilities between it and existing analysis and design tools.

In the third tier of the framework is a set of tools for developing application objects for the ComponentBroker environment, along with the CORBA IDL compiler. ComponentBroker services run in the runtime framework; they are not called. Finally, this tier features tools for remote debugging and testing of ComponentBroker applications.

As you might have guessed, all this functionality requires a large system to run on. Unfortunately, because, as noted, we were unable to do our own evaluation of the development process, we cannot list the requirements for such a system, nor the skills necessary to manage it (though it's probably safe to say that developers will need strong experience in distributed

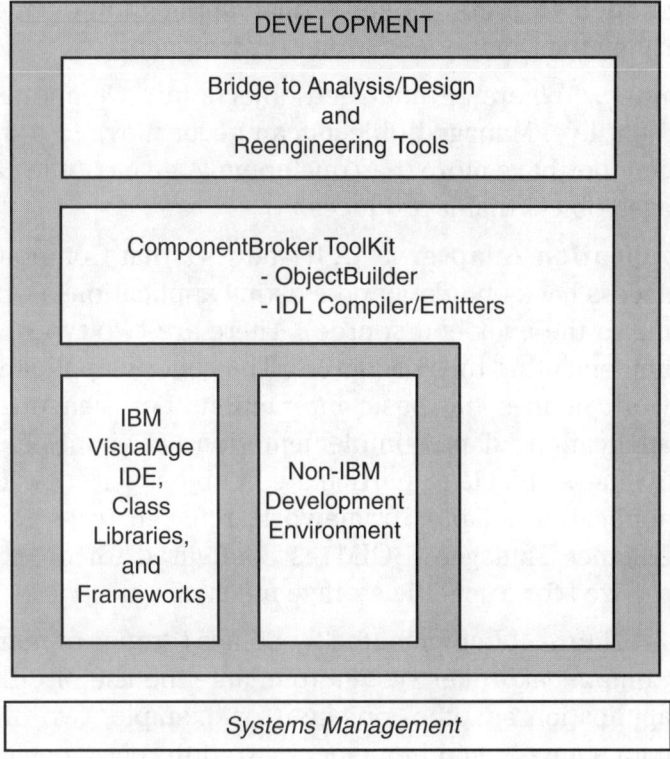

Figure 10.2 ComponentBroker development framework.

system and object-oriented design). But it might help to know that Object-Builder looks very similar to IBM's VisualAge development tools.

Today, ComponentBroker is available only in conjunction with IBM Consulting Services, which we assume is required for the initial configuration of the product, which is, in our opinion, positioned for very large environments with numerous users and back-end systems. For these types of applications, ComponentBroker offers almost limitless possibilities for setting specific policies that determine how objects and groups of objects react.

IBM Terminology

Before we go any further, it is important that you get some IBM definitions under your belts so that you can better understand how ComponentBroker applications and services are implemented:

Managed Objects. User-defined application or business objects that run in the ComponentBroker environment.

Homes. Where all managed objects in a ComponentBroker environment live. Managed objects can never move to a different home, nor can they have more than one home. A given home can locate any managed object that it produces.

Application Adapters. A framework that ComponentBroker uses to access back-end data and existing applications (which varies according to the back-end source). There are two types of frameworks for implementing these adapters: The generic application adapter framework defines the basic interactions between business objects and application adapter implementations; it simply defines a means for business objects to participate in object services. The second type of application adapter framework, referred to as the Business Object Instance Manager (BOIM) is configured for or extended to be customized for a specific storage mechanism.

Containers. Implemented by homes (groups of managed objects) in a ComponentBroker system to enable the use of different instances of application adapters objects (for example, two of the same type of data source; or to implement two different types of transaction policies for the same data source). Object administration in a ComponentBroker system is focused on this level—policy administration such as how transaction policies or security is handled—is established through setting policies for these containers. It is important to note that defining the use of services is accomplished at the container level—not the home level—so if you want to have different policies for different homes, you must create a container for each one.

Mixin Objects. Part of a BOIM application adapter framework called by a business object when required. The mixin object includes special "before and after" interfaces that allow methods to be invoked on the mixin object by other objects. The mixin object is called to provide a high level of abstraction for the business objects that use it (business objects need not implement all their own services, rather they call a mixin object to do it for them). The mixin object can integrate object services, manage persistence, externalize managed object keys, and participate in memory management activities all on behalf of the business objects that call it.

ComponentBroker applications are not portable. In contrast, all CORBA products on the market today have some proprietary extensions, and companies have the option not to use these services if they want to make the applications portable to other CORBA products. In ComponentBroker, on the other hand, the frameworks are making these decisions for you, so a company has no choice other than to use them.

Application Architecture Considerations

IBM's ComponentBroker is designed to provide a solid object-oriented foundation for mission-critical environments and large systems architectures. ComponentBroker meets a multitude of application needs through the combination of services from multiple frameworks. But to achieve all this means that ComponentBroker is a very complex environment, so hold onto your hats in this section, and keep in mind (or go back to refer to as often as necessary) the terms we introduced in the previous section.

 Due to limited platform support for this product, we were unable to evaluate IBM's ComponentBroker via an internal product review. The architecture information in this section is based on knowledge of similar products in this market and IBM documentation and vendor interviews. We therefore cannot guarantee our conclusions, but to the best of our knowledge, they are accurate.

Number of Concurrent Users

ComponentBroker achieves scalability by assigning a combination of policies for multithreaded objects. Client object requests go through the ComponentBroker runtime framework; they do not directly interact with server-side objects. Consequently, ComponentBroker maintains control over these connections, and will find an instance of the correct object class. Administrators do have control over how ComponentBroker will handle the *absence* of a specific instance, including the ability to create new instances on demand (the number of instances that can be created is also configured). All of this is managed through the configuration of the ComponentBroker Workload Management Framework.

ComponentBroker is not limited to a particular instance of an object because the product is able to take advantage of multithreading policies. As the client load increases, ComponentBroker issues available threads first; when all available threads have been used, it can create a new instance of another multithreaded object, and so on. This capability to combine the benefits of both multithreading and multiplexing enables true unlimited scalability.

And if ComponentBroker's Workload Management Framework is configured, the product offers additional capabilities for managing a pool of objects, such as load balancing across multiple object instances. It is through the definition of these policies that ComponentBroker can be configured for scalability even in very large environments.

User Session Length

ComponentBroker has a variety of session management services, which can be configured to meet specific application requirements, such as the predicted length of a user's session. For long client sessions, ComponentBroker allows for specific workflow semantics as defined through the use of mixin objects. Using these facilities, a developer can specify a complete session life cycle. Within the scope of this session, policies can be defined to propagate the session context to each object contained therein; and in turn, each object can then be aware of which portion of the session it is involved in. This level of control will not be necessary for every application, obviously, but it's very useful for applications that require longer sessions.

NOTE   **ComponentBroker is the only product in the OM market that offers this type of "workflow-like" control over sessions.**

User Population Changes

ComponentBroker makes it possible to define policies for the customized control of groups, or pools, of objects, so the system can be configured to optimally handle rapid changes in user populations. Not only can policies be defined for the creation of new instances of multithreaded objects for peak loads as necessary, these policies can optionally be set to create objects *only* during heavy loads, therefore making optimal use of resources during slower periods.

NOTE   **As with many ComponentBroker services, this capability is not automatic; the product must be configured to deal with rapid population changes through set policies. These can be defined at the administration or development level.**

Data Access

Access to data sources is managed by specific application adapters according to the type of back-end system. Objects that will call these sources are mapped to the appropriate system using the Component-Broker Toolkit.

As noted in the definition list earlier, these application adapters are responsible for providing system capabilities such as caching, recovery, and persistence for the managed objects that call the adapters. When these adapters are built on a foundation adapter framework, each adapter is specific to a particular data source. Whenever possible, the adapter delegates many of its object services to the existing resource.

ComponentBroker uses a very high level of abstraction for choosing data sources, and it has a common way to access these sources. But before ComponentBroker can take advantage of these adapters, they must first be created for each type of back-end system the application will call. In the current implementation, IBM offers adapters for DB2 and Oracle Corporation's Oracle DBMS, as well as for IBM legacy environments. Optionally, customers can create their own application adapters (this will require the customization of the base adapter framework, a nontrivial operation).

Methods for dealing with load balancing among multiple back-end sources are configured using the ComponentBroker Workload Management Framework. These workload-managed objects take advantage of ComponentBroker services that check for policies and institute load balancing based on this configuration information. Managed objects can be configured to always use the same server (unless unavailable) or to alternate between servers using a round-robin algorithm. Predefined bind policies determine which server should be selected; they apply to specific instances according to instructions from the ComponentBroker Systems Administration tools. These bind policies are called, and server instances can be chosen based on a controlled server group—each server is ranked and weighted, and the lowest rating is selected. This round-robin policy enables ComponentBroker's system to automatically rank the weight of these servers, although developers can choose to code specific policies.

Legacy Systems Integration

Legacy systems are accessed using IBM-supplied application adapters. These systems are selected as data sources in the same way a relational database application adapter is chosen: using the ComponentBroker Toolkit. Currently, IBM provides access to CICS and IMS systems through the Procedural Application Adapter (PAA).

PAA enables ComponentBroker applications to indirectly access data on these environments using existing transaction programs (direct access is not provided in the current implementation). This is done via a "screen scraping" or RPC mapping to an existing transaction monitor.

Included with the PAA package are two additional IBM products: the IBM CICS and IBM Connection (CICON), and IBM's VisualAge for Java development tool. These tools provide screen-scraping functionality in combination with IBM Host Demand (HOD), based on TCP/IP Telnet/3270 or the CICS client product.

> **NOTE** **In its current implementation, ComponentBroker does not support two-phase commit coordination with legacy systems.**

Response Time

Although we were unable to run in-house performance tests, we believe it is safe to make some assumptions regarding response time based on the architecture of the product. As described, ComponentBroker has several layers of functionality, many of which are not tightly integrated within the product but which use existing IBM technology. This could certainly have a negative effect on performance. We do believe that installing ComponentBroker in an environment that does not have sufficient resources will likely result in poor performance for this product.

However, we must stress that ComponentBroker was designed primarily to meet the needs of very large client and server configurations. In this type of systems environment, the product can be configured to provide a multitude of services which are specifically geared to very precise application requirements. This level of sophisticated customization can improve response time and resource utilization when implemented properly. Therefore, we believe that, in the right setting, ComponentBroker can provide very good response time and will be able to sufficiently handle massive loads on the system.

Messaging

ComponentBroker provides an implementation of a CORBA-compliant event service that can enable asynchronous communication among groups of objects using event channels. Similar to publish and subscribe, suppliers of event information push information to consumers, or vice versa. The event service is configured through the use of the Component-Broker ToolKit.

IBM is expected to release an adapter to IBM's message-oriented middleware product MQSeries in the second half of 1999. MQSeries supports message passing, queuing, transactional messaging, database access, multicast, guaranteed delivery, and fault-tolerant messages.

State Management

There is an infinite number of possibilities for managing state in ComponentBroker, thanks to the capability to configure the environment based on specific application requirements. With the ComponentBroker Toolkit, developers can define how specific objects should save state in persistent storage. When a client object makes a call to a server object, the ComponentBroker system will invoke these user-defined policies to restore and save state information. This is possible through the use of mixin objects, to alter policies for different classes of objects (which in turn means you could define a different way to deal with state based on specific application requirements).

The system can also be configured to allow for predefined session management so that developers can define exactly how state information is saved and restored, not only on an object basis, but on a session basis as well. This is accomplished through workflow semantics, which let each object within a session know where it is for the duration of the session. Each object can then save and restore state in real time (rather than holding all state for each object throughout the session).

High Availability/Fault Tolerance

ComponentBroker high-availability/fault-tolerant attributes account for these potential failures:

Client Failures.   Every time a client accesses the system, predefined policy options can direct the system to a back-up instance.

Server and Network Failures. Users can specify servers or entire domains of servers to act as back-up in the event of server or server domain failures.

These options can be defined by administrators, and can include multiple back-up systems that are prioritized based on system load and attribute availability.

Security

ComponentBroker currently offers support for Distributed Computing Environment (DCE) and Kerberos security for interactions between client and server objects in the ComponentBroker environment. Alternatively, clients can communicate with using Secure Sockets Layer (SSL) security, which calls the Kerberos security mechanism resident in the server-side ComponentBroker framework. (Note: For Internet-based applications you will have to use the SSL-to-Kerberos option, because the complete Kerberos implementation requires a DCE client for each client machine.)

Additional Object Services

In addition to the object services described throughout this chapter, ComponentBroker offers these additional services via the Component-Broker Toolkit:

CORBA Naming Service. Allows names to be associated with a CORBA object so that each object can be located without requiring a client binding to a specific server. The server institutes names-to-object mapping through the repository. Using this service means that clients do not have to be concerned about the server object's location. The ComponentBroker implementation of this service is based on the Distributed Computing Environment's Cell Directory Service (DCE CDS).

CORBA Life Cycle Service. Designed to help in the creation of objects that support a particular interface; manages these objects' lifetime (ComponentBroker uses mixin objects for this service).

CORBA Externalization Service. Moves and copies objects in a ComponentBroker network through a streaming mechanism.

CORBA Query Service. Makes it possible to locate object instances based on the state of attributes.

Systems Management

All objects derived from the ComponentBroker framework are by default managed; therefore, the system can manage the state, location, and instantiation. The ComponentBroker Systems Management (CB/SM) tool provides additional management facilities through a GUI interface that includes local installation and definition of host machines, servers, server groups, and an application's relationship to servers.

The product also includes basic operational and monitoring utilities: startup and shutdown of both servers and applications, and monitoring of server operational state, performance statistics and error, activity, and trace logs.

The Verdict

As you have no doubt realized, IBM's ComponentBroker is an incredibly feature-rich product whose wide array of services can be used with new applications as well as to access numerous existing software products in an organization. And, not surprisingly, it is well suited for accessing IBM legacy environments and other IBM middleware products (such as MQSeries, CICS, and Encina).

The opposite side of the wealth of features is, however, complexity, requiring developers to have significant skills in distributed systems if they are to configure it properly (which is why it's currently offered with IBM consulting services).

Its richness also means that ComponentBroker is not for environments that do not need such a wide range of configurations, nor for those whose resources are insufficient to install, configure, and run the ComponentBroker client and server libraries.

In Table 10.1, we recap the best application configuration and major application considerations.

Because we could not perform internal testing of ComponentBroker, we did not rate the product against the pattern applications detailed in Chapter 4. However, we restate that ComponentBroker does provide very extensive service functionality, so we believe the product may be ideally suited to *all* of the application patterns introduced in this book.

Table 10.1 ComponentBroker Application Considerations

BEST APPLICATION CONFIGURATION	MAJOR APPLICATION CONSIDERATION
Large to very large numbers of clients and servers in a heterogeneous environment	ComponentBroker is positioned for large-scale environments, with many clients, servers, and possibly legacy systems, providing a wide array of services for managing and configuring the system for optimal performance and scalability. For smaller environments and applications, ComponentBroker is overkill.

That said, it is essential to recognize the technology implications: ComponentBroker will require significant configuration before it will achieve desired objectives. Conversely, not setting up the system properly could result in massive performance degradation. Table 10.2 lists ComponentBroker's support for a variety of application requirements and their concomitant technology implications.

Table 10.2 Evaluation Results

APPLICATION REQUIREMENT	TECHNOLOGY IMPLICATION	PRODUCT SUPPORT
Number of concurrent users: small to medium	Maximize minimal system resources through multithreading.	**Yes.** Through multithreading support.
Number of concurrent users: medium to large	Maximize performance and system utilization through multiplexing of client requests.	**Yes.** Through both multithreading and multiplexing (configuration required).
User session length: short	Support short requests and responses	**Yes.** ComponentBroker can be configured for multiple short requests and responses even in very large environments.
User session: long	Manage connections to maximize resource utilization.	**Yes.** Connections between client and server objects can be configured for long sessions and invocation workflow.
User population changes:high number of sign-on/sign- off variances	Pool objects to maximize resources.	**Yes.** ComponentBroker can be configured to manage a pool of objects for rapid population changes.

Table 10.2 *(Continued)*

APPLICATION REQUIREMENT	TECHNOLOGY IMPLICATION	PRODUCT SUPPORT
Number of data sources: small	Maximize performance to a small set of back-end data sources.	**Yes.** The ComponentBroker Application Adapters are specifically created for each type of data source, allowing for close interaction.
Number of data sources: large	Effectively distribute the load across many data sources to maximize performance.	**Yes.** ComponentBroker allows for numerous customized load-balancing options through configuration variables.
Object database integration	Provide for interoperating with object database management systems.	**No.** ComponentBroker does not provide automated tools for connections to ODBMSs.
Legacy system integration "in the box"	Access legacy system information without the need for an additional product.	**No.** (See next row.)
Legacy system integration available from addition product: from the same vendor	Purchase an additional legacy systems integration product from the same vendor.	**Yes.** IBM sells legacy system Application Adapters for CICS and IMS (current implementation does not support 2PC coordination).
Average chain of distributed calls: simple	Statically define interaction among components.	**Yes.** Through CORBA technology, developers can define static interaction among components.
Average chain of a distributed calls: complex	Support workflow semantics among objects.	**Yes**. ComponentBroker makes it possible to configure the system for specific session and state management, which can be invoked based on workflow semantics.
Communication among objects: synchronous	Provide request/response communication model.	**Yes.** ComponentBroker natively supports synchronous communication.
Communication among objects: asynchronous	Guarantee delivery of send-and-forget messages.	**Yes.** ComponentBroker provides an implementation of the CORBA Event Service for asynchronous communication.
Communication among objects: "publish and subscribe"	Provide services for objects to publish and subscribe event information.	**Yes.** ComponentBroker includes an implementation of the CORBA Event Service that provides a service similar to publish/subscribe functionality.

Continues

Table 10.2 Evaluation Results (Continued)

APPLICATION REQUIREMENT	TECHNOLOGY IMPLICATION	PRODUCT SUPPORT
Advanced messaging functionality through interoperability with additional message-oriented middleware products	Interface to MOM products.	**No.** Not currently available, but IBM expected to provide an adapter to IBM's MQSeries.
Automatic maintenance of state between sessions	Support automated state management facilities.	**Yes.** ComponentBroker can be configured to fully automate state management of objects.
Response time: small environment (one server, smaller number of clients)	Ensure rapid response time for small client environments accessing one back-end resource.	**No.** ComponentBroker is not optimized for this type of environment, so it may provide good response, but will use unnecessary amounts of resources.
Response time: medium-size environment (four or fewer servers, manageable number of clients)	Ensure reasonable response time for an average size application environment with a manageable number of clients accessing the system concurrently.	**Yes and No.** ComponentBroker may provide good response rates for medium to large environments, but may use unnecessary amounts of resources.
Response time: large to very large environments (more than four servers, hundreds to thousands of clients)	Ensure average response time for a large application environment in which many clients are concurrently accessing many back-end resources.	**Yes.** ComponentBroker is ideally suited to large and very large environments and so promises very good response times even during major increases in the number of clients and/or servers.
High availability/fault tolerance: objects	Provide failover to back up objects in case of failure.	**Yes.** In the event of client object failure, the ComponentBroker can provide failover to a back-up instance.
High availability/fault tolerance: server system	Provide failover to back up resources in case of failure.	**Yes.** ComponentBroker allows for user-defined replicated server processes that automatically take over in case of server failure.
High availability/fault tolerance: network	Provide mechanisms for switching to back-up network domain in case of network failure.	**Yes.** ComponentBroker can be configured to partition a network into two domains and provide failover and recovery services.
Security through authentication	Provide security services to ensure authentication control of objects.	**Yes.** ComponentBroker provides SSL-based authentication security.

Table 10.2 *(Continued)*

APPLICATION REQUIREMENT	TECHNOLOGY IMPLICATION	PRODUCT SUPPORT
Security through access control lists	Provide security services for control of access privileges for specific application components.	**Yes.** ComponentBroker provides Kerberos-based access control lists for security.
Security through encryption	Provide encryption security for interaction between components.	**Yes.** ComponentBroker uses SSL for encryption security among objects.
Security through integrity of data checking	Provide for the detection of data modification during transmission.	**Yes.** ComponentBroker uses SSL for integrity of data-checking security.

Based on our study of the ComponentBroker materials and interviews with IBM personnel and users of the technology, we feel confident that it offers a number of very strong application services. As we've said repeatedly, the product is most appropriate for large systems environments that require mission-critical application services and that can take advantage of its customization capabilities.

Up Next

This concludes our product review. Up next is Part Three, which summarizes all our investigative work. It consolidates all the information on the state of the market and what to look for in the future; you'll also find supplementary information to assist in further product evaluations.

PART THREE

The Big Picture

Well you've come a long way to understanding what the Object Monitor market has in store for you. So far we've covered some very complicated subjects in a fairly brief time. You should now be able to answer questions about what middleware is good for, what the difference is between CORBA and DCOM and even the functionality of the current Object Monitor products available in the market today. So what else is there to know?

Well, now that you've learned so much, it's time to get a look at "the big picture". Chapter 11 will sum up the state of the entire Object Monitor market. We'll cover where the products are positioned across types of applications, standards support and ease of development. We'll also give you a start in understanding where these particular products are headed.

Chapter 12 will bring us back to our short list tools and give you some information on how to evaluate Object Monitor products in the future and how to continually re-evaluate the products we've covered dependent on your particular application requirements. If you're looking at product today, you should definitely take a look at this information.

Chapter 13 is, in our opinion, the most important chapter in the book as it takes all the information we've provided so far to explain the future of distributed systems and the products that will take us there.

We recommend everyone read at least Chapter 11 and Chapter 13, if only to impress your friends with your amazing ability to grasp the Object Monitor market and forecast the future of distributed systems technology!

The Merger Effect

Almost daily we hear of banks, retailers, phone and software companies, and many other businesses merging with their competitors. A side effect of this "merger effect" is the need to also merge disparate computing systems.

Mergers and acquisitions force companies to think about the way they have been developing applications. Fortunately, the Object Monitor products being introduced today are designed to handle the requirements for this new way of business life. They are created to establish a standard backbone, to which companies can "plug in" new applications and application services that are available to the entire corporate information systems architecture.

But these products themselves are experiencing their own merger effect. What does this mean for the state of the technology today—and tomorrow? This is the question this chapter will attempt to answer.

It is a common belief that combining two products will result in a functional compromise of both technologies. Object Monitor vendors are trying to prove this assumption wrong. However, the market is still in its infancy and all the currently available products lack key features that would make them appropriate to all applications.

Still the goal of the merger of these products is to deliver a cohesive and carefully thought-out combination that does not sacrifice the best of the individual products. Let's take a look at how far we've come.

What Have We Learned?

As with any new technology, there are bound to be issues and problems that can only be resolved through widespread adoption, resulting in user requirements for change. But how does this help you today in your choice of an Object Monitor product? The answer to this really depends on your goals in moving to an object paradigm and your current requirements for the applications you are developing today.

Distributed Object + Transactions

The distributed object model addresses three primary distributed system considerations: reduced user overhead, reduced transaction overhead, and maximum throughput. In this model, end users, the clients, no longer perform operations directly against databases; rather, they communicate necessary data to server components. The server component then performs the operation and returns a reply to the client. Operations are called services; each service is identified by a name, and a server component is a distributed object that offers one or more services. A service request travels to a server component that offers the named service.

A distributed object architecture has these benefits that directly impact a transaction processing application.

- *Reduces overhead per user.* End-user processes do not have to carry around all the code necessary to perform operations; for example, clients do not need to contain SQL libraries. User requests contain only the code to make a service request; they do not contain the code for database access.

- *Uniform control of processes.* Maximizes application throughput because requests to the database are serialized. This increases the overall efficiency of the database. The net result is that interaction time is reduced.

- *Natural expansion of systems.* Systems can be distributed across different computers. Because the end user (client) is separate from the database access (server), there is no reason the activities of the two must occur on the same computer.

- *Modular application design.* Clients make the requests and servers do the database accesses. This makes for easier development and maintenance, and the database is protected from any errors in the client.

- *Easy application extension.*   As the application grows, more client and server processes can be added to handle the increased load or to provide new functionality. New nodes and terminals can be added as needed.

We believe a distributed object model is the solution that will take us forward and can provide companies with the right technology for the Internet age and beyond. But it's not all good news.

Not a Cure-All

We said it several times throughout this book: No current product in the Object Monitor market is ideal for every type of application. Vendors still have a lot of work ahead of them before any one product can meet the vast list of today's distributed system requirements. In time, as these products mature, this list of complaints will become shorter.

Don't Rely on MOM

Most of the products covered in this book do not provide a good variety of options for enabling objects to share information. The basic premise seems to be that every time a client sends a message, a request must be issued. In practice, of course, this is not always the case. Objects and their applications need reliable, guaranteed ways to pass information without holding up processing of further requests by waiting for an often unnecessary response. At a bare minimum, objects should be able to "send and forget" pertinent information to other objects. At the same time, the developer should be confident that an application service is in charge of ensuring the delivery of these messages and the integrity of their content.

Currently, Object Monitor products offer only two approaches to this application requirement, neither of which is elegant or ideal. The products use remote procedure calls (RPCs) in a synchronous communication model. And though it is possible to "fake" an asynchronous communication model, this is not the most efficient use of resources.

The only other option available is to interface to an existing message-oriented middleware product. This solves the guaranteed-delivery problem, but the product passing information to the MOM still uses the synchronous communication model to extend the information to the additional MOM product. In addition, a company must have both an Object Monitor and a separate product to accomplish the task, which imposes an additional administrative burden and requires yet another set of skills to properly configure the system to produce the desired effect.

Make Products Easier to Use

There is no doubt that Object Monitors can help companies deliver applications faster, through their capability to reuse services cross-application style. And object-oriented development can reduce time and money expenditures, which often limit the introduction of new corporate services.

But why are·these products so hard to use? With the exception of Microsoft Transaction Server, none of the current Object Monitor products is easy to develop with or configure. Every product currently available on this market requires significant skills in both object technology and distributed systems.

To make these products worthy of widespread adoption we must move beyond the implication that mission-critical means difficult to use. Thanks to the advancements made in the capabilities of development tools, coupled with the proliferation of standard application programming interfaces and open database connectivity, we are ready to move on. It is not impossible to make middleware easier to work with—just ask Microsoft.

The Standards Way of Life

The industry is still debating the value of standards, specifically whether or not they will ever really work. On one side of the argument are proponents for the "standards way of life," who propose that through standards, companies will have a greater choice of products courtesy of the capability to easily integrate technology and swap products. Their opponents contend that standards do not work, and are based on ideals not reality.

So where does the Object Monitor market stand with respect to the portability of products? In short, both sides of the argument have a good case. Some of the products in this market have portable applications, enabling the use of an alternate product at any given time. It is also possible to use services from third-party companies to add functionality to the existing products through standard API support. However, to do so, users must resist the urge to use any proprietary product extensions.

The problem is that today many of these proprietary services are very compelling. If a specific application requires the services that one of these proprietary mechanisms can provide, it may be difficult to resist the temptation. In fact, some of the products in the market today make it impossible not to use their proprietary offerings.

The solution is the continual evolution of the standards process so that vendors can provide these extra features while maintaining strict adherence to object architecture standards. If a main objective for your company is to make sure that you are building standards-based applications, you will no doubt get involved in this process. CORBA enthusiasts can become members of the Object Management Group's program that encourages active participation in the standards process for CORBA-enabled products. DCOM users can take advantage of Microsoft's interactive feedback facilities on the company's Web site and through a standards organization known as The Open Group.

The State of the Products

The way products in the Object Monitor market are evolving is very interesting: On the one hand, you have the ORB-based products, which initially were mechanisms that enabled two objects to communicate transparently. Over time, companies have added services to work within this model—naming, events, and security, to mention just a few—all the while working toward the common goal to find the way to mix and match best-of-breed application services. These newer products don't have a track record for use in large mission-critical environments, which leaves them needing additional scalable, reliable, and often, performance enhancements. We call these products *ORB-like*.

ORB-Like Object Monitors

Typically, an ORB-like product is one whose primary architecture has not changed at all; rather, services are offered that feed off this common base. The Object Monitor paradigm enables these products to offer transactional integrity for object-oriented applications and enhancements for better database access. The benefits these products bring to market are:

- Standard architecture, mimicking object architecture specifications (CORBA or DCOM).
- Services that offer standard APIs.
- A lightweight product that is easy to install on a variety of platforms.
- Guaranteed transaction integrity through two-phase commit coordination (typically making use of or based on a proven transaction manager).

ORB-like products are ideally suited to companies that probably will not need the full-fledged services required for larger applications. But as these products enhance their services, you will be able to work in a truly standardized environment, using a product that will eventually be appropriate for even your biggest, most critical business applications. Products in this segment include IONA's OTM, Inprise's ITS, Microsoft's MTS, and Hitachi's TPBroker.

ORB-Like Object Monitor Essentials

This subsection addresses the essential features that we believe should be added to ORB-like Object Monitor products. The good news is that the architecture of the products makes it easy for vendors to add new functionality.

State Management.

To make the transaction management features of this new breed of Object Monitors effective, we need a clean easy way to save and restore the state of our objects. And in the interim we at least need the capability to add save and restore statements to our server objects so they can then be saved in persistent storage, without having to write all the code ourselves. The issue of state management may not look pretty on the data sheets, but it is very important when building applications.

Availability.

Object Monitor products are ideally suited to Internet-based applications; they're lightweight, easy to use with browsers, and adopt security services well. But in order for these applications to be useful, they must be available at all times. We need to move beyond the primitive ways of achieving availability by writing custom code or using a proprietary mechanism to failover to back-up objects.

If a Web server crashes, this can't bring down the company. Vendors must work on providing automated failover capability. Primitive mechanisms for downed objects are helpful, but there must also be a way to deal with network failures.

Load Balancing.

Companies building huge applications with many back-end objects must have the capability to balance the load of client requests across many servers. A round-robin approach is all right for medium-size systems, but are not sufficient to handle a large environment. Customers should be able to adjust their load-balancing capabilities as an application demands. Ideally, this capability would be fully automated, but it should at least be manageable from the nice graphical user interface management systems now offered.

Large Environments.

None of the products in this market segment is appropriate for large-scale environments. Object Monitors must be able to create new instances of objects on demand when the number of clients accessing the system increases. This functionality should be fully automated so that the system does not overuse or misuse resources during downtime.

All of these products support multithreaded objects, combining request multithreading and multiplexing could be the solution. And this functionality will instantly increase the capacity these products can handle.

TP-Like Object Monitors

If you've been developing object-oriented applications for a while and must have the services of a fully fledged mission-critical product, you have a different set of requirements that today can be filled using products we call TP-like Object Monitors. They already have many of the features necessary for large business-critical applications, and they are adding the benefits of the object paradigm. While not fully "objectized," they are better suited for large applications with many clients and servers.

Products in this market bring the following benefits:

- Best-of-breed business-critical platforms proven over many years of use.
- Numerous customers with good reference sites.
- Heavy-duty services including load balancing and state management.
- Transactional benefits including two-phase commit and more.
- The capability to develop transaction processing applications with object technology.

Over time, these products, too, will adapt to take full advantage of a more mix-and-match architecture that will enable these companies to enjoy standards-based distributed object technology. Products in this market include BEA's M3 and IBM's ComponentBroker.

TP-Like Object Monitor Essentials

The following are the essential features that we believe should be added to TP-like Object Monitor products. They must be extended to take full advantage of all the object model of computing has to offer.

Standards.

One of the fundamental requirements of an Object Monitor product is that it allows for the mixing and matching of products and application code, regardless of platform. The premise is that by hiding low-level operating system and communication protocols with standard application service software, customers can effectively handle such tasks as updating applications and merging business services. To accomplish this, we need products that fully support emerging object architecture standards such as CORBA and DCOM. Without this support, the applications created with the current TP-like Object Monitor products will not be portable or allow for cooperation with third-party services, thereby diminishing the benefit of the standards in the first place.

Bidirectional Scalability.

TP Monitor-like Object Monitors generally provide many features for scaling *up;* what they lack is the capability to effectively scale *down.* If an application does not have numerous clients and servers, these products will most assuredly be overkill. These products are intended to support a wide variety of applications, so they must be able to work in both small and large environments without the need to add bigger hardware.

True Object-Oriented Capabilities.

These products frequently use existing products as-is, then add a layer of object functionality over them to allow for object-oriented development practices. This may be acceptable at this early stage of this market's evolution, but over time, we predict that these "not quite" integrated solutions will cause performance problems that will not be easy to fix. Unfortunately, it will be quite a challenge for vendors to take existing products and rewrite them for a complete object-oriented architecture.

Object Monitor-Like Object Monitors

We define Object Monitor-like OMs as a combination of the two previous approaches, whereby their architectures integrate the benefits of ORBs, MOMs, and TPMs. This will bring about the right balance between the mission-critical services and the object architecture benefits. Currently, there is no product available that offers this combination.

We predict that the next step in the evolution process of this technology will be toward the integration of message-oriented middleware. The market may even see "MOM-like Object Monitors," probably into the early part of the new millennium.

Subsequently, we predict that the true Object Monitor-like OMs will be out shortly thereafter. We'll even go out on a limb and say that 2002 will be the year of the Object Monitor. Until then, you will have to choose products based on specific application requirements, which brings us the state of the market today.

State of the Market

We appraised each of the products in this book based on a number of factors. We first looked at the number of concurrent users they support and those appropriate for intensive database access (see Figure 11.1). Those products at the top in these regards are primarily suited to very large environments with many users and servers, and are optimized for

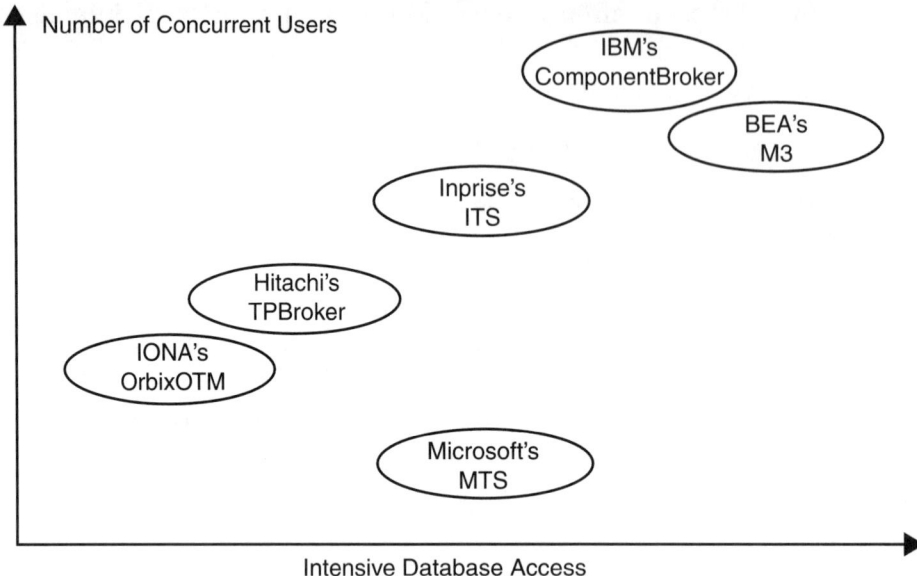

Figure 11.1 State of the market based on number of concurrent users and intensive database access.

a complex systems architecture. They also offer the features necessary for intensive database access requirements.

Smaller applications are advised not to make use of these products, as they will be unable to conserve minimal system resources and often require a great deal of initial configuration work, unnecessary in a smaller setting. Products with a small footprint are ideally suited to smaller client and server configurations, for which they can promise a reasonable performance rate and optimization of resources.

Next we looked at the ease of development, operation, and portability (see Figure 11.2). Toward the top are those products that are easiest to develop with. Those positioned to the right strictly adhere to standards and allow companies to create more portable applications. As you can see, none of the products, with the exception of Microsoft's MTS, is truly easy to use; however, all products are still evolving.

Next we accounted for the "Internet factor." Figure 11.3 shows where the products fit with respect to Internet *enablement* (how well the product is designed for use in Web-based applications) versus the scalability of the product (how it handles peak loads).

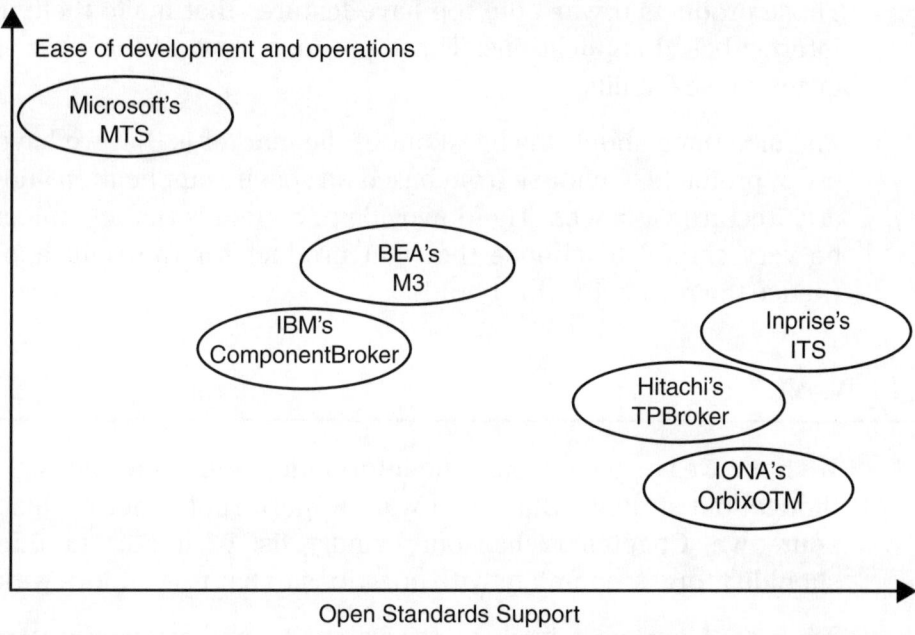

Figure 11.2 State of the market based on ease of development and standards support.

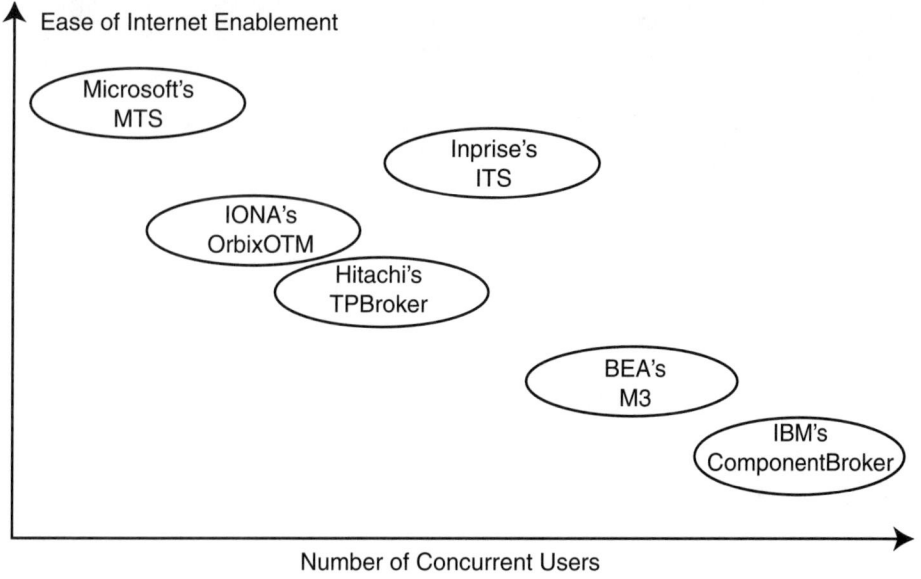

Figure 11.3 State of the market based on Internet use and scalability.

Those products toward the top have features that make them ideal for Internet-based applications. Those products toward the right are optimized for scalability.

The nice thing about this breakout of the market is that we have a variety of products to choose from based on specific application and system architecture variances. The downside of course is that customers must be very careful to choose the right product for the right application (hence the reason for this book!).

Up Next

We hope we've given you all the information you need to design a well-thought-out strategy. But if you want to perform further evaluations on your own, Chapter 12 has our laundry list of important things you shouldn't forget, complete with questions to harass vendors with.

The rest of you can skip ahead to Chapter 13, where we present our final thoughts on the market and preview what's coming soon from a vendor near you.

CHAPTER 12

Updating Your Shortlist

For those of you who have decided to do some product evaluation on your own, we offer the following list of essential questions you should not forget to ask on each topic. This information will help you not only to investigate new products that emerge in the marketplace, but to stay up to date on the products covered in this book.

Of course, because every application has its own specific requirements, the following information should be regarded as guidelines, to serve as a base; these questions can be modified or expanded to learn what you need to know for your business. Don't forget to rate the feedback you get, because no product can give you everything.

Evaluate Interoperability

Object Monitors are intended to enable both object and nonobject resources to transparently send and receive responses independent of language, operating system, and location. To effectively achieve this, it is important that the product support standard APIs or common interfaces for the invocation of resources and services.

You must do a bit of research to ensure that you are aware of the most recent standards in any given area. For object architecture standards, you can contact the Object Management Group for CORBA or consult Microsoft for COM/DCOM specifications.

Ask the Right Questions

To validate a product's adherence to this philosophy, ask the following questions based on your company's object architecture choice (CORBA or DCOM):

1. Does the product support the most recent interface language standards?
2. Does the product support the most recent language bindings (based on application requirements)?
3. Does the product support the most recent standard protocol interfaces?
4. For each object service: Does this service conform to the most recent specifications for service APIs?

In addition to object architecture standards, the product should support interoperability with existing nonobject resources. This may include relational and object database management systems, legacy systems, or other corporate architecture choices (such as the Open Software Foundation's Distributed Computing Environment, DCE). Validation questions include:

1. Which database versions does the product support (applicable for direct connection options)?
2. What does it take to integrate with legacy systems (CICS, IMS, etc.)? You may also want to ask the price of such integration options, as this varies greatly and can be extremely expensive.
3. Is it possible to propagate the transactions across these different systems?
4. What does it take to integrate with packaged applications (SAP, BAAN, PeopleSoft, etc.)?
5. Does the product interoperate with other in-house middleware solutions, including open transaction processing monitor products and message-oriented middleware solutions?

6. What tools are available for this integration (e.g., GUI- or text editor-based)?

For applications that may run in a heterogeneous environment, it is very important to make sure that the vendor software supports your system with the right version! Often for example, software vendors may delay porting to new versions of a database. (We learned this the hard way when we updated our systems to Oracle8.) The same is true for operating systems (while Solaris 2.X may look nice on a data sheet, it won't help if you require version 2.6).

Evaluate Scalability

In general, distributed software systems must be designed on a flexible and scalable architecture to enable quick response to changes in a company's technology and market needs. Scalability in distributed systems is a multidimensional characteristic. You can define scalability as how capable a product is of increasing/decreasing its capacity under varying workloads. When looking at scalability, it is also just as important to be sure the product can maximize a company's often limited resources.

Ask the Right Questions

To validate the scalability of a product, consider the overall architecture of the product and get definitive answers to the following questions:

1. How does the product handle the increase/decrease in the number of host machines?
2. How does the product handle the increase/decrease in the number of active processes per machine?
3. How does the product handle the increase/decrease in the number of active components per process?
4. How does the product handle the increase/decrease in the number of active threads per object (or per process)?

Don't forget to take into account different host configurations, as this may greatly affect how the product will react in your particular environment.

Evaluate Availability

Multiple discrete resources in a distributed system introduce many potential points of failure, and Object Monitors can be used to help to redistribute work to available resources until failed resources are available again.

Ask the Right Questions

Obviously, the level of availability required will vary according to application requirements, but in general, it is important to determine the following:

1. What are the consequences of server failure to the completion of business transactions?

2. What does it take to switch to another server in the event a failure occurs?

3. What information could be lost in case of server failure?

4. How does a server failure affect clients working with this server (how long will they need to wait)?

5. What extra code must be written for making an application system fault-tolerant (if required)? Can the system offer hot standby (if required)?

Once, high-availability attributes were seemingly only for mission-critical applications, but the growth in the number of businesses working over the Internet has increased the need to maintain applications availability. It is very important for these types of applications that you understand the effect of a failed client or server process on the user.

Evaluate Distributed Application Services

Two points make distributed technology applicable to distributed application services: technology itself and distributed services. Object Monitor vendors should be able to provide a list, with descriptions, of current distributed service offerings.

Ask the Right Questions

In this regard, ask the following questions as a start to determining the level of vendor support:

1. Which directory/naming services does the product provide?

2. Will the product integrate/interoperate with existing in-house directory services (if required)?

3. Does the product provide support for notification of events in a distributed system? If yes, how is this configured/manipulated by the user?

4. Does the product provide for state management? If yes, does the approach to state management coordinate with the requirements for the application?

To provide for portability of applications to other software products in the future, it is equally important to understand whether these services provide standard APIs and whether the implementation of the services does not exclude the capability to extend functionality via third-party products if required.

Evaluate Rapid Response Time

Performance in distributed systems is a complicated issue, as it is affected by many systems characteristics. We define performance as the capability of the product to execute the transaction set that is defined as its workload under full load testing. Our goal in performance testing is to measure the capability of each of the distributed systems to scale to required workload ranges; that is, up to 200/tps while providing the required response.

Ask the Right Questions

In conducting your own in-house tests for performance comparison between distributed systems, the answers to the following questions can serve as a template for checking the effect of application variances:

1. Was a single client run against a single server (object)?

2. Was the same test (as number 1) run with varying proportions between clients and servers (e.g. 1:1, 4:4, 10:10, and so on)?

3. Did multiple clients execute against one server (multithreaded with multiple objects)?

4. Did multiple clients execute against multiple servers (multithreaded with multiple objects)?

5. Did tests 3 and 4 compare the effect of various threading policies (e.g., pool of threads in comparison to thread per call)?

If possible, it is helpful to run these tests on various hardware configurations, as the product's response time may be different on other platforms. If you are unable to run these more sophisticated tests, ask your vendor for such performance test results.

Evaluate Robustness

We define product robustness as its capability to continually operate in all environments that may be encountered in a production scenario. How well the product operates is considered to be vital to its overall robustness. To account for a variety of attributes in your distributed system, however, it is important to understand how the product deals with specific application requirements, such as rapid population changes, long sessions, or the distribution of a user to a new location.

Ask the Right Questions

To determine a product's robustness, ask:

1. How well can the system handle dynamic load changes? In other words, what specific types of load balancing does the product support?

2. Does the product allow for various load-balancing scenarios; and how easy is it to configure the system to provide these capabilities?

3. How difficult is it to configure new hosts (or remove existing hosts) in real time? What effect does this have on the application environment?

4. What does it take to start, stop, or change runtime parameters to application services and system-related services in real time?

5. What kind of logging facilities are available with the product (including what information is in the logs; how to access this information; etc.)?

Evaluate Security

Object Monitors must ensure not only secure object invocations but also secure interaction among objects and nonobject resources. Therefore, in addition to finding information on specific security services, it is also important to learn the requirements for implementing the security features (e.g., software required on client and server machines). This is particularly important for Internet-based applications, which should minimize the need for customers to download a lot of software.

Ask the Right Questions

After you determine your application's specific requirements, ask these questions:

1. Which security standards does the security implementation support (CORBA or DCOM)?

2. Can the product be integrated with/interoperate with third-party security implementations (if required)?

3. Are security APIs available to the user for enhancement or modification?

4. Which authentication mechanisms does the product support?

5. Which authorization mechanisms does the product support?

6. Does the product have features for ensuring the privacy of distributed information?

7. What process does the user go through to establish a secure interaction with server systems?

8. Which tools are available for security administration?

Individual corporate and application needs for security obviously vary, therefore be prepared to add questions that apply to your particular requirements.

Evaluate Manageability

Manageability is defined as the product's capability to maintain the production environment. Object Monitors should offer services for managing the object/components known to the middleware. Where required, Object Monitors should also work with existing in-house systems management products.

Ask the Right Questions

To validate a product's management features, ask the following questions:

1. Does the product have the capability to dynamically reconfigure the system (start, stop, change distributed components)?
2. Does the product support "proactive management" (problem determination and recovery before fatal results)?
3. Does the product offer APIs for creating managed objects?
4. Does the product provide tools for distributed application deployment?
5. Does the product provide tools for distributed resource monitoring?
6. Does the product provide tools for distributed deployment?

It is also essential to determine how usable the product is, as this varies widely, from very primitive text editor functions with no automated functionality to fancy GUI tools and automated services.

Evaluate the Development Environment

Understanding how a developer will use the middleware product can go a long way in determining the required skill sets needed and the speed at which new applications can be developed. Previous middleware products often provided no rapid application development options, but today, companies have a variety of possible solutions, including integrated tool sets and/or the capability to work with major development tools of third-party companies.

Ask the Right Questions

One of the first things to consider with respect to the development environment is the programming language support of the product for both client and server programming processes. Access to other development tools and client interfaces through support of standard options (JavaBeans, ActiveX/COM, etc.) is also extremely important. Some major features to ask about include:

1. Is there a true GUI-based integrated development environment (IDE)?
2. Is there support for team development?
3. Does it have the capability to provide full project cycle (requirements, modeling, design, testing, and deployment)?
4. Is there support for multiple language development?
5. Is there support for configuration management?

Products vary widely as to how many programming languages they support, and may be dependent on client versus server languages, so it is very important to get as much information as possible so that you can determine whether you have the proper skills in-house to deal with requirements.

Evaluate Vendor Information

The long-term vendor-client relationship is an important factor to the success of any effort. The last thing a company needs is to build its mission-critical applications on a product that may be discontinued two years down the road.

Ask the Right Questions

A third-party resource can help in answering the following questions:

1. What is the history of the company in the application services market?
2. What is the vendor's strategic direction?
3. How strategic is this product for the vendor?

4. How does this product fit within the company's overall product line?

5. How likely is the company to survive long term?

Building distributed system applications is hard work, and it is very likely that customers may need ongoing support. This is particularly important for mission-critical applications or those that will run on a continual basis (such as Internet commerce applications). To learn about these issues, determine the following:

1. What is the cost for maintenance contracts?

2. What hours is support available?

3. How can support be notified? (Watch out for e-mail-only support as this often incurs a long wait time for a response.)

4. Is on-site support available when required; and what is the typical wait time for such service?

5. Does the company provide a Web-based user support group? (This can be very helpful so that you can share questions with other users.)

6. Does the company offer consulting services to assist with specific implementation issues? What is the cost for these services?

A vendor should also be able to provide you with a list of references and contact information. To be sure you talk to the right user for your project, ask for the following information:

1. What is the biggest installation (in terms of clients, hosts, servers, objects, and transactions)?

2. Which installations are similar to yours?

3. What are typical customer hardware, software, and network configurations? (This is very important, as it will vary depending on the vendor and will affect the funding required for the installation.)

We urge you to check references assiduously before committing to any product that will be used for evaluation. And one final word to the wise: Be aware that case studies offered by vendors may be more fiction than fact, sometimes more optimistic than truthful. Not checking references has been the cause of many a bad technology choice.

Up Next

Chapter 13, the final chapter, will tell you what you can expect in the near future from players in the Object Monitor market, and will introduce you to others that may play a key role in shaping that future. You'll also learn how the information you've learned thus far can be used to understand many other product types as well, because Object Monitor technology is having an impact on the entire technology landscape.

CHAPTER 13

The Future of Object Monitors

I n the Introduction for this book we told you we had been asked a very simple question, "What is middleware anyway?" But, we didn't tell you about the follow-up question, "Why do we need a separate product; doesn't the operating system give us all that?" Good question.

The short answer is no. Even after years of improvements to our operating systems, they still don't give us what middleware does.

We believe the OS will eventually have another layer over it in the form of middleware. Companies may call this layer an *application system*. Much like the operating system, it will be largely invisible to the developer. Luckily, we are approaching this new technology in such a way that there may only be two choices: CORBA and DCOM.

The application system will be required to handle the demands resulting from the way companies are now developing applications, through direct customer access via the Internet, interactive telephone services, and interactive television, to name a few. The goal of this chapter is to explain how companies will handle this interaction using Object Monitor products and alternative approaches to achieving the functionality of Object Monitor technology.

Application System versus Operating System

Today's distributed operating systems have some very important features that provide system-level transparency to users. These services allow many users to share other equipment in a distributed system. For example, a PC user can share a printer or database with another user, without the two aware of their mutual access. Likewise, neither user needs to know where the back-end resource they are accessing is located, whether it is replicated across two or more machines, or even whether one machine is inoperable.

In addition to this transparency, the administrators of an operating system can build in operating-level services such as:

Security. Setting access rights to a specific machine for a specific timeframe.

Availability. Sending requests to another machine if one machine goes down.

Scalability. Defining how many users the hardware system can handle and queuing multiple requests to the same machine to allow for many users.

These built-in services give companies great control over how hardware systems communicate and how users access these machines.

In contrast, an application system builds in this functionality at an application level, and is therefore much more software-specific. Developers of an application system can create the following business-driven services without having to create their own application-level services:

Security. Setting user access rights to a specific application for a specific timeframe.

Availability. Sending a request to another application component if the current application component goes down.

Scalability. Defining how many users can access an application, and providing new instances of application components to handle many users (regardless of the hardware they're running on).

These built-in services give companies great control over how application components communicate and how users and developers access these applications.

The proliferation of products supporting the object-oriented concept of many small application components communicating with each other in a distributed manner has increased the demand for application system services. In the future, the same system communication benefits we expect from our operating systems will be in demand at a higher application level through an application system.

Database versus Middleware

For years, database vendors have argued that middleware, including transaction processing monitors, was unnecessary, claiming that the database was able to take care of all the data integrity features that applications would reasonably require. Therefore, there was no reason to provide this type of functionality outside of the database product.

These arguments focused on the TPM method of handling data integrity through a separate two-phase commit coordination mechanism versus a database proprietary mechanism for handling this same coordination across one brand of database through stored procedures. In the stored procedure model, customers used a specific database function for managing transaction integrity; they could not use this same process for dealing with transactions that spanned multiple types of databases. Middleware vendors tried to get across the fact that their products did more than two-phase commit, while database vendors tried to keep users focused on this specific portion of the TPM functionality.

But along the way came object technology, a new model of creating applications that just happened to fit very nicely with the premise of middleware: reuse of application logic to perform services on behalf of many applications. Suddenly, middleware vendors were in a very good position to provide this capability.

Today, database vendors are offering products that sound very familiar to middleware proponents. They have introduced grand plans to provide users with reusable application services (including standard two-phase commit coordination). Not surprisingly, these services make use of middleware technology.

Today, there are a couple of options in the works from the most popular databases, including Oracle's Network Computing Architecture, Sybase's Jaguar Product Set, and Microsoft's BackOffice. If you take a look at

One Database, Two-Phase Commit

Originally, the two-phase commit coordination model centered around the idea that a transaction will often need to access many back-end data resources. In a traditional application environment this typically meant several databases or other data sources, such as legacy systems.

The need to ensure data integrity across these multiple back ends was something that only applications involving more than one database had been concerned about. But in object-oriented applications, mulitple data sources are actually data objects, which may reside in the same database on the same machine. Handling all these interactions by hand-coding the coordination of the potentially numerous data objects could obviously be a developer's nightmare.

Two-phase commit coordination can make it possible to specify which data objects will need to be part of a transaction context, and allow the transaction manager to manage these intricate object communications while ensuring data integrity.

these offerings, you'll begin to see that much of the functionality behind these "corporatewide architecture offerings" is making use of middleware functionality, which has been included "in the box" with a database product. In fact, for most application services, these products use one of the offerings mentioned in Part Two of this book.

What is interesting about this trend is that these same services can be extended and incorporated within a new generation of database servers. The idea is to enable companies to customize their database functionality, not through proprietary features, but through embedded data management objects that support the same standards that Object Monitors support (CORBA or DCOM).

But this is only half of it, because to access this data, developers still have to design the snazzy screens with which users will access the data. That's where our development tools come into the picture.

Middleware with a Pretty Face

We'll be honest, using middleware is a pretty ugly proposition today. Sure, these products can give us numerous reusable application services, but does this mean that to take advantage of this functionality we'll have to use text editors or clumsy access methods? As long as we're discussing servers, what about the client side of the equation? At the same time our database vendors are adding functionality to the database, development tool vendors are hard at work trying to hide the complexity of middleware behind a graphical user interface. Some of these vendors are those we covered in Part Two. Vendors such as Inprise Corporation (for its popular Borland development tools) and IBM Corporation (with its VisualAge product offerings) are creating this same functionality. Many other vendors are also trying to get into the act through partnerships with existing tool companies.

It won't be long before customers will have a choice between a variety of easy-to-use middleware services. And what about those Web tools you've been using? What are you going to do with all those applications that were written with HyperText Mark-up Language (HTML)? Don't worry; there are a number of new companies coming out with Web products that take advantage of Object Monitor technology.

Middleware Hits the Web

Traditional applications were based on corporate personnel accessing computing systems to perform a prespecified set of tasks. If these same personnel found that the existing applications did not account for some customer needs, the IS staff would be asked to create a new application. This worked on a majority rule: new applications would be created based on an overwhelming corporate need. Requests that were not part of this majority were handled in some other manner, such as a customer service representative accessing multiple systems and arriving at the answer through some detective work.

This model was perfectly appropriate for its time because application environments were very predictable. IS staff took historical information and created applications based on the following factors:

- How many people will access the system? This was fairly easy to figure out, based on other similar applications accessed by the users.
- What will the application's peak times versus downtimes be? This was very easy to figure out, based on hours of operation and historical information.
- How long is an acceptable wait time for these personnel?
- What type of business needs do these users most often handle?

In contrast, customers accessing corporate applications directly create a much more unpredictable environment. The new applications have no historical information to fall back on. This often leaves companies unsure of what exactly their requirements are. Instead of having concrete numbers to rely on, they are left with a host of new questions, including:

- How many customers will want to use the application? This is very difficult to forecast, and has caught many companies unprepared.

- What types of services are these customers going to want to perform? This is very difficult to gauge, as most companies don't have any history with customers actually having direct interaction.

- What are the peak times versus downtimes?

- How long does the customer consider it a reasonable time to wait for a response?

Object technology naturally lends itself to this unpredictable environment. In an object world, each piece of an application survives on its own and handles its own data. Combining these self-managed pieces then generates an object-oriented application. The pieces each perform only their own specific functions. The nature of this model will eventually allow users to mix and match business functions as required, freeing developers from having to forecast what will be required.

What this technology still needs, however, is a way to combine the object middleware's capabilities with those of products designed for Web-based application development, and to handle Web-specific standards and protocols. Knowing this, it's no surprise that our Web servers are getting into the act with new products called "application servers." Not very original, yet certainly descriptive. These products use middleware technology combined with Web-specific services to meet the needs of Internet-based applications—often one of the Object Monitor products covered in this book. The value they add is the capability to make use of preobject Web standards such as HTML or HTTP (HyperText Transfer Protocol) and CGI (Common Gateway Interface). (Don't be surprised if the vendors we covered in Part Two release their own application servers for the Web.)

Final Advice

We've reached the end of our investigation into this fascinating market. But before we say goodbye, we'd like to remind you of the important points to consider when evaluating middleware technology in general, and Object Monitors in specific:

- No product is perfect for every application. Choosing the right product takes careful evaluation of your specific requirements and systems environment.
- Middleware can help save your developers (or you if you are a developer) time, money, and aggravation by eliminating the need to constantly reinvent application services with every new project.
- Stick to standard services and avoid the proprietary services of object middleware technology so that your company can create portable applications and avoid vendor "lock-in."
- Third-party sources, such as market research and consulting firms, can help you to decide on the right product for you.
- Object Monitor technology is permeating every spectrum of the software industry. Share your knowledge of its benefits.

Closing Remarks

We hope this book has made you one of the growing group of Object Monitor-literate people out there. We believe in the value of middleware products and hope you will come to the same conclusion.

We welcome your feedback. You can contact us at this book's accompanying Web site, www.wiley.com/compbooks/boucher. This site is also the place to go for updates on object market technology and products. These products will only improve, and we look forward to monitoring their progress for you. See you at the middleware trade shows!

Glossary

2PC. See Two-phase commit protocol.

Access Control List. Information associated with a file, directory, or other resource, which defines the permissions that users and groups have for accessing it.

ACL. See access control list.

Active Server Pages (ASP**).** Microsoft's alternative to CGI scripts for building dynamic pages. Allows Web pages to interact with databases and other programs. Provides Web page format that contains programming code written in VisualBasic Script or JavaScript. When a browser requests an Active Server Page, the IIS executes the embedded program. Active Server Pages use an .ASP extension.

ActiveX. Microsoft technologies based on its Component Object Model (COM), many of which are targeted for the Internet.

API. See application programming interface.

Application Programming Interface. A specific method format used by an application program to communicate with the operating system or other program or application system. APIs are implemented by writing function calls in the program, which provide the linkage to a specific subroutine for execution.

ASP. See Active Server Pages.

Asynchronous. Refers to events that are not synchronized, or coordinated, in time. In the case of ORB (CORBA), provides capability to invoke methods on remote objects without waiting for their completion.

Authentication. Process that verifies the identity of a user who is logging on to a computer system or verifying the integrity of transmitted message.

Authorization. Process where server checks whether client has privileges to perform specified operation over particular object (a database, routines, files, etc.).

Basic Object Adapter (BOA). Primary architectural component of an object request broker (ORB). The CORBA specification defines the BOA pseudo-object in IDL. The BOA's main purpose is to allow an object server to interact with the ORB. A server process uses the BOA to tell the ORB when an object is ready to perform operations.

BOA. See basic object adapter.

CBC/SM. IBM technology that provides systems management services for the ComponentBroker.

Centralized Transaction Management Model. Used in some implementations of OTM technology to provide a transaction semantic for application components involved in transaction. Microsoft (MTS) and Inprise (VisiITS) provide this model.

CICS. See Customer Information Control System.

COM. See Component Object Model.

Common Gateway Interface Protocol (CGI). Protocol that describes how a Web server can communicate with a program (CGI program or script) on the same machine. CGI programs can be written in any language (e.g., Perl).

Common Object Request Broker Architecture (CORBA). A standard for distributed computing promoted by the Object Managing Group (OMG). CORBA significantly simplifies heterogeneous distributed computing by introducing a high level of abstraction for distributed resources.

Component Object Model. Microsoft's framework for developing and supporting components. Its goal is to provide interoperation of components, including distributed environment components (DCOM).

COMTI. Integration technology from Microsoft that provides tools for integrating COM-based applications with legacy system such as CICS and IMS. In COMTI, CICS and IMS transactions are presented as COM objects to other COM applications.

CORBA. See Common Object Request Broker Architecture.

Customer Information Control System (CICS). An online transaction monitor from IBM, originally created for mainframe environment. In the last two decades, the combination of CICS/COBOL has become a synonym for business applications in the world of large enterprise mainframe computing. Today, it is also available on nonmainframe systems, including UNIX, WindowsNT, OS/2.

Daemon. A special program that runs in the background, ready to perform a specific operation when required. Initially, daemons were introduced in the UNIX operating system. Daemons are usually extensions to the operating system initiated at startup.

Data Integrity. The notion of keeping database(s) in a consistent state.

DCE. See Distributed Computing Environment.

DCOM. See Distributed Component Object Model.

Directory Service. Provides capability to map logical names to physical addresses (similar to name service).

Distributed Component Object Model. An extension of Microsoft's Component Object Model (COM). Provides capability for client program objects to request services from server program objects on other computers in a network.

Distributed Computing Environment (DCE). Software system from the Open Group (formerly Open Software Foundation, OSF), that embodies and implements concepts for total distributed computing across different platform and operating systems.

Distributed Transaction Coordinator. Windows NT service that handles two-phase commit for MTS- (and SQL server-) based applications.

Distributed Transaction Management Model. Used in some implementations of OTM technology to provide transaction semantic for application components, where transaction monitor is a part of application server. IONA (IONA/OTM), BEA Systems (M3), IBM Corporation (ComponentBroker), and Hitachi (TPBroker) provide this model.

Distributed Workflow. Automatic routing of work unit to the component responsible for working on it. Workflow is concerned with providing the information required to support each step of the business cycle.

DTC. See Distributed Transaction Coordinator.

EJB. See Enterprise JavaBeans.

Embedded SQL. Used when programmer needs to process SQL statements from programs that are written using a high-level programming language such as C or C++ (the SQL statement is embedded into your program).

Encryption. Method of converting data into a special form that cannot be easily intercepted or understood by unauthorized people. The antonym of encryption is decryption, which converts encrypted data back into its original form so it can be understood.

Enterprise JavaBeans. Extension of initial JavaBeans component technology. Defines a component model for the development and deployment of Java server-side applications, allowing implementation of multitier, distributed object architecture.

Event Service. CORBA service that allows CORBA objects to be notified when particular event happens during system execution.

Fault-resilient. A distributed system that can recover quickly from a failure. Implies servicing a component in the system without shutting down the entire operation. Different from fault-tolerant, in which redundant components are designed for continuous processing.

Framework. Complete architecture in which a collection of objects work together. Rather than explicitily defining the flow of an application (how one object calls another, in what order it should be called, etc.), the framework defines both the execution flow and how objects that are part of the framework perform their functions.

HyperText Markup Language (HTML). The document format used on the World Wide Web.

HyperText Transport Protocol (HTTP). The communications protocol used to connect clients to servers on the World Wide Web.

IDL. See Interface Definition Language.

Implementation Repository (IR). Implementation repository defined in CORBA standard. Contains information about classes supported by specific server implementations.

Information Management System (IMS). Hierarchical database system created by IBM in the '70s for mainframes running under MVS. It has two major components: IMS/DB (IMS/DataBase) is the database for a batch processing environment, and IMS/DC (IMS/Data Communications) is the component required for online applications.

Interface Definition Language (IDL). An international standard for defining software interfaces.

Internet Information Server (IIS). Microsoft Web server software that runs under Windows NT.

Interoperability. As used in this book, the capability of a programming system (e.g., CORBA implementation) to work with other systems (e.g., another CORBA implementation) without the need to develop extra translation layers.

IR. See Implementation Repository.

JavaBean. Platform-independent component model written in the Java programming language, primarily used for developing GUIs (see also Enterprise JavaBeans).

Java Transaction Service (JTS). Specification for transaction management within Enterprise JavaBeans environment, targeted to vendors providing the transaction system infrastructure required to support transactional application runtime environment.

JTS. See Java Transaction Service.

Kerberos. Security system developed at MIT, primarily to authenticate users and establish their identity at logon time, which could be used throughout the user session.

Load Balancing. Technique that tunes a computer system to enable a more even distribution of load between different components.

LU6.2. SNA protocol developed by IBM, primarily to allow session-oriented peer-to-peer communication between two programs. Also used for interaction between programs running in the host with PCs.

Message. In general, a set of data sent from one program to another. In object-oriented programming, a message is the means by which one object communicates with another, including action and information passing to server object.

Microsoft Interface Definition Language (MIDL). Microsoft's version of DCE IDL, provided by COM (DCOM) and COM+ technologies.

Microsoft Message Queuing (MSMQ). Microsoft implementation of communication system that provides distributed components (programs) with loosely coupled and reliable network communications services based on a messaging queuing model. Runs on Windows NT.

MIDL. See Microsoft Interface Definition Language.

MQSeries. IBM implementation of a communication system that provides distributed components (programs) with loosely coupled and reliable network communications services based on a messaging queuing model. Runs on multiple platfroms, including Windows NT, UNIX, mainframes.

MSMQ. See Microsoft Message Queuing.

Multiple Virtual Storage (MVS). One of the major operation systems for IBM Mainframe computers (the others are VM and DOS/VSE). MVS provides batch processing-oriented operating system that manages large amounts of memory and disk space. CICS and TSO could be used for providing online operations.

Multithreading. Programming technique whereby a thread is an execution unit that serves one user or particular service request.

Naming Service. As defined by CORBA specifications, a service that provides capability to bind a name of object relative to naming context.

Notification Service. Extends CORBA event service by providing structured event.

Object. Programming module that combines data and its associated processing. Objects are the major software building blocks of object technology.

Object Activation Daemon. Program created by Inprise Corporation that activates server objects automatically when they are needed by a client application. Often works cooperatively with another Inprise program called the OSAgent.

Object Database Management System (ODBMS). A database management system that provides the means for managing an object's persistence.

Object Linking and Embedding (OLE). Extension of Microsoft Component Object Model (COM) for managing compound documents. OLE allows the embedding of different objects, such as a spreadsheet or audio, into a document, called the container application.

Object Management Group (OMG). Formed in 1989 by a group of vendors with the goal of creating a standard architecture specification for distributed objects in networks. The major element of this architecture is a location-independent communication mechanism between client and server objects. The result was a specification: the Common Object Request Broker Architecture (CORBA).

Object Monitor. Software product that provides application services for interacting objects.

Object Request Broker (ORB). Technology that provides for the communication of messages from a requesting object (client object) to a server object, along with any return values from the object back to the calling object.

Object Transaction Monitor (OTM). An ORB that provides support for the two-phase commit protocol.

Object Transaction Service (OTS). CORBA specification for distributed object transaction service.

ODBMS. See Object Database Management System.

OLE DataBase (OLE DB). Microsoft technology that allows access to different types of data (not only to SQL databases, as in ODBC).

OMG. See Object Management Group.

Oracle Call Interface (OCI). Interface developed by Oracle for accessing Oracle database using high-level languages, such as C and C++.

ORB. See Object Request Broker.

OSAgent. Program developed by Inprise for providing basic functionality of discovering and connecting server objects to the clients.

OTS. See Object Transaction Service.

Performance. The total effectiveness of a computer system, including throughput, individual response times, and availability.

POA. See Portable Object Adapter.

Portability. Software capability to be moved from one type of machine (system) to another. If a program (application system) can be easily ported from one machine type to another, it is considered portable.

Portable Object Adapter (POA). Portion of a CORBA ORB provided in contrast to a traditional basic object adapter (see BOA). The POA uses information on the class of a requested object to locate this class. (This results in a more flexible and portable system than a traditional BOA implementation.)

Proxy Object. A proxy is a local client representation of a server object. Local calls to proxy objects (located on the client) are intercepted and routed to a remote server. This provides location transparency (clients believe they are conducting a normal local call, when in fact the object middleware is passing the request to the appropriate object located anywhere on a network).

Publish/Subscribe. Programming paradigm that allows decoupling of two programs by enabling one (producer) to publish some events without specific knowledge of who the client is and for another program (consumer) to subscribe to events that are in interest without specific knowledge as to who published it.

RDBMS. See relational database management system.

Relational Database Management System (RDBMS). Technology that allows easy manipulation of data in many different ways without changing the structure of the database tables. SQL (Structured Query Language) is used for data manipulations in RDBMSs. Developed by E. F. Codd at IBM in 1970, based on relational concept where collection of data items are grouped as a set of formally described tables.

Remote Procedure Call (RPC). Technology that provides capability of one program to invoke services of another program in a remote machine.

RPC. See Remote Procedure Call.

Scalability. Capability of a computer system to handle increasing (scale up) or decreasing (scale down) service requests in predictable and manageable way.

SCM. See Service Control Manager.

Secure Socket Layer (SSL). Major security protocol on the Internet.

Security. Protection of data and business transactions against unauthorized access.

Service Control Manager (SCM). Windows NT service that launches background tasks.

Session. The active and identifiable connection between a user and an application system.

Simple Network Management Protocol (SNMP). Protocol for monitoring and managing networks. Allows for monitoring of different types of hardware and software resources, such as hubs, routers, bridges, communication software, etc.

Systems Network Architecture (SNA). Network architecture for mainframe systems, introduced by IBM in 1974. Originally provided only centralized architecture for connecting multiple terminals to the host; latest releases have peer-to-peer communications.

SQL. See Structured Query Language.

SSL. See Secure Socket Layer.

State. Status, or condition, of particular resource within a computer system. In distributed object systems, state relates to the value of attributes for distributed components.

State Management. Maintenance of state and state changes for different resources.

Structured Query Language (SQL). Programming language for working with data in a relational database.

Synchronous. Refers to events that are synchronized, or coordinated, in time. For example, when client objects invoke methods on distributed server objects, the client's execution is postponed until the server has finished its method and returns results to client object.

TM. See transaction manager.

TPC. See Transaction Performance Council.

TPM. See transaction processing monitor.

Transaction. A unit of work comprising a sequence of related activities (such as database updating) and that provides data integrity.

Transaction Manager (TM). Portion of a transaction processing system responsible for two-phase commit coordination.

Transaction Performance Council (TPC). Organization that supplies benchmarks for transaction processing systems.

Transaction Processing Monitor (TPM). Programming system that controls sequence of events that comprise a transaction and manages its completion. When a transaction completes successfully, all changes to databases are committed; otherwise, the TPM rolls back all changes.

Transmission Control Protocol/Internet Protocol (TCP/IP). De facto standard protocol for Internet communications for connecting different systems. Widely supported on all known hardware platforms.

Two-Phase Commit Protocol (2PC). Technique for ensuring that a transaction successfully updates all appropriate distributed resources. All resources involved in the transaction first confirm that the transaction has been received (prepare phase). Then each resource is told to commit the transaction (commit phase).

WAI. See Web Application Interface.

Web Application Interface (WAI). Programming interface based on CORBA paradigm that enables the extension of the functionality of Netscape Web servers. WAI defines object interfaces to the HTTP request/response data and server information. C, C++, and Java can be used to write WAI programs that accept an HTTP request from a client, process it, and return a response to the client.